INTERIM MEASURES OF PROTECTION IN INTERNATIONAL CONTROVERSIES

Interim Measures of Protection in International Controversies

PROEFSCHRIFT TER VERKRIJGING VAN DEN GRAAD VAN DOCTOR IN DE RECHTSGELEERDHEID AAN DE RIJKSUNIVERSITEIT TE LEIDEN OP GEZAG VAN DEN RECTOR-MAGNIFICUS DR. J. J. BLANKSMA, HOOGLEERAAR IN DE FACULTEIT DER WIS- EN NATUURKUNDE, VOOR DE FACULTEIT DER RECHTSGELEERDHEID TE VERDEDIGEN OP VRIJDAG DEN 17 JUNI 1932 DES NAMIDDAGS TE 3 UUR

DOOR

EDWARD DUMBAULD

GEBOREN TE UNIONTOWN

'S-GRAVENHAGE

MARTINUS NIJHOFF

1932

TABLE OF CONTENTS

FOREWORD

The author hopes that the present work may be of value to his colleagues in the legal profession who in one way or another are called upon to take part in the administration of international justice according to law. By a happy coincidence it was concluded on the tenth anniversary of the establishment of the Permanent Court of International Justice.

The author is conscious of divers shortcomings. In particular he wishes that the survey of national law in Chapter II were more comprehensive and complete, and regrets that he was not permitted to examine the original documents in the case of Countess Széchenyi before the Czechoslovak-Hungarian Mixed Arbitral Tribunal. Investigation of the briefs and records of cases before the United States Supreme Court might bring to light information not found in the reports.

The author desires to thank his family and the authorities of Harvard University for enabling him to continue his legal studies until this book was written, and to thank for their stimulating suggestions the multitude of friends in many lands with whom he has had the benefit of valuable discussions *in rem*, not to speak of purely personal courtesies and indirect help. If there exists such a thing as international intellectual co-operation, this study may be regarded as one of its fruits.

For furnishing useful material, the author wishes to thank Professors Hudson, Neuner, Verdross, Guggenheim, Chiovenda, Collinet, Levy-Ullmann, Niboyet, Pagenstecher, Goldschmidt, Del Vecchio, Balladore-Pallieri; Dr. Schüle of the Berlin *Institut*; MM. Krno and Toombs of the League Secretariat; and, more especially, M. Hammarskjöld, Registrar of the Permanent Court of International Justice. The codes of civil procedure of the Swiss cantons, unavailable in any single publication, were placed at the author's disposal by Dr. Heinrich Bueler of Zürich. What the author says of the law of Hungary and Czechoslovakia he owes to the kindness of Professors Szladits and Hora, being himself unable to read the languages of those countries. His colleague Albert A. Roden, of the Princeton Politics Department, has helped read proof.

The author makes grateful acknowledgement of his indebtedness for library facilities he has enjoyed in Cambridge, Vienna, Geneva, Rome, Paris, Hamburg, Berlin, Leyden and the Hague.

E. D.

ABBREVIATIONS

Works included in the Bibliography are cited by the author's name, followed by a catchword if necessary.

A	See Bibliography *s.v.* Permanent Court of International Justice. (Also *ibid. s.v.* League of Nations, for citations beginning with A or C followed by figures and other letters and figures).
A/B	See A *supra.*
ABAJ	American Bar Association Journal.
ABGB	Allgemeines bürgerliches Gesetzbuch (Austrian civil code).
AJ	American Journal of International Law.
Am. Pol. Sc. Rev.	American Political Science Review.
B	See A *supra.*
BG	Bundesgesetz (federal law).
BGB	Bürgerliches Gesetzbuch (German civil code).
BYB	British Year Book of International law.
C	See A *supra*; Codex, in the Corpus Juris of Justinian.
CC	Code civile or Codice civile (civil code).
C Com.	Code commerciale or Codice commerciale (commercial code).
CPC	Code de Procédure civile or Codice di Procedura civile (code of civil procedure).
Cor. LQ	Cornell Law Quarterly.
D	See A *supra*; Digest, in the Corpus Juris of Justinian.
E	See A *supra.*
EO	Exekutionsordnung (Austrian).
F	See A *supra.*
Geo. LJ	Georgetown Law Journal.
G	Gesetz (statute law).
GH	Gerichtshalle (Vienna).

Grünhuts Zt.	Zeitschrift für das Privat- und öffentliche Recht der Gegenwart.
GZ	Gerichtszeitung (Vienna).
HLR	Harvard Law Review.
Inst.	Institutes, in the Corpus Juris of Justinian.
Int. Aff.	International Affairs, journal of the British Institute of International Affairs.
Int. J. Eth.	International Journal of Ethics.
J.Br.Int.Int.Aff.	See Int.Aff. *supra*.
JW	Juristische Wochenschrift.
Krit. Viert.	Kritische Vierteljahresschrift für Gesetzgebung und Rechtswissenschaft.
LNTS	League of Nations Treaty Series.
LQR	Law Quarterly Review.
Malloy	Treaties, Conventions, International Acts, Protocols and Agreements between the United States of America and other powers.
Mich. LR	Michigan Law Review.
Niemeyers Zt.	Niemeyers Zeitschrift für internationales Recht.
OJ	Official Journal of the League of Nations.
PAW	Princeton Alumni Weekly.
PB	Pasicrisie Belge.
Proc.Am.Soc.Int.Law.	Proceedings of the American Society of International Law.
RDI	Revue de Droit international.
RDILC	Revue de Droit international et de Législation comparée.
Rec.	Académie de Droit international de la Haye, Recueil des Cours.
RGDIP	Revue générale de Droit international public.
RGZ	Entscheidungen des Reichsgerichts in Zivilsachen (German).
Riv.	Rivista di Diritto internazionale.
Riv. di dr. pr. civ.	Rivista di Diritto processuale civile.
RM	Rechtsgeleerd Magazijn.
R.O.	Recueil officiel des Arrêts du Tribunal fédéral suisse (Swiss).
St.	Statutes at large of the United States.
TAM	Recueil des Décisions des Tribunaux arbitraux mixtes.

TV	Treaty of Versailles.
UPLR	University of Pennsylvania Law Review.
US	United States Supreme Court Reports. (Other American and English decisions are cited, as is customary, by the abbreviation for the name of the State or of the reporter).
W	Weekblad van het Recht.
WPF	World Peace Foundation pamphlets.
Yale LJ	Yale Law Journal.
ZGB	Zivilgesetzbuch (Swiss civil code).
ZPO	Zivilprozessordnung (code of civil procedure).
ZR	Blätter für Zürcherische Rechtsprechung.
Zt.f.aus.öff.Rt.u.Vrt.	Zeitschrift für ausländisches öffentliches Recht und Völkerrecht.
Zt.f.aus.u.int.Privatrecht.	Zeitschrift für ausländisches und internationales Privatrecht.
Zt.f.öff.Rt.	Zeitschrift für öffentliches Recht.
Zt. f. Vrt.	Zeitschrift für Völkerrecht.
Zt.Sav.St.Germ.	Zeitschrift der Savigny-Stiftung, Germanische Abteilung.
ZZP	Zeitschrift für deutschen Civilprozess.

INTRODUCTION

§ 1. This book represents the results of the author's reflections since reading an article by Professor Philip Marshall Brown published Armistice Day, 1927, in the Princeton Alumni Weekly. Although admitting at the outset that „force is thoroughly discredited as a means of justice" [1]), Professor Brown proceeds to urge the necessity of assuring immediate protection and redress, in case of emergency, for the precious and vital interests of nations, (such as American interests in Haiti or China) [2]). Mere willingness on the part of a delinquent state to arbitrate should not stave off recourse to arms by the aggrieved nation under those circumstances [3]).

Such a statement strikes one at once as odd. If, as Grotius held [4]), war is a substitute for judicial procedure, *ubi judicia deficiunt incipit bellum* [5]), one would suppose, conversely, that willingness to make use of arbitration or judicial settlement would as a natural consequence exclude resort to hostile measures of self-help. *Ubi judicia incipiunt deficit bellum.*

„We may grant that every state wishes to see its own interests protected; yet to believe that states actually prefer the protection of their interests by extra-legal means rather than by law, if the choice is offered, would be an exaggerated cynicism for which

---

1) New Thought and War, 28 P.A.W. 193.

2) In a recent pronouncement Professor Brown declares that „the right of the United States under international law and accepted usage to act in a sudden emergency for the immediate defense of its citizens and of the recognized standards of international conduct must always remain intact". 26 A.J. (1932) 121.

3) Consequently Professor Brown declared himself an opponent of the then mooted Briand-Kellogg pact for the renunciation of war. Professor Borchard, for other reasons, also opposed that treaty. „The Kellogg Treaties Sanction War", 1 Zt.f.aus.öff.Rt.u. Vrt., Teil 1, (1929) 126—131.

4) De Jure Belli ac Pacis Libri Tres, II, i, 2. See note 3, p. 30 *infra*.

5) Contesting the soundness of the view which regards war as a means of settling disputes similar to judicial procedure, see Lasson, Princip und Zukunft des Völkerrechts, 1871, 67; Sir John Fischer Williams, Treaty Revision and the League of Nations, 10 Int. Aff. (1931) 343.

there is really no warrant to be found in the behavior of states" [1]).

Perhaps, then, one of the „shortcomings of international law" is the absence of adequate legal remedy safeguarding jeopardized interests when circumstances permitting no procrastination call for immediate action, before final judgment on the merits of a dispute can be pronounced. But to what extent does this imperfection in fact exist? Do the rules of procedure prescribed by international law for the pacific settlement of international controversies afford protection *pendente lite?*

§ 2. Research revealed an aspect of international jurisprudence which is becoming increasingly important and useful. Yet it is not an overnight innovation. It is framed along lines familiar to the lawyer, and founded on well established international practice.

Certain obligations respecting conduct of the parties *pendente lite* arise as a logical consequence of the very act of submitting a dispute to a tribunal [2]). Express provisions are found in American treaty law as early as 1902. Especially significant were the Bryan „cooling off" treaties concluded by the United States with many other countries [3]).

According to those treaties, all disputes whatever were to be referred to a commission of enquiry, pending whose report the parties agreed to abstain from all acts of force. Three of the treaties contain provisions that the commission shall indicate what measures to preserve the rights of each party should be taken pending its report. These provisions furnished the basis for article 41 of the Statute of the Permanent Court of International Justice [4]).

The Bryan treaties likewise inspired the network of post-war arbitration treaties designed to complement the Covenant which Switzerland, after becoming a member of the League of Nations, took the lead in negotiating. Many of those treaties embody articles dealing with interim protection [5]).

Indeed, the Covenant itself was at the outset hardly more than

---

[1]) Brierly, The Shortcomings of International Law, BYB (1924) 7.

[2]) See p. 182 *infra.*

[3]) See p. 99 *infra.* According to Dr. James Brown Scott in Proc. Am. Soc. Int. Law (1929) 171—5, paying a well-deserved tribute to Secretary Bryan, the existence of such a treaty with England prevented war between that country and the United States over violation of the latter's rights as a neutral. Germany had refused to sign such a treaty. The „cooling-off" idea came from Bryan's practical experience in labor disputes, not from theoretical ratiocination about international law.

[4]) See p. 144 *infra.* [5]) See p. 125 *infra.*

a collective „cooling-off treaty", providing a temporary moratorium on hostilities [1]). At that time no one dared to demand outright prohibition of war [2]). The Covenant as adopted did not speak of provisional measures, but in practice the League has often had occasion to resort to them. Preliminary proposals on the part of American and English writers had envisaged League organs possessing the powers of a court of chancery to issue temporary injunctions. The Phillimore committee, however, professed doubt whether outside Anglo-Saxon law such procedure was familiar [3]).

Nevertheless a survey of procedural legislation and literature reveals a general recognition of the need for interim protection during litigation. A number of monographs are to be found dealing with remedies *pendente lite* in different legal systems [4]). But although the importance of our topic for international law [5]) has often been referred to incidentally [6]), no study dealing *ex professo* with the subject has been published until 1931 [7]).

---

[1]) Cf. G. Lowes Dickinson, The Choice Before Us, 1917, 176.

[2]) Gilbert Murray, The Ordeal of this Generation, 1929, Eng. ed. 228.

[3]) See p. 104—5 *infra*. Likewise Magyary 163 considered article 41 of the Statute of the Permanent Court of International Justice to be something of an innovation.

[4]) Outstanding among these are the works of Muther, in the field of Roman law; Wach in mediaeval Italian law; Planitz and Kisch in Germanic law; Stern in modern German law; Druart in French law; Ott and Bonnard in Swiss federal law; Rintelen in Austrian law, which he compares with the German; and Coniglio in Italian law. Perhaps most useful of all is the last-named treatise, which traces the development of Italian law to date from its origins, and compares it with other modern legislations.

[5]) Strupp in 15 Zt. f. Vrt. (1930) lists it as „besonders behandlungsbedürftig".

[6]) See, e.g., Lowell, Dickinson and Phillimore, note 3, p. 103 *infra*; Brown, La Conciliation internationale, 1925, 89; Scott, Sovereign States and Suits, 1925, 102; Madariaga, Disarmament, 1929, 144, 175; Descamps, in 56 RDILC (1929) 199; Borel in 27 Rec. 1929—II, 575; Dumbauld in 40 Int. J. Ethics (1929) 98—9, and 18 Geo. L. J. (1930) 88; Sir John Fischer Williams in 34 Rec. 1930—IV, 105.

[7]) Guggenheim, Les Mesures provisoires de Procédure internationale et leur Influence sur le Développement du Droit des Gens, 1931; reviewed in 58 RDILC (1931) 635—6, and 25 Am. Pol. Sc. Rev. (1931) 1089—91. That author's treatment differs from ours *inter alia* in that he does not deal with the topic as one falling within the domain of procedural law, in the light of comparative law; but is preoccupied with the repercussions of provisional measures upon substantive international law through the extension of the jurisdiction of „collective organs of particular juridical communities existing in the bosom of the society of states", and the corresponding diminution of the *domaine reservé* left to the domestic jurisdiction of states. The schematic structure of the book is admirable. Having laid down a distinction between provisional measures of legal and political character, the author proceeds in logical sequence from the former towards the latter. Over two-thirds of the book is devoted to political measures, in connection with various aspects of League activity. Only 9 pages are given to the Permanent Court of International Justice. The same tendency to consider the jurisdiction of international bodies as a means of effecting surreptitious changes and amendments in substantive law recurs in Guggenheim's article, Völkerrechtsprozessrecht und materielles Recht, 11 Zt. f. öff. Rt. (1931) 555—578. Cf. Arnold 640—3.

§ 3. What is included within the designation remedies *pendente lite* or interim measures of protection? It is evident that the measures in question form part of remedial or procedural law, dealing with legal protection of the rights of parties. It is likewise clear that the protection thus afforded is purely provisional. Definitive relief must be sought in subsequent proceedings.

Law protects interests by laying down rules of conduct imposing obligations and granting rights. But it also extends protection by prescribing rules regarding the procedure by which such rights and obligations are enforced [1]. Except under primitive conditions [2], the procedure so established involves deliberation by impartial officials charged with the task of deciding in individual cases whether or not to grant requests for protection which they have power to give. When such decisions are not based simply on considerations of expediency or equity, but the tribunal is legally bound to grant the relief prayed for in all cases where the application fulfils the requirements laid down by law, the procedure is judicial [3].

An application for legal protection must conform to certain rules of form or it will be altogether ignored and have no effect at all. If it is made in due form, the tribunal will inquire whether the relief requested falls within the scope of that which it is the func-

[1] In the case of internal law, it would be possible to say that the state, not the law, performs these tasks. But such a statement would lead to confusion in its application to international law. So too, in §§ 9, 10, *infra*, the concept of the right of action as a public-law right against the state, must be understood *mutatis mutandis*. It is not necessary here to discuss Kelsen's theory which identifies law and state, or the view that regards law as the product of the state and hence holds that if there is international law there must be a world-state. Such nomenclature does not obscure the fact that such a „state" differs in important respects from the entities we usually call states. Sir John Fischer Williams, in 45 H.L.R. (1931) 227; van Vollenhoven, De Iure Pacis, 1932, 186. Our treatment assumes the legal validity of international law norms, and classifies them with respect to the functions or purpose they fulfil. See Dumbauld, The Place of Philosophy in International Law, (MS).

[2] It is possible for the prescribed procedure to be self-help, mutual help, or collective help. A remedial right usually, but not necessarily, carries with it a jurisdictional body to apply and interpret the remedial norm. See pp. 9, 93, 127 *infra*.

[3] The distinction between power to decide and rule of law applicable (*Entscheidungskompetenz* and *Entscheidungsnorm*) is brought out clearly by Roden, La Compétence de la Cour permanente, 58 RDILC (1931) 757—773; and Gordon, The Observance of Law as a Condition of Jurisdiction, 47 LQR (1931) 386—410, 557—587. Note the difference between a body which does what seems good in its own sight when exercising its powers, and a body exercising them in accordance with a legal requirement that its discretion must be satisfied. Note also that it is possible to have a perfectly satisfactory and just substantive law in force for unlitigated transactions in a given community, while the law of procedure may be arbitrary, ill-administered, or too technical.

tion of the tribunal to afford. If it finds in favor of its competence, it will consider whether, in the particular case, the application has merit, i.e., presents all the requirements laid down by law for giving protection [1]).

This culminating act toward which the whole procedure moves, the decision which accords the sort of protection which the tribunal is instituted to furnish, we call final judgment. Other proceedings and decisions, prior to final judgment, are interlocutory proceedings or decisions (*jugements d'avant dire droit*).

Some interlocutory decisions are designed simply to facilitate and direct the course of the procedure, to prepare the way leading up to the final judgment. Such decisions are called preparatory decisions (*mesures d'instruction, jugements préparatoires, provvedimenti istruttorii*).

Other interlocutory measures are designed to supplement the protection afforded by the final judgment by affording protection against injury to the interests of a party against which the final judgment, by reason of the delay involved in the course of procedure leading up thereto, affords no protection. Unlike the measures mentioned in the preceding paragraph, these measures are not a preliminary phase of that procedure, but are necessitated precisely because of its inadequacy. [2]) They constitute an independent and additional remedy, directed against prejudice from the delay required to obtain a final judgment. These are the measures of interim protection, the remedies *pendente lite*, with which we are concerned [3]).

[1]) Vizioz (1930) 97—8: „Si la demande est présentée en dehors de certaines formes préscrites par le droit procédurel, le juge ne sera même pas tenu de l'examiner. Si ces formes sont respectées, le juge devra se prononcer au moins sur la recevabilité. Le requérant ne remplit-il pas les conditions de recevabilité: sa demande sera declarée irrecevable, mais la fonction juridictionnelle aura été mise en mouvement, il aura été rendu un jugement.... Ainsi, suivant que telles ou telles conditions sont réalisées, la demande ne sera suivie d'aucun effet, ou aboutira à un simple jugement sur la recevabilité, ou à un jugement de rejet sur le fond, ou enfin à un jugement favorable". Cf. the system of Hellwig set forth at the end of § 9 *infra*.

[2]) Arrondissements-Rechtbank te Rotterdam, 3 December 1906, W. 8607; Glasson-Tissier, 3 ed., III, 5: „Ici les juges prescrivent une mesure, non dans le but de s'éclairer, mais pour sauvegarder des intérêts menacés par l'effet même du procès et éviter un préjudice à l'un des plaideurs. Le jugement provisoire a un caractère d'urgence et se détache complètement de l'affaire".

[3]) See Mortara, Commentario, III, 471. Hence the expression „interlocutory proceedings in international disputes", employed by Sir John Fischer Williams in 3 J. Brit. Inst. Int. Aff. (1924) 300, was too inclusive to serve as the title of this work. „Interim measures of protection" seems to be preferred to the more cumbrous „measures for the preservation in the meantime of the respective rights of the parties" as a trans-

The essence of such a measure is that it precedes the final judgment[1], but has no effect on the tenor thereof; and that it is not merely preparatory, but is remedial, affording protection against harm due to delay. The intrinsic content of the measure is immaterial, and varies with the nature of the substantive law right which it safeguards[2]. Not its content but its relation to the ultimate relief toward which the whole procedure moves, which the tribunal is instituted to furnish, stamps it as a measure of interim protection[3].

§ 4. Notwithstanding the maledictions contained in Magna Carta[4], which classified „the law's delay" along with venality and denial of justice as abuses to be abjured by the king, it is inevitable that considerable time must often elapse after a dispute has been referred to a tribunal before final judgment on the merits of the case can be pronounced[5]. A complicated controversy is not to be decided without prolonged judicial deliberation. Disputed questions of law and fact demand thorough investigation, especially where important interests are at stake. Indeed, it is of the essence of judicial proceedings that every party be fully and fairly heard, and that the tribunal conscientiously consider every pertinent factor in the case before giving its decision. The high responsibilities of a judge's office[6] are incompatible with cursory or off-hand action; reasoned reflection and sober consideration are indispensable.

lation of „mesures conservatoires" by the Permanent Court of International Justice, though the question was left open. D no. 2, 2d addendum, 253—4.

[1]) It may also precede the institution of proceedings, under many systems of procedure. In such cases provision is usually made that action must be brought within a certain period.

[2]) Thus if the ultimate relief tends to be of political character, the interim measure will also be likely to be political. See p. 26 *infra*.

[3]) The very same measure may be interim protection in one case and final judgment in another, according to the object of the action. Wenger 101, 234, 235. Cf. Pound in 27 Int. J. Eth. (1917) 164. In a suit to recover possession, possession is the object of final judgment; in a petitory action based on ownership, possession would be an interim question. Cf. Italian CPC § 444; Glasson-Tissier, 3 Ed., I, 494.

[4]) Cap. 29: „Nulli vendemus, nulli negabimus, nulli differemus, justitiam vel rectum". Lord Coke's commentary, in 2 Co. Inst. is as follows: „Hereby it appeareth that justice must have three qualities, it must be Libera, quia nihil iniquius venali Justitia; Plena, quia Justitia non debet claudicare; & Celeris, quia dilatio est quaedam negatio; and then it is both just and right".

[5]) Respecting the necessity of judicial delays, see the vigorous remarks by Secretary of State Jefferson to Mr. Hammond, the British minister, 7 Works of Thomas Jefferson, Federal ed. 69.

[6]) When the king demanded that the judges consult him before deciding a case, if he should so request, Lord Coke alone replied that in such an event he would do that which should befit a judge. See Pound, The Spirit of the Common Law, 1921, 61. It is to be hoped that no judge of an international tribunal has ever had occasion to repulse in like fashion the improper advances of a government, seeking to influence his decision.

All that has just been said applies *a fortiori* with respect to international litigation [1]). But international tribunals, in addition, are beset by reasons for procrastination from which ordinary courts are exempt. Judges may be required to travel, or documents to be transmitted, over long distances. There are difficulties of language. The parties are states, and the procrastination inherent in governmental action is proverbial [2]).

Yet in the meantime vital interests may be jeopardized. Immediate action may be necessary to ward off irreparable injury threatened by intervening circumstances. The final judgment may prove nugatory and futile if measures of interim protection are not taken at once.

How are these conflicting necessities to be reconciled? The problem is not one peculiar to international law, but is common to all legal systems where procedure for judicial determination of controverted rights has been established and private war abolished. Practically every legal system wisely institutes, in some form or another, remedies *pendente lite*. In ancient legislations as well as in modern codes, and above all in the familiar preliminary injunction of Anglo-American equity practice, provision is made for interlocutory relief. To what extent are similar safeguards available in international controversies?

Remedies *pendente lite* are expressly established by many international agreements, including the Statute of the Permanent Court of International Justice. In addition to analyzing these, it will be necessary to consider the effects flowing from the very act of submitting a dispute for settlement according to a regularly established judicial procedure, and from the „general principles of law" which for the Permanent Court of International Justice, as for other international tribunals having similar competence, constitute a source of the international law to be applied.

---

[1]) „This, you will see, is extremely deliberate procedure, but nothing could be more important than deliberateness and thoroughness in the disposition of international controversies, where not the fortunes of individual litigants are at stake, but the future course of Governments which have been unable to reach an accord as to their mutual obligations". Chief Justice Charles Evans Hughes, The World Court as a going Concern, 16 ABAJ (1930) 156, BYB (1930) 181.

[2]) Scott, Sovereign States and Suits, 178—9; R. I. v. Mass., 13 Peters 23, 24 (1839); Holmes, J. in Va. v. W. Va., 222 U.S. 17, 19—20 (1911): „But a State can not be expected to move with the celerity of a private business man; it is enough if it proceeds, in the language of the English chancery, with all deliberate speed".

CHAPTER I

INTERIM PROTECTION IN PROCEDURAL SCIENCE

§ 5. (*a*) Substantive and procedural norms (*Recht und Rechtspflege*).

Without at length going into the perennial problem of jurisprudence respecting the nature and definition of law, we may take it as agreed that law contains norms [1]), which claim to be binding and call for enforcement and realization in the external world [2]). Moreover every legal system has its remedial or procedural norms [3]), that is to say, that part of the law which treats of the procedure by which legal rights are protected and duties enforced and controversies in regard thereto settled.

These norms may be of various content. In primitive law they

---

[1]) By norms is meant propositions which do not purport to state facts but to set up standards to which conduct *ought* to conform. That law is normative is generally agreed; controversy is confined to dispute with respect to the *differentia specifica* between law and other social norms. Verdross, Verfassung 1. But see Laun, Recht und Sittlichkeit, 2ed. 1927; Radbruch, Grundzüge der Rechtsphilosophie, 1915, 54, who regard law unsupported by moral obligation as a mere threat that force will be exerted under certain specified circumstances. See also Pollock, Essays in Jurisprudence and Ethics, 1882, 49—50; Sander in 10 Archiv. d. öff. Rt. (n. F.) (1926) 193; Holmes, J. in Am. Banana Co. v. United Fruit Co., 213 U.S. (1909) 347, 356.

[2]) Kelsen, Allgemeine Staatslehre, 1925, 125; Schultze 52; Sir John Fischer Williams, Chapters, 1, 2. Chiovenda 44—5: „Le norme giuridiche tendono ad attuarsi. La coazione è inerente all'idea del diritto, non nel senso che per aversi diritto si debba poterlo effetivamente attuare, ma nel senso che esse tende ad attuarsi con tutte le forze che sono *di fatto* a sua disposizione". E. Huber, Recht und Rechtsverwirklichung, 1921 242: „Nun ist die Rechtsordnung ihrem Wesen nach dazu bestimmt, verwirklicht zu werden". Scholten, Algemeen Deel Assers Handleiding, 1931, 130: „Uit zijn aard vraagt het recht om verwerkelijking".

[3]) Just as Jèze maintains that every state has an administrative law. Principes généraux du Droit administratif, 1925, I, 1. This does not mean that the *science* of procedure is developed in every legal system. *Prozessrechtswissenschaft* as we now know it did not arise until the middle of the nineteenth century in Germany. Neuner 11; Binder 1—4. It has since flourished in Italy, but more feebly in France. Vizioz (1927) 165 ff., Millar 5. For the contrast between international law and its science, see Verdross, Règles, 30 Rec. 1929—V, 275. According to Kunz, On the theoretical Basis of the Law of Nations, Transactions of the Grotius Society (1925) 10 : 115, there has always been international law but the science began with Grotius.

comprise regulations of self-help [1]. In modern times, self-help is permitted only in certain exceptional situations, and administration of justice is effected by means of proceedings before impartial officials acting under public authority. For the most part, therefore, procedural or remedial law is made up of rules governing the constitution and organization of tribunals for the administration of justice, obligations to resort to such tribunals, the types of remedy which they have capacity to grant, the forms they observe in administering such relief, and the mode of giving effect to their decisions [2].

§ 6. It should be noted that the remedial law of a particular legal system may provide: (1) A simple *norm* respecting the remedial right. (2) A norm plus a *police jurisdiction* to enforce it. (3) A norm plus a *judicial jurisdiction* to define and apply it in concrete cases. (4) A norm plus both judicial and police jurisdiction [3].

In situation (1) the norm may be implied or express. Situation (1) occurs where there is no remedy for violation of the remedial norm except self-help (unless the view is preferred that self-help is a *jurisdiction* exercised by the aggrieved party).

In situation (2) public power is brought into play in order to establish a situation of fact corresponding to a given legal situa-

---

[1] A legal system might forbid self-help, but furnish no judicial remedy whatever. (That is in fact the case if interim protection is not available, and the ordinary judicial procedure is too cumbersone to be of value to plaintiff). A similar situation would arise in international law if war were renounced without any provision for pacific settlement of disputes. Abandonment of war as a means of settling controversies does not necessitate establishment of an alternative mode of settlement. Pollard, The League of Nations, 1918, 50; Sir John Fischer Williams, in 10 Int. Aff. (1931) 343. Nevertheless prohibition of private war and provision for the administration of justice should go hand in hand. Kunz 47; Telders 7. Otherwise injustice with impunity would be permitted. Dumbauld, Automatic Arbitration, 12 World Tomorrow (1929) 72. The peace movement in its early stages concerned itself with promoting pacific settlement, and did not demand outright renunciation of war. Dumbauld, in 30 P.A.W., November 1, 1929, 152.

[2] All French treatises treat in turn *organisation judiciare, compétence, procédure proprement dite.* Pigeau, the first professor of procedure and collaborator in drafting the code, wrote: „Pour obtenir la justice, il faut la réclamer; on doit ensuite instruire le juge de la justice de sa prétention; lorsqu'il est éclairé, il doit décider. Si les juges se sont trompés ou ont été trompés, le condamné doit avoir le droit de demander la réformation de leur décision. S'il ne le fait ou si, l'ayant fait, la décision est maintenue, et qu'il ne veuille pas l'exécuter, il faut l'y contraindre. La procédure est donc composée de cinq parties principales: la demande ou réclamation, l'instruction, le jugement, les voies à prendre contre le jugement, et l'exécution du jugement". Pigeau considered this order as established by the nature of things; and „depuis plus d'un siècle, les processualistes français n'ont pas cessé de transmettre pieusement cette révélation". Vizioz (1928) 29—31.

[3] Cf. Schüle 57.

tion, the legal situation being accepted without any investigation of controversial contentions by the organ taking action. Situation (2) occurs where a ruler's task is envisaged as that of enforcing the dictates of an immutable customary law of supposed divine origin [1]; or in proceedings for the execution of judgments [2]; or in summary procedure for vindication of uncontested rights [3]; or in action by the Council of the League of Nations to suppress admitted aggression [4].

In situation (3) the remedial norm is objectified, by reason of the tribunal's power to supervise its interpretation and application in concrete cases. Subsidiary disputes tending to confuse the issue are avoided. Situation (3) is the normal rule in international affairs, where there is no international *Vollstreckungsorgan* charged with the duty of enforcing either international law in general or the execution of judicial decisions in particular [5]. Situation (4) is the normal condition in internal law.

In all of these situations the remedial norm may afford either interim protection or definitive relief, as the case may be. In order to comprehend the nature of remedies *pendente lite* as related to other remedial rights, it will be necessary to investigate the character and content of procedural norms.

§ 7. (*b*) Character and content of procedural norms.

1. The nature of rights of action.

The remedial law of a given legal system might ordain that all action to enforce the law must be commenced by a public official, a sort of guardian *ad litem* at large, as is usually the case in criminal prosecutions. On the other hand it might provide for nothing

[1]) Pollock, Essays in Jurisprudence and Ethics, 1882, 58—9; Millar 94—5, 145; Schultze 88.

[2]) Rules as to execution form part of remedial law, whether the proceeding is entrusted to the courts as in Austria (Exekutionsordnung § 3) or to the executive branch of government, as in the United States, where on a celebrated occasion the President, Andrew Jackson, displeased with a decision rendered by the eminent Chief Justice is reported to have said: „John Marshall has made his decision; now let him enforce it". Warren, The Supreme Court in United States History, 1922, II, 219. See Schultze 534.

[3]) Such as *Mandatsverfahren*, or the Swiss procedure „zur schnellen Handhabung klaren Rechtes". See p. 56—7 *infra*; Zürich ZPO § 292 (1).

[4]) Where a plain, downright violation of international law is committed, it serves no useful purpose to apply to a court of law and justice for a decision as to what the law is. What is needed is a police jurisdiction to repress the wrongful conduct. When there are no doubtful or disputed questions at issue, arbitration is of no value. van Vollenhoven, The Three Stages in the Evolution of the Law of Nations, 1919, 43—4. Cf. Arnold 633.

[5]) See however § 13 of the Covenant.

but self-help. As a rule it will envisage action to be taken by a tribunal after proceedings are instituted in due form by the aggrieved party. Since a right is a legally sanctioned capacity to act or to demand that other persons act, it would seem proper to speak of a „right of action" only where the remedial law requires and permits action by the aggrieved party in order to set in motion the remedial procedure.

Since the remedial right has its *raison d'être* in the fact that the pre-existing substantive right is inadequate to furnish sufficient protection for the interests of the aggrieved party, it is evident that the law does not consider the remedial right as a mere repetition of the substantive right. On the contrary, it regards the new right as more efficacious in achieving the purpose of the legal order. Otherwise, if the two rights were identical, there would be an endless *regressus in infinitum*, a series of succeeding rights each born of the failure of its predecessor to accomplish its task.

But what is the nature of remedial rights, in their relation to substantive law rights? Divergent views are taken. According to one view, the substantive right reappears in a new form; according to another, the remedial right is entirely independent, and is a right to demand that action be taken by public authority with a view to protecting the substantive right of the aggrieved party. We shall examine these views more closely.

§ 8. α. Civilistic view.

As civilistic we class those writers who maintain that rights of action constitute part of private civil law (i.e. substantive law), and that procedural law deals only with the *forms* of proceedings (*Verfahren, procédure proprement dite*). The action is conceived of as being the substantive right in a state of activity, in motion instead of at rest, in combat instead of at peace. Procedure is confined to a study of externals, is a practical forensic art and not a science at all; or at best is but a commentary on the code in force and fails to grasp the true substance of this branch of law. The civilistic view, dating from Demolombe, still prevails in France, and was upheld in Germany by Puchta and Savigny [1].

In its modern form this view recognizes the existence of a gen-

[1]) Vizioz (1927) 165—70, 260; Binder 1; Savigny, System des heutigen römischen Rechts, V (1841) 2, 4; Bethmann-Hollweg 208—9.

eral principle affording a remedy wherever there is a right [1]. *Ubi jus ibi remedium.* Instead of various forms of action, there is only one civil action. To have abolished the various forms of action known at common law was hailed as a noteworthy achievement of procedural reform. Some states adopting code pleading even proclaimed a fusion of law and equity [2].

Windscheid declared that it was difficult for modern civil law jurists, accustomed to the system just described where an action is the automatic appurtenance of a substantive right, to comprehend the Roman law system with its multifarious forms of actions [3]. The Roman *actio* did not correspond to the action as understood by modern civilists, but was in fact the substantive right itself. The Roman law, due to its practical nature and the position of the praetor, did not grant rights otherwise than by granting actions. A right apart from an action did not exist.

Windscheid's position did not escape criticism [4]. Muther declared that Windscheid misunderstood the conception of the action held in modern times. Modern doctrine did not consider the right of action (*Klagrecht*) as mere procedure (*Klaghandlung*), as Windscheid asserted, but as a public-law right (*publizistischer Natur*) quite independent of the right it protected. The two rights were directed against different obligors: the substantive right against the defaulting debtor of that right; the right of action against the state [5]. Muther's declaration that the *Klagrecht* is a

---

[1]) Binder 118. So in C. J. Can. § 1667: „Quodlibet jus non solum actione munitur, nisi aliud expresse cautum sit, sed etiam exceptione, quae semper competit et est suapte natura perpetua". But even in a developed legal system some rights may have no remedy, because the injury may be too trifling, or enforcement impracticable. Cf. Pound, The Limits of Effective Legal Action, 27 Int. J. Eth. (1917) 150—167; Hahl v. Sugo, 169 N.Y. 109 (1901); Jèze, in 35 RGDIP (1928) 82—3, citing Principes I, 279, 280 (3ed. 1925). As to *naturalis obligatio*, see Scholtens, De geschiedenis der natuurlijke verbintenis sinds het romeinsche recht, 1931.

[2]) See Morgan, Introduction to the Study of Law, 1926; Maitland, Equity and the Forms of Action, 1909; Chitty, Pleading and Parties to Actions, 1809; Ames, Lectures on Legal History, 1913; Shipman, Handbook of Common Law Pleading, 3ed. 1923; Clark, the Code Cause of Action, 33 Yale LJ (1924) 817—837; Mc Caskill, Actions and Causes of Action, 34 Yale LJ (1925) 614—651.

[3]) Windscheid 3, 229. Roman law was thus akin to the English common law system of forms of action before the modern reforms.

[4]) Bruns pointed out that it held good in Roman law only for praetorian law but not for the *jus Quiritium*. When the *lex* said *ita jus esto*, it created rights directly, and not actions. An action was of course the corollary of such a right. But when the praetor granted an action not founded on a law, it was an action and nothing more. There was no right apart from the action. Binder 21—22.

[5]) Muther, Actio 11, 48.

right to the help of the state in maintaining the legal order, and not the substantive right metamorphosed as Savigny held, marks the birth of the modern theory of the *Rechtsschutzanspruch*, which we shall consider further on [1]).

Windscheid's theory of the Roman *actio* has recently been adopted and extended by Binder [2]). The latter holds that not only in Roman law but as a general principle rights do not exist unless a remedy or action is available. A right *is* nothing but the protection granted by the might of the state. The rules governing the right to protection (i.e., the right of action) therefore constitute private civil law. The law of procedure contains nothing but the formal rules governing the manner, rather than the content, of judicial decisions upon claims for state protection.

It will be seen that this view differs from the civilist view of Demolombe and Savigny in that the right of action is not merely a part of private civil law, but the whole thereof. The action is not the right in a transformed condition, but the right *überhaupt*.

§ 9. β. Processualist views.

As processualist we class those writers who maintain that rights of action do not constitute part of private civil law, but fall within the domain of procedural law, a branch of public law. Purely formalistic rules of *Verfahren* (*procédure proprement dite*) do not make up the whole of procedural law [3]); but constitute only the *development* of a legal relation (*Prozessverhältnis, rapporto processuale*)[4]). Recognition that pendency of proceedings creates a legal relation under public law [5]), and that the action is a right independent of substantive law [6]) are the main doctrines of the science of procedure which grew up in the nineteenth century [7]).

[1]) Binder 115. [2]) Binder 33, 280.

[3]) Chiovenda 101: „La norma che concede l'azione non è certo *formale*, perchè garantisce un bene della vita". But it is a *norma processuale*. Just as *Kriegsrecht* includes not only *Recht im Kriege*, but also *Recht zum Krieg*, so *diritto processuale* includes more than *procedimento*. [4]) Chiovenda 662; cf. Bülow 2.

[5]) Goldschmidt declares that this idea is unfruitful, because no rights or duties arise out of the relation itself. Zivilprozessrecht 4. See also Schultze 290. Morelli 175 considers the concept inapplicable in international law, but Salvioli 65 ff. adopts it.

[6]) Chiovenda 46: „L'azione è un bene e un diritto per sè stante". Kohler, in 33 ZZP 218: „Wir haben das Zivilrecht als wirkendes Element aus dem Prozess hinausgetrieben". Mortara, Commentario, 2ed. II, 561: „L'Azione è un diritto, vale a dire un diritto per se stante, che non si confonde con la pretesa che ne forma oggetto... si può definire l'azione....: il diritto di provocare l'esercizio dell'autorità giurisdizionale dello stato, *o in genere degli organi all'uopo abilitati*, contro le violazioni che stimiamo patite, per qualsiasi fatto altrui, positivo o negativo, da un diritto che noi affermiamo appartenerci". (Italics ours). [7]) Binder 2; Chiovenda ix.

Although we have seen that Muther's reply to Windscheid involved the seeds of the modern outlook, Bülow's epoch-making work *Die Lehre von den Prozesseinreden und den Prozessvoraussetzungen* marks the conscious rise of a science of procedure independent of substantive civil law [1]). He there for the first time expounded the doctrine of the procedural legal relation and distinguished between defenses which merely hindered the course of proceedings once under way, and those which raised the objection that the legal relation was not validly created.

The requirements necessary to establish the *Prozessverhältnis* are called *Prozessvoraussetzungen.* Is the right of action identical with those requirements? Since it is the right to set in motion the machinery of justice with a view to enforcing rights, it would be possible to hold that the right of action is identical with the right to establish the legal relation (*Prozessverhältnis*). This view is perhaps the extreme logical consequence of the separation of the province of procedure from that of substantive law [2]). The *Klagrecht* is regarded as *abstract,* as a right to institute proceedings without regard to the actual legal situation prescribed by substantive law [3]).

Plósz and Degenkolb maintained this doctrine. The latter considered as the important feature of a law-suit the compulsion put upon the defendant by the state to participate in the proceedings (*Einlassungszwang*), whether or not the claim put forward by the plaintiff was well-founded [4]). The merits of the case, the existence or non-existence of substantive rights, is not known until the termination of proceedings. The right of action, however, must exist when proceedings are begun; it can not, therefore, be identical with the substantive right. For a plaintiff who loses his case had the right to bring the action. Substantive law likewise re-

---

[1]) Binder 1; Degenkolb 2.

[2]) Binder 6, 125; Bekker II, 252: „Wo Aktion und Anspruch beide völlig selbständig auftreten, muss ihr Zusammensein als Zufälligkeit gelten".

[3]) Morelli 182—3 accepts the „abstract" view of the action for international law, because disputes between states may be decided in accordance with standards differing from the law in force.

[4]) Modern civil procedure regards defense against an action as a privilege of the defendant, not a duty. „*Einlassungszwang*" really does not exist. Wach, in 14 Krit. Viert. (1872) 605; cf. Wach, Defensionspflicht und Klagerecht, 6 Grünhuts Zt. (1879) 515—558. Kunz 49 sees an „*Einlassungszwang*" in the duty of members of the League to bring their disputes before the Council. League procedure thus differs from judicial proceedings. See p. 27 *infra.*

cognizes, according to Plósz, a right on the part of an aggrieved party to his legal remedy; but this right belongs only to a party really having a substantive right [1]). For procedural law, on the other hand, it is sufficient that a legally relevant right be *alleged*; it need not exist. The right of action is merely that of demanding that the judge decide the case [2]).

But what of the rules of law requiring, not merely that the judge, observing certain forms, decide a case, but also that he decide it in a certain way? [3]) Does not procedural law include all rules governing the decisions of tribunals in proceedings? It may be formal, relating to the organization of the court and the types of relief given in general, without regard to the decision to be rendered in a particular case; or material, which comprises the rules dictating the content of a particular decision. But wherein does the latter differ from substantive law?

Goldschmidt's theory distinguishing *materielles Justizrecht* from *materielles Recht* attempts to maintain the complete independence of procedural and substantive law as established by the modern science of procedure, without recognizing the former as capricious and abstract, unrelated to the actually existing substantive rights of the parties. According to Goldschmidt, procedural law for the administration of justice (*Justizrecht*) comprises all rules directed to the tribunal. In addition to purely formal rules of *Verfahren* governing the manner of procedure, there are rules which yield the concrete decision of individual cases. These substantive rules (*materielles Justizrecht*) are not identical with substantive law (*materielles Recht*), because they are directed to the *tribunal*, not to the *parties*. Goldschmidt's theory involves the duplication of substantive law [4]), in order to maintain the separate status and dignity of procedural law.

It would seem possible that under Goldschmidt's view as well as that of the abstract *Klagrecht*, the law as well as the facts serv-

---

[1]) Cf. Star Busmann, I, 149.

[2]) Cf. Duguit, Traité de Droit constitutionnel, 2ed. 1922, II, 322: „L'action, c'est la possibilité de demander au juge de résoudre une question de droit et de prendre une décision qui soit la conséquence logique de la solution qu'il donne à la question de droit".

[3]) The existence of such rules we have seen to be a characteristic mark of judicial, as distinguished from political or administrative, discretion. See p. 4 *supra*.

[4]) Neuner 10. Normally the second class of rules is identical with substantive law, except for the limitations mentioned in note 1, p. 12 *supra*.

ing as the foundation for the tribunal's decision may not correspond with actually existing law and facts [1]).

Further removed from the abstract theories of pure procedure for its own sake regardless of the existence or non-existence of substantive law is the doctrine of the *Rechtsschutzanspruch* [2]) originating with Wach, and adopted by Hellwig [3]) and Stein. According to this system, the right of action is a public law right against the state to demand protection for the plaintiff's rights. It is a right to a *favorable* decision, and hence is available only to parties entitled to protection. The right to establish the *Prozessverhältnis* by instituting proceedings is not a *right* of action (*Klagrecht*), but a mere *possibility* of bringing an action (*Klagmöglichkeit*), which is open to almost anyone (since modern law does not impose to any great extent disabilities such as those of slaves under Roman law restricting the *jus standi in judicio*) and hence cannot be said to be a peculiar right of the party entitled to protection.

The litigious relation (*Prozessverhältnis*) must be establisshed in order for the court to proceed to a decision *in merito*. If the requirements for establishing that relation (*Prozessvoraussetzungen*) are not present, a decision refusing to entertain the proceedings (*Prozessabweisung*) results. But when the relation has been validly created, it remains for the court to examine whether the conditions laid down by the law for granting protection (*Klagevoraussetzungen, Rechtsschutzvoraussetzungen*) are present.

These conditions are of two kinds, processual and material. The former are those requirements whose absence results in a binding decision against the plaintiff's claim (*Klageabweisung*, not *Prozessabweisung*), but without involving any examination of his

---

[1]) Miscarriage of justice by reason of impossibility to ascertain the true facts is a perennial peril. But it is also possible for a tribunal to be bound to decide a case according to a rule of *law* (*Entscheidungsnorm*) which in fact is not the law governing the case. Thus a common law court without equity powers can not give equitable relief, though the rules of equity be in fact part of the law of the land; a national court may be obliged to convict a foreigner for a crime committed abroad, where the national law was not in force; article 38 of the Statute of the Permanent Court of International Justice, according to Strupp, leads to a decision based on law different from that applicable to the case before submission to that tribunal. Note 1, p. 177 *infra*.

[2]) Star Busmann I, 159 considers this doctrine to be of slight utility.

[3]) For an appraisal of Hellwig's rigorously logical system of procedural science, see Binder 4; Stein, in Der Zivilprozess: Vier Vorträge, 83.

substantive rights. Such requirements are capacity to sue, admissibility of judicial as opposed to administrative remedy, showing of special circumstances required for special forms of relief, such as declaratory judgment or action on a claim not yet due when there is fear of non-performance when due (German ZPO § 259). These requirements manifest the independence of procedure from substantive law, but in modern times tend to disappear. As a rule few restrictions are imposed upon the right of a party whose substantive right is endangered to appeal to the procedure established by law for his protection [1]).

The substantive or material *Klagevoraussetzungen* come from substantive law, being incorporated by reference, as in Goldschmidt's *materielles Justizrecht,* but without being given a new name. They are borrowed outright from substantive law. An unfavorable decision for lack of these requirements means that in the judgment of the court plaintiff has no substantive right.

§ 10. γ. Summary.

Certain conclusions of interest for us may be drawn from the *mélange* of opinions just reviewed. For the most part, the controversies there revealed are over questions of intra-systematic classification within the law of a single state. With these questions of *finium regundorum* and delimiting the respective provinces of civil law and the law of civil procedure, of private law and public law, we are not concerned. Those divisions are largely matters of academic convenience [2]).

Our classification of international law norms, as has been remarked already [3]), is based on function. Remedial or procedural law is law about law-enforcement [4]). Remedial and substantive law are part of the same system of international law, are equally

---

[1]) See note 1, p. 12 *supra.*

[2]) Thus the Swiss federal court, which has separate sections for public and private law cases, in a recent decision (R.O. 56-II, no. 55, 1 July 1930, 318, at 322) adhered to the present practice of the court in treating as a private law case (*Zivilsache*) a question of procedural law regarding interim protection, though two pages further on it speaks of „den *publizistischen* Rechtsschutzanspruch auf vorsorgliche Verfügungen", recognizing that in theory the topic would be classified under public law.

[3]) Note 1, p. 4 *supra.*

[4]) P. 8 *supra.* What we call procedural law deals with what Anzilotti treats in vol. 3 of his Corso, and now describes as „attuazione del diritto nella comunità internazionale". Corso, 3ed. 1928, v. Morelli 208—9 rejects the maintenance of law or rights as the function of international jurisdiction. He lays stress on solution of controversies, whether in accordance with law or otherwise.

positive, are equally law, just as medicine and food are equally physical objects of commerce inserted into the human body. Just as both have different functions, while both are intended to maintain health, so both types of law differ in function while maintaining the health of the social order. Similarly, just as in a modern community medicine is usually furnished only on a physician's prescription, so do legal remedies generally require a judge's decision.

We therefore recognize the distinction between (1) Substantive rights, (2) Rights of action, and (3) Formalities, the process of action itself (*Verfahren, procédure proprement dite*). The object to be obtained, the right to obtain it, and the act of obtaining it are obviously distinct. We include (2) and (3) in procedural law, because they both presuppose the possibility of litigation, while substantive law does not.

Moreover admissibility of the action may be considered as an important formal requirement. *When* or *why* proceedings may be instituted and *how* they may be instituted are inquiries not far removed from each other.

In any case it is clear that, in the words of Chiovenda, the action is a thing of value and a right standing by itself [1]).

Civilistic views admit that the original right is *transformed*. Processualist views declare the independence of the new right; and differ only with regard to its relation (or lack of relation or connection) with substantive law. They declare that it is a right under public law, a right against the state, a right to protection. Insofar as the right calls for protection by public action, which is usually the case in modern law, it would seem justified to use that mode of expression.

The same mode of expression is admissible in international law under our functional classification insofar as the content of the right calls for action on the part of other organs than the party invoking the remedial procedure [2]). We do not find it necessary or desirable to investigate what, if any, significance the concepts of „public law", „public order", „public law of Europe", etc., have

---

[1]) See note 6, p. 13 *supra*.

[2]) Anzilotti, Corso, 3ed. 1928, 270 contends that international organs are organs of the states concerned. Nevertheless they are created by an agreement based on international law, and the view of Verdross, Verfassung 79 is to be preferred.

in international law [1]. For our purposes, the idea contained for international law in the statements of processualists that the right of action is a public law right is: that the right of action is different from the substantive right; and (to the extent that it is true in positive international law [2]) that the procedure prescribed involves action by organs not controlled by the litigants [3].

§ 11. 2. Types of remedy.

Not only is the action a thing of value and a right standing by itself, but the action with a view to security (*Sicherungsprozess, azione assicurativa*) is an action standing by itself [4].

The task of procedural law in maintaining the legal order is threefold: to ascertain, to execute, and to secure rights [5]. Execution, usually the culminating point toward which procedure aims, is the application of such physical force as the law can command in order to bring about a situation desired by it. Such extreme consequences require strong reasons in their justification; consequently execution is not accorded unless there is a good reason for believing that the situation sought to be enforced is one in accordance with the very right of the matter as prescribed by substantive law. What the law considers as affording sufficient ground for such belief is contained in the enumeration of titles justifying execution; as a rule these are decisions of tribunals or

---

[1]) Telders 10 regards article 11 of the Covenant as a provision of public order, exacting peace in the interest of all nations, even if the two parties fighting have agreed voluntarily to disregard an arbitral award and resort to war. But this hardly means that article 11 is different in quality from other rules of international law. It merely modifies former practice in that it gives members of the League a legally recognized interest, not only in wars immediately concerning them, but in all wars or threats of war. Just as a state may possess rights in territory not adjacent to its own, so it may have rights that peace be preserved in territory far from its own.

[2]) International law admits self-help to a much greater degree than the law of any modern civilized state. Anzilotti, Corso, 3 ed. 1928, 44: „un *apparato istituzionale per la realizzazione coattiva del diritto*.... manca in gran parte o è rudimentale.... (divenendo così normale quel fatto dell' *auto-tutela*, che nelle organizzazioni statali è una figura rigorosamente eccezionale)". See p. 9 *supra*.

[3]) See Mortara, in note 6, p. 13 *supra*.

[4]) Chiovenda 226: „Il potere giuridico d'ottenere uno di questi provvedimenti è una forma per sè stante d'azione (azione assicurativa); ed è *mera* azione, che non può considerarsi come accessorio del diritto cautelato, perchè essa esista come potere *attuale* quando ancora non si sa se il diritto cautelato esista; e mentre il convenuto non ha alcun obbligo di cautela prima del provvedimento del giudice".

[5]) Hellwig 1; Rosenberg 3; Schulte 181; Rintelen 4; Muck 3. Cf. Chiovenda 58. Another classification of actions is into declaratory, executable, or constitutive (*Feststellungsklage, Leistungsklage, Rechtsgestaltungsklage*). The action with a view to security then falls in the third group, as it modifies the existing situation by creating new rights of security. Stein, Grundriss 25—6.

formal admissions by the party against whom execution is sought of the validity of the claim in virtue of which execution is requested [1]). Moreover before a court renders a judgment, upon which execution may be had, it demands that after full hearing of both parties sufficient evidence be at hand to justify its decision. It is obvious that as a rule considerable time is consumed before a party can secure his remedy by means of the normal procedure of judicial cognition and execution.

But it is a general principle of the law of procedure that the passage of time should not prejudice the plaintiff whose case is ultimately upheld [2]). Circumstances may often be such that a decision in favor of the successful party will be nugatory and valueless unless appropriate action is taken in the meantime. By means of such measures, which are often the only effective means of providing that the endangered party will not have won his case in vain [3]), procedural law fulfils the third great function which falls to it in upholding the legal order.

It is a general principle in modern civil procedure, says Wach [4]), that rights endangered *pendente lite* should be protected by an action with a view to security. Another writer considers this general principle as „one of the main pillars of modern procedural law" [5]).

In a notable pronouncement by an international tribunal [6]) it is declared that by measures of interim protection the courts strive to remedy the delays of justice, so that so far as possible the result of the case will be the same as if it could end in a day.

Procedure with a view to security employs the same means and methods as procedure with a view to satisfaction, namely judi-

---

[1]) See, e.g., Austrian EO § 1.

[2]) Chiovenda 137: „La sentenza che accoglie la domanda deve attuare la legge come se ciò avvenisse al momento della domanda giudiziale: la durata del processo non deve andare a detrimento dell'attore".

[3]) Bellot 23; Walker, Grundriss des Exekutionsrechtes, 1913, 48; Muther, Sequestration 274. [4]) Arrestprozess 79. [5]) Kisch 76.

[6]) German-Polish Mixed Arbitral Tribunal, 29 July 1924, 5 TAM 459: „Par les mesures conservatoires les tribunaux cherchent à rémédier aux lenteurs de la justice, de manière qu'autant que possible l'issue du procès soit la même que s'il pouvait se terminer en un jour". Cf. Glasson-Tissier, 3ed. 1925, II, 17: „La juridiction des référés aide ainsi à réaliser en partie ce principe idéal de la procédure d'après lequel le demandeur doit, s'il triomphe, avoir la situation qu'il aurait obtenue par une justice rendue immédiatement. Elle est un remède à la lenteur des procès. Grace à elle on obtient une protection provisoire qui souvent devient définitive parce que le litige se trouve supprimé; la mesure ordonnée a déjoué la fraude, paralysé la mauvaise foi".

cial cognition and application of available force by way of execution [1]). Of course the forms of proceeding (*Verfahren*) are more rapid and summary. But it is the grounds upon which action is taken (*Rechtsschutzvoraussetzungen*), the danger against which the applicant seeks protection, which chiefly differentiate the two types of relief. The content of the right of action with a view to security (*Rechtsschutzanspruch auf Rechtssicherung*) is not the same as that of the other actions [2]).

§ 12. (*c*) Remedies *pendente lite* distinguished from similar legal institutions.

1. Interlocutory measures. That interim protection is only one function of interlocutory measures has already been noted [3]).

2. Self-help. Like the judicial procedure which has for the most part replaced it, self-help may or may not be a provisional remedy. Where it is confined by the law to cases of emergency and must be followed by judicial justification, as in the German BGB § 229 [4]), it may be considered as a measure of interim protection.

3. Measures of pure preservation or conservation. While preservation and impartial custody of property in dispute, pending adjudication of conflicting claims, is of frequent occurrence as a measure of interim protection, it must not be forgotten that mere acts of administration *in loco domini* undertaken by a custodian designated by law in order to prevent dissipation or dilapidation of property for want of an owner capable of seeing to its proper management do not constitute interim measures of the sort with which we are concerned. [5]) Mere uncertainty in a legal situation is not sufficient. The uncertainty must arise from controversy or litigation [6]); there must be a particular peril which makes it likely

---

[1]) Schulte 25. *Sicherungsverfahren* is partly *Erkenntnisverfahren* and partly *Vollstreckungsverfahren*. The indication and execution of interim measures should be carefully distinguished, especially in international law, where tribunals have no power to execute their decisions. See § 13 *infra*.

[2]) See Hellwig 13—15.

[3]) P. 5 *supra*.

[4]) The analogy is mentioned by several writers. van Leer 19; Schulte 30; Goldschmidt, Zivilprozessrecht 320; Hellwig, Klagrecht 15: „Inhaltlich ist dieses privatrechtliche Notrecht des § 229 keineswegs ein Recht zur Selbstbefriedigung.... Ist der Arrest eine provisorische Sicherung, so stellen jene Selbsthilfehandlungen also nur ein Provisorium des Provisoriums dar".

[5]) Pasquier 59 distinguishes „actes conservatoires" (actes d'administration") from „mesures conservatoires". If there exists a controversy, what would otherwise be a pure measure of conservation or administration becomes a measure of interim protection. Austrian ABGB § 932 (*a*), Italian C. Com. § 71, sale of defective animal or perishable commodities *pendente lite*.

[6]) Muck 5—6.

that the results of contentious judicial procedure will be vain. Thus the appointment of guardians, executors and receivers, or measures such as those prescribed in the German BGB § 966 respecting the care of lost property by the finder, do not interest us [1]).

4. Summary procedure. We have already observed that, far from being identical with procedure designed to secure a speedy decision of the question at issue, interim protection is necessary precisely for the very reason that such a decision is not possible [2]). Of course applications for protection *pendente lite* must be disposed of by summary procedure; otherwise interim relief would be obtained no sooner than the final judgment, and would be superfluous. But summary procedure includes any deviations from ordinary procedure which make for rapidity [3]), and applies to many other matters than applications for provisional measures [4]).

5. Summary or anticipated execution of a claim for substantive law security. Procedure with a view to security differentiates itself from other summary proceedings by reason of the different purpose in view, the different *Rechtsschutzvoraussetzungen* [5]). We have seen that the action with a view to security is an action standing by itself, independent of the main action. Its function is to afford security, not satisfaction [6]). But this right to security must be distinguished from a substantive law right to security [7]). Many writers take pains to point out that the right in question comes from procedural law [8]), because Wach in his famous study of the

[1]) See Pomeroy, Equity Jurisprudence, 4ed. IV, § 1483 ff.

[2]) See p. 5 *supra*. For this reason it has been contended that where a rapid procedure is ordinarily available for cases requiring celerity, as in French commercial courts, resort to interim measures is thereby precluded. Mérignac-Miguel, II, 46. Both modes of procedure might be rendered unnecessary in some cases by making the ordinary procedure more rapid. Cf. Klein, in GZ (1911) nr. 41, p. 324.

[3]) It was introduced by Alexander III in canon law, who ordered „simpliciter et de plano, sine figura judicii, absque judiciorum et advocatorum strepitu procedere", and developed by the Clementine „Saepe contingit" in 1306. Briegleb 15. Long before the latter, according to Wach 180, there was also a rapid procedure in Germanic law. Moreover *cognitio summaria* existed in Roman law. Roth 102.

[4]) Besides cases of *periculum in mora*, summary procedure applied to trifling claims, incidental and subsidiary points, cases *nullo jure justificabili*, commercial cases, those involving shipwrecked persons, poor people, domestic relations and employment. Bayer 6—14.

[5]) Schmidt 583; Ott, Zur Lehre 328—9.

[6]) P. 19 *supra*.

[7]) Such as that of a fiduciary for performance of his duties, of a husband for the security of his wife's dowry. Examples are German BGB §§ 232, 1051, 843 and are enumerated in Hellwig 24, Stern 17, Seuffert 644, Wach 100, Chiovenda 225, Stein Grundriss 25. Such a claim may coexist with a right to procedural security. Schulte 16.

[8]) Thus Kohler 62.

Italian *Arrestprozess* regarded it as summary or anticipated execution of a right to substantive law security [1]).

6. Provisional or anticipated execution of the principal claim. Interim measures involve execution of an interlocutory judgment authorizing such protection. It may well occur that the content of this preliminary decision is in fact identical with that of the final judgment. [2]) Nevertheless such congruence is altogether fortuitous [3]). The distinction between interim protection and provisional or anticipated execution of the final judgment is very clear. The purpose of the two sorts of measures is quite different. Provisional execution is an instalment or anticipated grant of the very thing which is to come later; the final judgment brings only the confirmation and assurance that no condition subsequent will take it away [4]). Provisional execution is provisional *satisfaction*. Interim protection is always, in the eye of the law, a measure of *security*, even though in practice it may sometimes virtually amount to satisfaction [5]).

---

1) Wach 100. This view was later abandoned by its author. Schulte 16. It would seem peculiarly inadequate to explain measures of security to secure specific performance of a non-pecuniary claim.

2) This is apt to occur when the principal proceeding is purely an exercise of police jurisdiction (§ 6 *supra*) to restrain the commission of an unlawful act. As in this case the only object of the final judgment is to forbid the wrong definitively, and that of the interim order is to forbid it provisionally, the two decisions are factually equivalent in content. See p. 164 *infra*; and Neumann II, 1164; Schmidt 598; Stern 14; Jahn in JW (1930) 1161; Enger 37.

3) Indeed, the mistaken view is often advanced that a certain measure of interim protection is not permissible, because it is identical in content with what will be obtained on final judgment. See pp. 57, 87 *infra*. Of course that fact is an important element to be taken into consideration, but it is not decisive. Interim measures must go no further than is necessary to fulfil their purpose. P. 185 *infra*. But they may go as far as is necessary to fulfil that purpose, and if justified on consideration of all the pertinent elements in the case, they may not be precluded by reason of their coincidence in content with the final relief, note. See note 3, p. 186 *infra*. The rule that an interim measure has no influence on the final decision is a rule regarding the *effect* or consequences of the interim order, not a rule respecting the conditions or circumstances in which the order may be made. RGZ 9 : 336; P.B. 1904, 2e partie, 109; Gerechtshof te Amsterdam, 2 June 1922, W. 10941; Caroli 17, 47, 365 ff.; Star Busmann I, 77; Mérignac-Miguel, 2ed. II, 188.

4) Cf. the similar distinction between *arrha* and *pignus*. Muther Sequestration 374.

5) Thus when under German BGB § 1716 a needy mother obtains an order against the *probable* father of her illegitimate child for support during its first three months, this payment is not provisional anticipation of the duty of the father of an illegitimate child to support it until it reaches the age of 16 (BGB § 1708). The preliminary payment to relieve immediate distress may be smaller than would be required by the scale of support later to be adjudged under § 1708. It is a separate obligation imposed because the legislator has found that since in many cases, the *prima facie* father will be found to be the real father, it is better that he should relieve the urgent need than that the community should do so.

It will be noted that codes of procedure deal with provisional execution in passages distinct from those treating the measures of security with which we are concerned [1]). Likewise the jurisprudence of national [2]) and international [3]) courts distinguishes the two concepts.

§ 13. The relation between execution and interim protection is a source of frequent misunderstanding. Often the provisions relating to the latter are improperly placed in codes. Thus in the German ZPO *Arrest* and *einstweilige Verfügung*, measures of security, are treated in the 8th book, dealing with execution (*Zwangsvollstreckung*) [4]). In Austria *einstweilige Verfügung* is not treated in the ZPO at all, but in the *Exekutionsordnung*; where, however, it appears in the second part, which deals not with execution but with security [5]). Among the excellencies [6]) of the code of civil procedure of the canton of Geneva of 29 September 1819 may be numbered the fact that it puts in their logical place the articles dealing with „*mesures provisoires*" [7]). Many Swiss codes, quite properly, treat the topic under the heading of exceptional proceedings (*ausserordentliches Verfahren*). The Statute of the Permanent Court of International Justice is extremely excellent in this respect. Article 41, which deals with interim protection, immediately follows the article dealing with institution of proceedings by special agreement or unilateral application. Both articles are found in the chapter on „procedure". Recognition is thus given to the fact that jurisdiction to grant interim protection is

---

[1]) German ZPO §§ 708—9; French CPC § 137; Italian CPC § 363. Guggenheim 9 therefore improperly compares § 137 of the French CPC with the *einstweilige Verfügung* of German ZPO §§ 935 and 940, although his conclusion is correct, that French law is casuistic, like Roman law and Hungarian law. Fragistas, Das Präventionsprinzip in der Zwangsvollstreckung, 1931, 47. See pp. 33, 62, 80 *infra*.

[2]) German RGZ 15 : 377, 13 Nov. 1885; ZR 27 nr. 193 (Swiss, 1928).

[3]) A no. 12. §71 *infra*.

[4]) This arrangement is criticised in Stein-Jonas II, 885; Schulte 113. Merkel 20 justifies it because of the function of interim protection in ensuring execution of *Individualleistungen* (specific performance). The practical importance of execution of the interim orders is advanced as the explanation by Stein, Grundriss 25 and Roth 3. Schulte 5 points out that there is an inner relation between the two concepts in that if execution is impossible, security is likewise impossible, whereas the possibility of obtaining a purely declaratory judgment remains unaffected. See p. 26 *infra*.

[5]) The full title of the Austrian law, criticised by Muck 3, 4 and defended by Ott, Zur Lehre 328, is Gesetz über das Exekutions- *und Sicherungsverfahren*.

[6]) Kohler 40; Meyer, Beiträge zur Geschichte des Zürcherischen Zivilprozesses im 19. Jahrhundert, 1927, 67—8.

[7]) See p. 58 *infra*.

part of the jurisdiction of the Court [1]), and that such protection should normally come soon after proceedings are commenced, before the merits of the case are considered.

The German *Staatsgerichtshof*, in support of its conclusion that it had power to grant *einstweilige Verfügungen* although its rules made no provision therefor, referred to the fact that its decisions were not mere expressions of opinion but judgments to be executed by the President of the *Reich*. Critics of its conclusion accepted the same mistaken test, and argued that the Court had no right to grant such measures because it did not have power to execute its own orders. That power was vested in the President and could only be exercised for violation of a constitutional duty, while no such duty to obey interim orders existed [2]).

Likewise the Phillimore committee seemed to think that the League of Nations should have no power to make interlocutory awards or decisions because its final awards or decisions were not to be enforced [3]). Similarly the „Committee on Procedure" drafting the rules of court of the Permanent Court of International Justice deemed it unnecessary to prescribe detailed regulations in regard to the method of indicating interim measures, since the Court had no power to enforce its decisions [4]).

It is difficult to perceive the relevancy of such arguments. As Judge Fromageot pointed out later [5]), they prove too much if the prove anything. The Court would thereby be precluded from rendering final judgments as well as interim orders, for in neither case has it power to execute its decisions. If in the one case it must pronounce its opinion and trust that the parties will conform thereto, it should do so in the other.

The *indication* of interim measures and their *execution* are quite distinct proceedings [6]). It is of course true that such measures would have little practical value if not put into effect [7]). In cases

---

1) Cf. § 17 (3) of the Regulations of the Central American Court of Justice of 2 December 1911. 8 Am. J. Sup. 183.

2) See pp. 84, 90 *infra*. 3) See p. 104 *infra*. 4) See p. 146 *infra*.

5) D no. 2, 2d add. 183.

6) This is made very clear in Swiss law of attachment, where different authorities are competent for granting the order and executing it. Ott 68—9; p. 52 *infra*. So in France civil courts alone are competent in matters as to execution of judgments, though the judgment may have been rendered by a commercial court. CPC § 442.

7) „Die einstweilige Verfügung setzt begrifflich voraus, dass entsprechende Sicherungsmassregeln tatsächlich getroffen werden". Jerusalem 185; cf. Schmidt 583; p. 21 *supra*.

where the harm has already been done and no benefit will be derived from an order prescribing interim protection, doubtless the order will be refused, in accordance with the rules *non vivitur in praeteritum* and *lex non cogit ad vana* [1]). But in such cases, though the *executability* of the measures may be of importance, it is the objective *physical or factual* impossibility of execution and not the tribunal's lack of power to enforce execution which causes it to refrain from exercising its jurisdiction to indicate such measures.

§ 14. (*d*) Types of measures *pendente lite* [2]).

1. *Jurisdictionis fundandae causa.* In proceedings against non-residents, or persons without a fixed and known domicile, it may be difficult or impossible to pursue effectively one's claim in the normal way. Consequently there grew up the rule that, in addition to the courts usually competent, the court of the district where the person or property of such a *debitor suspectus* was found (*forum arresti*) had jurisdiction. Arrest or attachment in such cases not only served to ensure execution of the judgment to be rendered, but to establish the jurisdiction of the court to take cognizance of the case [3]). *Missio in bona* against an *indefensus* in Roman law [4]), and measures in English law such as foreign at-

---

[1]) The German-Polish mixed arbitral tribunal made an order granting interim protection where it was not clearly proved that the Polish government had already taken the action in question, and hence that the tribunal's order would come too late. „Est-il besoin d'ajouter que, si l'Etat polonais a déjà vendu le bien du requérant, la mesure conservatoire arrivera trop tard et que le présent arrêt sera dépourvu d'objet? Mais, étant donné l'incertitude où le défendeur a laissé le Tribunal de ses intentions, le Tribunal ne croit pas devoir s'abstenir d'une mesure qui est juste si elle est utile et qui ne peut faire aucun mal si elle est inutile". 9 TAM 324, 30 July 1924. So 6 TAM 327, 4 March 1925. On the other hand, where the order would have been of no effect, it was denied. 6 TAM 332, 3 July 1926. It is incompatible with the dignity of a judicial tribunal to make an order which will have no effect. A no. 24, 14; La Abra Silver Mining Co. v. U.S., 175 U.S. 423, 457 (1899), citing opinion of Taney, C.J. in Gordon v. U.S., 117 U.S. 697.

[2]) Guggenheim 13 makes a classification of provisional measures into political and judicial, a fruitless distinction in that it merely reflects the content of the decision and the nature of the procedure of which it is a part. P. 6 *supra*. The distinction tends to coincide, however, with that between *einstweilige Verfügung* to preserve peace and to ensure execution of a judgment (p. 44 *infra*), and that made by Judge Negulesco between measures to preserve the status quo and those to preserve the rights of the parties. D no. 2, 2d add. 192—3. The conclusion there reached that article 41 of the Statute of the Permanent Court of International Justice admits measures of the former sort seems to be based on the thought that since it protects the respective rights of *both* parties it wishes to maintain as a totality the existing status of their mutual rights. It obviously authorizes measures of the second sort. See pp. 137, 150, 165—6. 187 *infra*.

[3]) van Kuyk 366; Bort 467.

[4]) Wenger 101.

tachment, *capias ad respondendum*, outlawry, or *peine forte et dure* were employed to coerce a defendant into appearing before the court and submitting to trial [1]).

There would seem to be little if any occasion for measures of this type in international litigation. International courts [2]) do not attempt to increase the amount of business brought before them, but pass upon the cases duly submitted for their decision [3]). Even the „optional clause" does not make it „compulsory" for parties to submit disputes to the Court if they prefer not to; it merely authorizes the Court to decide the case in the absence of action by one party if the other party invokes the Court [4]). And if an arbitration treaty should expressly provide that certain disputes were to be submitted to a particular international court, the court would have no „right to decide the case" authorizing it to proceed *ex officio* to deal with the dispute.

2. To facilitate the conduct of proceedings (*Sicherung der Prozessführung*). Such measures, for the most part, consist in perpetuating proof or otherwise facilitating the task of the tribunal. Obviously they are desirable in international procedure as well as internal [5]). Particular mention should be made of the frequent

[1]) Jenks 52, 171; Patton, Foreign Attachment in Pennsylvania, 56 UPLR (1908) 137. *Peine forte et dure* is a curious proceeding. When a defendant will not put himself upon the country and stand trial by jury, he is bound hand and foot, with one limb extended toward each corner of the room, and on his chest are placed weights as heavy as he can bear and heavier, while his diet is musty bread and brackish water. Defendants have died in this way rather than stand trial where they would certainly have been found guilty of crimes working corruption of blood, involving confiscation of their property by the crown and disherison of their heirs.

[2]) Unlike organs of the League of Nations, which is bound to bestir itself to safeguard the peace of nations, even if thereby settlement of disputes by League machinery becomes necessary. A system is thinkable in which the mere *existence* of a controversy, without invocation of the court's jurisdiction by either party, would suffice to set the wheels of justice in motion. Morelli 181.

[3]) The Central American Court of Justice on one occasion offered its services to disputant states. See p. 96 *infra*. The Permanent Court of International Justice extends its jurisdiction when possible so as to prevent gaps in the available judicial organization. „The Court, when it has to define its jurisdiction in relation to that of another tribunal, cannot allow its own competence to give way unless confronted with a clause which it considers sufficiently clear to prevent the possibility of a negative conflict of jurisdiction involving the danger of a denial of justice". A no. 9, 30.

[4]) This distinction is clearly brought out by the practice of the Supreme Court of the United States. Scott, Judicial Settlement 181; Mass. v. R.I., 12 Peters 755, 761 (1838): „The practice seems to be well settled, that in suits against a State, if the State shall refuse or neglect to appear, upon due service of process, no coercive measures will be taken to compel appearance; but the complainant, or plaintiff, will be allowed to proceed *ex parte*".

[5]) Habicht, Post-war Treaties for the Pacific Settlement of International Disputes, 1931, 1019: „Guaranties against Disturbance of Proceedings. A promise of the

exhortations by the League of Nations to its members to abstain from any action likely to hinder pacific settlement of a dispute; apparently such injunctions are not confined to conduct with respect to the particular controversy, but cover all disturbance of good relations between the parties whatever if likely to aggravate the dispute and impede its pacific settlement.

3. To regulate the status quo of the subject matter of the dispute *pendente lite* [1]). The law does not always speak with such a clear voice that *bona fide* differences of opinion are rendered impossible. Until it has been approved and established by a judicial decision having force of *res judicata*, no party is obliged to accept his opponent's view of the law as correct. Is he free to act upon his own view as correct, or must he act upon the assumption that his opponent may possibly be right? The former alternative applies in the absence of provisions authorizing interim protection; [2]) the latter if the law has introduced such remedies. A party then may require the immediate creation of a state of facts not inconsistent with his ultimate victory; and must therefore show the likelihood of such victory and the futility thereof as an effective means of protecting his interests without the help of interim measures.

It is thinkable that a tribunal may be authorized to decide a question, and to indicate measures of protection necessary to ensure execution of the decision, but not to regulate the interim

---

parties not to disturb the course of the procedure is generally expressed". The Council recommended that parties to the Albanian frontiers dispute „strictly.... abstain from any act calculated to interfere with the procedure in course" (s'abstenir rigoureusement de tout acte qui pourrait troubler la marche de la procédure), OJ (1921) 725; and on another occasion recognized that „when a question is submitted to the Council for its examination, the parties should take whatever steps are necessary and useful to prevent anything occurring on their respective territories which might prejudice the examination or settlement of the question by the Council" (compromettre l'examen ou le règlement de cette question par le Conseil). OJ (1928) 909—910.

[1]) „In diesen.... Fällen hat die einstweilige Verfügung nicht die Aufgabe, die spätere Prozessführung oder Exekution zu ermöglichen, sondern sie will den Berechtigten vor den Nachteilen schützen, die in der durch die Prozessführung bedingten Verspätung der Exekution liegen". Rintelen 15; cf. Wrede 354. („Den anscheinend Berechtigten vor den Nachteilen zu schützen, die in der durch die Prozessführung bedingten Verspätung der Rechtsverwirklichung" is the object of all interim protection. Impossibility of executing the judgment is only one species of prejudice; but stands out by reason of the fact that it not only injures the aggrieved party but offends against the dignity of the court and renders ridiculous the authors of the judicial proceeding. Hence an intention to provide protection against this species of prejudice is more readily to be implied from the very act of resorting to judicial procedure, whereas protection against all harm resulting from modification of the status quo must be more clearly sanctioned by the texts governing the tribunal's activity. Cf. Schüle 54. See pp. 181—182 *infra*.) [2]) Cf. Schüle 51.

situation. However as a rule the law is not satisfied with taking steps to bring about ultimately a situation of fact in conformity with the law, but desires to approximate that condition as soon as possible [1]). Even though no particular arrangement may be urgent, it may be highly important that some *régime* or other be established *pendente lite* in order to eliminate uncertainty and inconvenience. Thus if two parties each claim to in be possession of a disputed territory, and hence to be entitled to defend it, *vim vi repellere*; or prudent economy requires that someone administer the contested region in order to prevent disorder, it may be desirable to settle the situation for the time being by an explicit decision. Since neither party is entitled to assume that its own position is correct, and since the exigencies of nature require that some one have temporary possession, or the exigencies of civil polity require that the temporary possessor, though a trespasser, not be violently molested with a view to contesting his status, intervention by the court is necessary. [2])

So far as requisite in order to give effect to the principle that

[1]) Kohler 145: „Viele Verhältnisse verlangen nämlich eine kontinuirliche Regelung, weil es sich nicht um eine einmalige Leistung, sondern um einen dauernden Zustand handelt, welcher rechtlich geordnet werden soll. In solchem Falle ist es möglich, dass für die Zeit nach dem Urtheil die Vollstreckung völlig versichert ist und dass daher die Verhältnisse nach dem Urtheil keinen Grund zu einer Sicherungsmassregel abgeben würden, aber die Zeit vor dem Urtheil ist möglicher Weise eine ungeregelte, und diese ungeregelte Zeit kann möglicher Weise unleidliche Zustände mit sich führen. Das Recht ist nun aber nicht schon damit befriedigt, dass in künftiger Zeit der Zustand dem Recht entspricht, sondern es soll auch in der Zwischenzeit eine dem Rechte möglichst nahe kommende Gestaltung der Dinge erzielt werden. Auch hier hat die einstweilige Verfügung ihre Stelle; sie soll nicht für die Zukunft den Eintritt des postulierten Zustandes garantieren, sie soll dafür sorgen, dass auch einstweilen ein leidlicher *modus vivendi* geschaffen wird. Wie die einstweilige Verfügung die Herbeiführung eines rechtmässigen Zustandes überhaupt garantieren soll, so soll sie bewirken, dass dieser rechtmässige Zustand nicht nur für die spätere Zeit ermöglicht wird, sondern dass auch schon in der Zwischenzeit ein Zustand entsteht, welcher leidlich den Postulaten des Rechts entspricht".

[2]) German common law, and statute law prior to unification, as well as the ZPO now in force, distinguish between measures to ensure execution and those which establish an interim regulation of the situation. Wach in 15 Krit. Viert. (1873) 372; Goldschmidt, Zivilprozessrecht 319; Schmidt 583—4, 589. The purpose of the latter type of measure is different from that of the first. „Dieser Erfolg ist nicht Schutz, auch nicht nur provisorischer Schutz des einzelnen *Privatrechtsanspruches*, sondern Schutz der gesamten Rechtssphäre der um ein Rechtsverhältnis streitenden Parteien, mit *Beziehung* auf dieses Rechtsverhältnis". Thus in the claim of an illegitimate child for support, the injury due to lack of support does not arise out of the claim itself, but out of the child's entire financial position; if it is in no danger of destitution, but has other sources of income, the father is not compelled to pay during the suit (Roth 50); „so wird damit ein *ausserhalb* des Privatrechtsverhältnisses selbst liegender Nachteil abgewendet". If however there is danger that the father will squander his means, the case is different. „Denn dann handelt es sich um Sicherung der Vollstreckung des

the final judgment when rendered must protect the winning party to the same extent as if it were rendered at once [1]), measures governing the temporary status quo may also be authorized as falling within the following class.

4. To ensure execution of the final judgment. This is the most frequent and important group of interim measures. Administration of justice would be a mockery if there were no means of taking timely steps to prevent frustration of the procedure and to guarantee its efficacy.

§ 15. (*e*) Application in international law. (*Das völkerrechtliche Prozessrecht*).

According to our definition of remedial or procedural law [2]), we may accept the view of Grotius which regards war as a type of procedure for the enforcement of legal rights, a substitute for judicial procedure. [3]) Similarly diplomatic action may be considered as a legal remedy [4]).

Privatrechtsverhältnisses selbst". Güthe 383 likewise emphasizes that in the interim regulation of the status quo it is the relation of the controverted claim to the other interests of the party entitled which constitutes the basis of the remedy. It is the „Beziehung der Anspruchsubstanz zu den sonstigen Interessen des Berechtigten" which is „die Grundlage der einstweiligen Verfügung". Such a measure furnishes a remedy where execution, though feasible after the judgment, would not be an adequate remedy because it would come *too late*, and irreparable injury to the applicant would already have occurred. Ibid. 370.

[1]) See p. 20 *supra*.

[2]) See p. 17 *supra*.

[3]) De Jure Belli ac Pacis Libri Tres, II, i, 1: „Causa justa belli suscipiendi nulla esse potest nisi injuria". II, i, 2: „Ac plane quot actionum forensium sunt fontes, totidem sunt belli: nam ubi judicia deficiunt incipit bellum. Dantur autem actiones aut ob injuriam non factam, aut ob factam. Ob non factam, ut qua petitur cautio de non offendendo, item damni infecti, & interdicta alia ne vis fiat. Factam, aut ut reparetur, aut ut puniatur". So Thomasius, Dissertatio III, c. lviii: „Remedium istud violentum si adhibeatur iis, qui vinculo societatis civilis eodem non nectuntur, ***bellum*** dicitur; si iis, qui sub civile societate vivunt, *actio*". Kunz 45 speaks of „der Krieg als Rechtsverfahren"; and Triepel, Völkerrecht und Landesrecht, 1899, 368 regards independent states as „Subjekte des völkerrechtlichen Aktionenrechts", apparently having in mind diplomatic protests, reprisals, war, and other means of making resentment felt and coercing states into acting in conformity with law. But might not such means be used for coercing conduct *not* in accordance with rights under international law? Reprisals presuppose a violation of international law, but may not the violations against which reprisals are directed be imaginary? War is not so restricted. Hold-Ferneck, Lehrbuch 104; Dumbauld, Legal Limitations on Warmaking, 18 Geo. L. J. (1930) 83. Strisower, Der Krieg und die Völkerrechtsordnung, 1919, takes the view that under common law war is permitted only for enforcement of rights and self-defense. That such a rule of customary law might arise in future, T. R. White, Limitations upon the Initiation of War, Proc. Am. Soc. Int. Law (1925) 102; that perhaps such a rule exists at present, Scott, Proc. Am. Soc. Int. Law (1931) 213—5, cf. Mausbach, Naturrecht und Völkerrecht, 1918, 130, (the argument here being that war is permitted only when no other remedy is available, and that it can no longer truthfully be urged in good faith that a nation has no other remedy).

[4]) Capitant-Trotabas in 35 RGDIP (1928) 39: „la voie diplomatique, seule voie de droit commun en matière internationale".

A recent writer stresses procedural rules of international law even to the extent of swallowing up the whole of international law therein [1]. The contention is that diversity of national customs and civilization prevents any unanimity of opinion with regard to matters of substance, but that common consent can and does prescribe procedural forms which must be observed [2].

Nevertheless it will be proper to consider the concept of procedure in its essential characteristics and its relation to substantive law as being the same in international law as in internal law [3], and to think chiefly of judicial remedies as applied by international tribunals [4]. The administration of justice (*Rechtspflege*) differs from other manifestations of state activity both in national and international life [5].

It is unimportant for the legal nature of an organ for the administration of justice that its competence is based on the consent of states who are the suitors before it, as well as legislators of the law it applies. Important only is the existence of such competence. If an international tribunal is the same as a national court except that the basis of its jurisdiction is different, its function will not necessarily be different [6].

In fact we notice that international law, since it has concerned

---

[1]) Cf. the similar effect of Binder's view, although he professes to vindicate substantive law from the encroachments of procedure. Binder 7, 46—7, 395. See p. 13 *supra*.

[2]) Stowell, International Law, 1931, 34. Cf. Radbruch, Grundzüge der Rechtsphilosophie, 1914, 172, 178; and Sir John Fischer Williams, Treaty Revision and the Future of the League of Nations, 10 Int. Aff. (1931) 338.

[3]) J. B. Moore, Law and Organization, in International Law and Some Current Illusions, 1925, 302.

[4]) Of course the peculiar nature of international law must never be ignored. Nippold 149: „Nicht nur das materielle Völkerrecht, sondern auch das formelle, auch das Verfahren in völkerrechtlichen Streitigkeiten muss als Teil des Völkerrechts dessen Eigenart aufweisen". The same author regards „Die Fortbildung des völkerrechtlichen Verfahrens" as „die höchste Aufgabe des heutigen Völkerrechts". Ibid. 64.

[5]) Stein, Grundriss 71 defines *Rechtspflege* as „die Aufgabe, das objektive Recht durch autoritätiven Ausspruch über konkrete Lebensverhältnisse oder durch ihre unmittelbare Regelung zu verwirklichen. Es gehört zum Begriff der Rechtspflege, dass sie ohne Rücksicht auf andere staatliche Interessen ausgeübt wird, d.h. nur nach Massgabe des Gesetzes, das den Willen zu einer bestimmten Gestaltung zum Ausdruck bringt. Sie tritt im Gegensatz zur *Verwaltung*, das ist die handelnde Betätigung der Staatsgewalt im Dienste der unmittelbaren staatlichen Interessen und Kulturbedürfnisse (d.h. zur Erfüllung der Staatsaufgaben): denn für die Verwaltung ist das Gesetz nur Richtschnur und Machtbegrenzung". In the international field it may be contrasted with conciliatory negotiations for the settlement of political disputes, where a simple decision according to existing law would be unsatisfactory. Morgenthau 142; Strisower 63—41; Sir John Fischer Williams, Chapters, 43—48.

[6]) Morgenthau 18; J. B. Moore, International Adjudications, I, li, lxxiv, lvi.

itself with arbitration, has had to deal with three questions: erection of tribunals, establishment of the obligation to use them, formulation of their rules of procedure [1]). These are the same three features which we have seen to be the staple of French treatises on the law of procedure [2]).

Procedure has been indicated as a fruitful field for the application of comparative law in order to deduce the „general principles of law" which form a source of international law for the Permanent Court of International Justice [3]). Application of law by means of judicial tribunals, and the rules governing the operation of such tribunals, are indeed likely to be more universal legal phenomena than any other juridical rules or concepts.

In the light of the general notions thus far developed, we proceed to an investigation of interim protection in various legal systems and in international law.

---

[1]) Morgenthau 1.
[2]) P. 9 *supra*.
[3]) Härle in 11 Zt. f. öff. Rt. (1931) 223.

CHAPTER II

INTERIM PROTECTION IN INTERNAL LAW

§ 16. (a) *Roman and mediaeval law* [1]).

One finds frequent statements that interim remedies were unknown in Roman law; but these statements are coupled with the qualification that prompt protection of endangered interests in certain cases was not an idea foreign to the Roman legal system [2]). The truth seems to be that Roman law in this respect does not contain a broad general principle of procedural law that whenever rights are jeopardized *pendente lite* an interim remedy is available, as in German and Austrian law, but is casuistic, like modern French and Hungarian law, affording protection only in certain specified cases. Before examining these, it will be useful to glance at the Roman judicial system and observe the function of the praetor therein during the classical period.

The praetor was a magistrate having *imperium*. He did not as a rule himself decide cases, but made the parties enter into an agreement (*litis contestatio*) submitting their dispute to the decision of the *judex* in accordance with the *formula*. The Roman law suit was thus a form of compulsory arbitration in two stages: procedure *in jure* before the praetor, leading up to award or refusal of the formula; and procedure *apud judicem*, where the *judex* decided the issues submitted in accordance with the terms of reference contained in the formula [3]).

1) In an ancient Greek code, the law of Gortyn, it is provided: „Whoever is going to contend about a freeman or slave, shall not lead him away before trial". 2 LQR 142.

2) Gianzana 7; Wach 1 (cf. 81); Mittermaier 223; Kleinfeller 539; Kisch 76, 82; Juster 426.

3) Conwell-Evans 128 distinguishes two stages in procedure before the Council of the League of Nations. The first is a general discussion out of which the questions at issue to be decided are formulated. The Council need not necessarily decide them itself. Ibid. 132. Its task is to preserve peace; it may prevail on the parties to submit the dispute to arbitration. The jurisdiction of an international tribunal, like that of the Roman judex is founded on consent of the parties.

In granting and denying actions, the praetor was not bound by the strict civil law (*jus civile, jus Quiritium*). He acted *juris civilis adjuvandi aut supplendi aut corrigendi causa* in accordance with his own discretion and the principles enounced in the edict he issued at the beginning of his term of office. The rules on the basis of which he acted constituted equity law (*aequitas, jus praetorium, jus honorarium*).

Among the powers of the praetor was that of compelling parties to conclude agreements called *stipulationes praetoriae* [1]). Such an agreement might exact security for the execution of the judgment or against threatening damage.

Another power possessed by the praetor was that of granting *bonorum possessio* or *missio in bona*, whereby he ensured possession of property to a party not the legal owner [2]). This weapon was available against a party failing to comply with the praetor's order to give security.

§ 17. [3]) *Cautio judicatum solvi*, security for execution of the judgment, was naturally regarded as a sufficient interim remedy in proceedings where the issue of the suit would yield plaintiff only money damages [4]).

Since an obligation, as against a right of property, is a right *in personam* and not *in rem*, the plaintiff as a rule in actions *in personam* was required to look to the person of the defendant. Se-

---

Likewise in early English law the king's judges concerned themselves only with breaches of the king's peace. Disseisin was a breach of the peace (2 Pollock and Maitland 44); in trespass *vi et armis* the allegation of violence was necessary in order to confer jurisdiction on the royal courts, though as time went on it did not need to be proved, and the defendant was not allowed to rebut it. English law likewise insisted on the presence of the defendant and his voluntary participation in the procedure. Instead of giving judgment by default, the procedure of outlawry was used to coerce an absent defendant to appear. If upon appearance he refused to „put himself upon the country" and accept trial by jury, *peine forte et dure* was applied. So too the jury decided the issue after it had been settled by the pleadings of the parties and the rulings of the court. Just as the parties before the praetor might haggle over what formula was appropriate to the case, so in early times when pleadings were oral the judge would tell a party advancing an insufficient plea to say something else.

[1]) D. 46, 5. An agreement in which the party to be charged uses the word *spondeo* is called a *stipulatio*.

[2]) In this way, by means of *bonorum possessio edictalis*, the praetor built up the equitable law of inheritance. Bethmann-Hollweg 739.

[3]) As to the matters treated in this section, see Bethmann-Hollweg §§ 119, 120 and Keller 6ed 391—2.

[4]) Specific performance was unknown in Roman law until the despotism of the empire. Muther Sequestratio 300.

curity was exacted of the defendant only in exceptional cases, by reason of the nature of the action (*actio judicati* or *defensi* or *judicium de moribus mulieris*), or by reason of the defendant's being an untrustworthy person (*persona suspecta*). But in actions *in rem*, it seemed just that the party enjoying possession during trial, when it was doubtful whether it belonged to him, should give security that in case of defeat he would return the property or its value [1]).

If defendant failed to give security, possession was transferred to plaintiff, on his giving the required security. If plaintiff failed to do so, defendant remained in possession by virtue of the maxim, *potior est conditio possidentis*. But what if the defendant in this case were *persona suspecta?* Such a contingency resulted in sequestration, where the property was placed in the hands of a third person as custodian [2]). During the formulary period, the transaction of transfer to the stakeholder probably took place by the mutual act of both parties at the praetor's order [3]).

Operis novi nuntiatio enabled one claiming a right to prohibit new construction (*jus prohibendi*), by means of a formal declaration made on the premises, to suspend such construction until security for damage caused by it had been given. If the builder went on with the work, he was compelled to remove the new construction, irrespective of whether it was rightly or wrongly erected [4]). The purpose of the remedy is to afford protection against

---

[1]) Gaius IV, §§ 89, 102; Inst. IV, 11.

[2]) Muther Sequestratio 151, 154. D. II, 8, 7, 2: „Si satisdatum pro re mobili non sit et persona suspecta sit, ex qua satis desideratur, apud officium deponi debebit, si hoc judici sederit, donec vel satisdatio detur vel lis finem accipiant".

[3]) Muther Seq. 161. This was the case in early times, when the transaction, originally a form of escrow, created a pledge (*pignus*) for executing the non-binding arbitral award as to ownership of the property. Muther 80. In the *actio sacramenti*, during the period of the *legis actiones*, the parties were struggling for possession. The praetor first commanded „Mittite ambo hominem", and caused both parties to give up possession. He then restored interim possession to one of them, on giving security; if neither gave security, he restored it to both of them, charging them to choose a *sequester*. In the time of the formulary procedure, the parties cannot scramble for possession, but must appear in clear-cut party-rôles: one must be defendant in possession, the other out of possession but having the right to possession. At this period the rule *melior est conditio possidentis* is applied, as stated above. Muther 147, 149.

As to the *actio sacramenti* see Gaius IV, 16; Maine, Early History of Institutions, London 1875, 272—5; Maine, Ancient Law, 14 ed. London 1875, 375—8; 3 Street, Legal Liability 14—5; and J. B. Scott, International Justice, 15 Geo. L.J. 37, where it is suggested that the Roman *album librum judicum*, containing a list of those who acted as arbitrators, is paralleled by the panel of the permanent Court of Arbitration at the Hague.

[4]) D. 39, 1.

anticipated damage from the new construction. It is in effect a form of security against *damnum infectum.*

The classification of cases falling under this topic might well be applied to interim protection in general. Action is taken *aut juris nostri conservandi, aut damnum depellendi, aut publici juris tuendi causa* [1]).

Cautio damni infecti was security against anticipated damage from the ruinous state of old buildings [2]).

The party entitled to security first demands it extrajudicially. If refused, he brings his demand before the prator (*postulat*), who passes upon it with summary procedure and orders that security be given. If the delinquent party still refuses, *missio in bona* is granted [3]).

In cases of *damnum infectum,* it is *missio in possessionem rei singularis* which is given, not of an entire estate. Legal possession is not transferred from the owner; the party entitled to security has only custody for safeguarding his interests, and possesses jointly with the owner. After hearing, his interest may become bonitarian ownership [4]).

Such joint possession of the whole property is given collectively to the creditors of an absent debtor in *missio rei servandae causa.* If the absence is unjustified, if the debtor is hiding in fraud of creditors, a *magister* is appointed and the property is sold [5]). If the absence is in the public interest, the measure is purely conservatory and a curator has charge of the property [6]).

Not dissimilar is *missio legatorum servandorum causa* for the protection of legatees against an heir who is insane or has an interval within which to deliberate whether or not to accept the inheritance [7]).

Another series of *missiones* are *hereditatis tuendae causa,* to secure the subsistence of an heir whose status as heir is contested,

---

[1]) D. 39, 1, 1, 16—17, & 19—20. See § 14 *supra.*

[2]) D. 39, 2, 4, 1. [3]) Bethmann-Hollweg 734.

[4]) Keller 394; D. 39, 2, 4, 4; D. 39, 2, 5, pr.; D. 42, 4, 12: „Cum legatorum vel fideicommissi servandi causa, vel quia damni infecti nobis non caveatur, bona possidere praetor permittit, vel ventris nomine, in possessionem nos mittit, non possidemus, sed magis custodiam rerum et observationem nobis concedit".

[5]) D. 42, 4, 7.

[6]) D. 42, 4, 6; D. 42, 5, 35; Tambour I, 186; D. 4, 6,21,2.

[7]) D. 36, 3, 1, 2; D. 27, 10, 3.

and final determination of the question is postponed for one reason or another. These cases may be: (1) *Ventris nomine,* where a pregnant woman declares that the fruit of her body will be an heir (*suus heres*) [1]. (2) *Ex Carboniano edicto,* where a minor's status as heir is contested and determination of the dispute is postponed in his interest to his majority [2]. (3) *Furiosi nomine,* where an heir is insane and there must be a curator until his death or a lucid moment when he may accept or refuse the inheritance [3]. (4) *Ex edicto divi Hadriani,* where an heir instituted in a *prima facie* valid testament is given possession pending decision of the controversy [4]. In the last named case, as well as where *translatio possessionis* occurs in favor of the adversary of an *indefensus, missio* serves to transfer legal possession and determine the party-rôles as plaintiff and defendant [5].

§ 18. In post-classical Roman law other remedies than *missio in bona* were developed [6]. In place of sequestration as a voluntary pledge to secure a voluntarily assumed obligation to obey the decision, the Theodosian code attained what Muther calls *Arrest* [7], where the judge by downright order created that obligation and ordered the object to be placed in the custody of an official [8].

So too, personal arrest upon failure to give security in cases where it was required existed under Justinian law. Sequestration was less harsh, and the order was couched in the alternative, for security or real or personal arrest. It was thus possible for the proceedings to begin with arrest [9].

But under Justinian law, the development of new forms of enforcement was paralleled by disappearance of the duty to give security for executing the judgment. *Cautio judicatum solvi* was replaced by *cautio judicio sisti* or *cautio pro sua persona quod in*

[1]) D. 37, 9, 1, 2.

[2]) D. 37, 10, 1, pr.; C. 6, 17.

[3]) D. 37, 3.

[4]) C. 6, 33.

[5]) Bethmann-Hollweg 739.

[6]) Imperial magistrates liked to make orders *pro sua potestate*; thus instead of *missio in bona* against an *indefensus, missio in possessionem rei petitae* was given. Bethmann-Hollweg 571; D. 42, 4, 7, 17—19.

[7]) Muther Seq. 304.

[8]) Muther Seq. 303. This explains why the term *apud officium* replaces *apud sequestrem* in the Justinian D. 2, 8, 7, 2 in note 2, p. 35 *supra*. The latter expression is reserved for cases of *sequestratio voluntaria* and does not apply to cases of *sequestratio necessaria*. Muther Seq. 359.

[9]) Muther Seq. 347—8, 360.

judicio permaneat usque ad terminum litis. The defendant was obliged to give security only for his appearance and participation in the case throughout the entire proceedings [1]).

It remained therefore for German common law, the modified Roman law system prevailing after the reception, to utilize the new modes of enforcement in support of an obligation to give security for execution of the judgment. The *usus modernus* applied both types of *cautio* in both real and personal actions. But exceptional conditions were required. *Cautio judicatum solvi* was required of a defendant suspected of inability to fulfil the judgment (*alienationis aut dilapidationis suspectus*; sometimes also *fugae suspectus*); *cautio judicio sisti* was required of non-resident or fugitive defendants (*fugae suspectus, recessurus*). Failure to furnish such security led to arrest [2]).

Wach, in his notable study portraying the development of the *Arrestprozess*, finds that the institute in question originated in the extra-judicial seizures (*pignoratio*) of Lombard law. At first a pure measure of self-help, it was subsequently subjected to judicial restraint after the fact by the requirement that it be justified before the judicial authority. The final stage was reached when previous judicial permission was required in order to execute a seizure. Thus from being an extra-judicial anticipated execution of the principal claim, it became a summary procedure with a view to security [3]).

This development took place only in Italy. Germanic arrest remained a pure and simple measure of execution until the reception of Roman law in Germany [4]). Thereafter the German *Arrestprozess* still differed from the Italian in that the principal claim as well as the justification of the arrest were considered at

---

[1]) Inst. IV, 11; Muther Seq. 315, 318.

[2]) Wetzell 196—7, 201.

[3]) Wach 37: „Wollte man daher die Eigenmacht soweit möglich verbannen, so musste man noch einen Schritt weiter gehen und von vornherein die Zulässigkeit der Pfändung der richterlichen Cognition unterwerfen. Das geschah, und zwar, wie es scheint, anfangs in der Form, dass der Gläubiger die Pfändung vornahm, aber alsbald deren Rechtmässigkeit vor der Obrigkeit nachweisen musste. Später lag die Beschlagnahme ganz in der Hand des Richters, von dem sie zu erbitten und vor dem sie zu rechtfertigen war. Sie selbst bildete jetzt eine auf einseitiges Gehör erlassene provisorische Dispositionsentziehung als Beginn eines prozessualischen Verfahrens. So hatte man *lediglich durch die Anticipation der Execution* eine ausserordentliche Procedurform gewonnen, welche auf den Namen eines Arrestprozesses wohl Anspruch machen konnte".

[4]) Kisch 45.

the hearing which followed the seizure; in Italian practice that hearing was confined entirely *ad dicendum contra arrestum* [1]).

Fugitive debtors and foreigners were subject to arrest [2]). Kisch maintained that a native who took to flight was treated as a foreigner [3]). For Planitz, on the other hand, fugitive-arrest was the fundamental form. He contended that extra-judicial seizure (*Pfandnahme*) could not be the source of *Arrest*, as Wach held, because the former applied only to chattels, while arrest was applicable to realty as well. Planitz asserted that arrest, both criminal and civil, was the reaction of the law against a wrong, was the consequence of the partial outlawry (*Friedlosigkeit*) of a debtor whose intent not to pay was considered equivalent to theft. Against a native, intention not to pay must be manifested by flight to escape the obligation; in the case of a foreigner, a demand and refusal sufficed [4]). Another writer concludes that both types of arrest have their root in distrust of foreign courts [5]).

In addition to the *Arrestprozess* [6]) whose function was to ensure

---

[1]) Wach 167; Planitz, Grundlagen 92.

[2]) There was also arrest by way of reprisals against all fellow-citizens of the debtor. This was done away with by treaties between different cities. Likewise arrest *ex pacto contrahentium* as a consensual pledge was known. Wach 48. These were not interim measures of security, and do not interest us.

[3]) Kisch 31. [4]) Planitz, 34 : 135; Grundlagen 12, 14, and elsewhere.

[5]) Alfred Schultze, review of Kisch in 37 Zt. Sav. Stift. (Germ.) (1916) 591—5: „In beiden Arrestfällen wirkt die Scheu vor der fremden Gerichtsbarkeit. Der Bürger, der in den fremden Gerichtsbezirk entweicht, vergeht sich gegen den Gläubiger; der Arrest gegen ihn ist deliktsrechtlicher Herkunft. Der Gast, der in der Stadt weilt, gehört von Rechts wegen unter die fremde Gerichtsbarkeit; der Arrest gegen ihn, unter Zurückdrängen des Satzes „actor forum rei sequitur" ist gästerechtlicher Herkunft". The sources show at least that Planitz is wrong, since foreign arrest is as early as fugitive arrest, though Kisch's converse proposition is not proved. Planitz's explanation that the foreigner is arrested for robbery is an ingenious *tour de force* („gesucht und künstlich").

[6]) Arrest was regarded as anomalous because the proceedings commenced with acts of execution, which ought to be the final step. It was permitted only when proper grounds (*causa arresti*) were present. *Sequestratio est odiosa et regulariter est prohibita.* Cynus, Super Dig. vet. 11, Super Codice 137; Durantis, Speculum judicialis, tertia pars, libri quarti particula secunda, rub. de sequestratione possessionum et fructuum; Kisch 92—3; C. IV, 4: „Quotiens ex quolibet contractu pecunia postulatur, sequestrationis necessitas conquiescat. Oportet suum debitorem primo convinci et sic ad solutionem pulsari. Quam rem non tantum juris ratio, sed et ipsa aequitas persuadet, ut probationes secum adferat debitoremque convincat pecuniam petiturus". Peckius, Tractatus de jure sistendi, c. 2, 4: „Creditorem ab executione, cuius species est arrestatione, inverso juris ordine non posse"; 2, 7: „Omnis recessus a jure communi est odiosus, et odiosa omnia sunt stricti juris"; 2,1: „Sic cum aequitas postulat, lex concedit, debitorem fugitivum, aut de fuga suspectum, capi et detineri". Merula, Manier van Procederen, 1741, 207: „Want *Arrest* is eene specie van Executie, van de welke te beginnen de Rechten niet toe laten".

Petrus de Ferrarriis, 1: „Frequens est hic tractatus saximentorum maxime in Monexecution of the judgment, mediaeval Roman law established provisions for interim regulation of the status quo, especially in respect to possession, in accordance with the principles of *vitium litigiosi* and *ut lite pendente nil innovetur* [1]. Prevention of armed combat by parties struggling for possession was a factor making for exercise of such control by the court [2]. A summary examination by the court (*possessorium summarissimum*) determined which party was in actual possession and entitled to the legal advantages which flowed therefrom [3].

§ 19. Canon law was influential in the development of mediaeval civil law. The *corpus juris canonici* was built up of the *Decretum* of Gratian dating from the middle of the twelfth century; the *Decretales* collected by order of Gregory IX and published in 1234; the *Clementinas* published in 1313, and the *Extravagantes*, or scattered texts.

In the *Decretum* [4] the doctrine of *vitium litigiosi* is found. The decretals in part II contain several titles of interest for our subject. Title XIII, *de restitutione spoliatorum*, deals with the principles governing the restoration of the status quo, violently disturbed, before litigation of issues on their merits. The principle *spoliatus ante omnia restituendus* is a rule of procedure, not of substantive law [5], to the effect that before any complaint could be heard against a clerk despoiled of his benefice, the party dispossessing him must first restore what had been taken away [6].

teferrato & quibusdam aliis partibus ubi jus et justitia ministrantur per boves et ignorantes qui multum sunt faciles concedere talia saximenta. Est igitur sciendum quod regulariter ista saximenta ante latam sententiam sunt omni jure tam civile quam canonico prohibita.... maxime lite pendente.... & est ratio: quod nemini auferenda est commoditas possessionis: que in fructuum perceptione consistit ante latam sententiam.... Sic ergo stat regula fallit in x casibus". The number of cases where the remedy is permissible is stated variously by different authors as 3, 5, 10, 15, 25 and 47. Cludius 110.

1) C. 8, 36; C. 2, 49. Wach 108.

2) Wetzell 202—4; Durantis, speculum, loc. cit: „ne partes veneant ad rixas et ad arma". Cludius 116: „ne litigatores a verbis ad verbera ac arma descendant".

3) Bethmann-Hollweg 377 considers this procedure less elegant than that where the praetor awarded possession to whichever party was the highest bidder. In the medieval procedure, the court must decide at once the same question which forms the object of the entire proceedings, but on less thorough examination and incomplete proof.

4) Secunda pars, causa XI, quaestio i, cap. 50.

5) Kohler, Gesammelte Beiträge zum Civilprocess, 1894, 27; Windscheid, Lehrbuch des Pandektenrechts, 9ed. 1906, I, 833.

6) II, xiii, 7: „Spoliatus etiam a judice, juris ordine praetermissa, ante omnia restituatur.. Mandamus.. si ita est.. praedicto clerico praefatam ecclesiam cum re-

Similarly spouses are entitled to resumption of conjugal cohabitation pending decision whether or not their marriage is valid. If, however, a wife would be endangered by her husband's cruelty, she will not be returned to him, but placed in the custody of a respectable and trustworthy woman pending decision of the case. Likewise, if a marriage is being contested on the ground of consanguinity within the prohibited degrees, a woman offering summary proof of the relationship and taking oath that her scruples are conscientious and not malicious, will be relieved of her obligation *quoad torum* [1]).

Title XVI, *ut lite pendente nihil innovetur*, presents an interesting case [2]). The Archbishop of Canterbury had obtained a papal privilege confirming all the rights exercised by his prececessors. Apparently in the past he had enjoyed the right of having a cross carried in front of him throughout all England, for he was permitted to continue that practice pending decision of the controversy in which his claim to such honors within the jurisdiction of the Archbishop of York had been challenged. There had been a previous order prohibiting his having a cross carried in front of him within the territory of the Archibishop of York *pendente lite*.

Title XV, *de eo qui mittitur in possessionem causa rei servandae* and Title XVII, *de sequestratione possessionum et fructuum*, are directly reminiscent of the secular Roman law which we have discussed above.

The *corpus juris canonici* as revised in 1917 contains provisions for sequestration and inhibition of exercise of rights [3]), as well as

---

ditibus inde perceptis restituas, et in pace eam possidere permittas. Restitutione autem facta, si quid adversus eum super praescriptam ecclesiam proponere volueris, coram.. delegato a nobis.. ordine judiciario poteris experiri". This chapter, as well as others in the titles under consideration, dates from Alexander III (1159—1181).

[1]) II, xiii, 8, 13. Cf. Gaill, cap. 12: „..ubi concludunt, quod scandali evitandi gratia, spoliatus ante omnia restituendus non sit.... Similiter si agatur de irreparabili praejudicio: quo casu paratae probationes dominii ad probandum admittuntur, & restitutionem interim impediunt. Exemplum adducunt de castro munitissimo, cuius executio difficilis foret, & multis scandalis, & homicidiis occasionem praeberet.. Ubi uxor, impedimentum consanguinitatis allegans, & paratam probationem offerens, marito non est ante omnia restituenda, ne ob peccati periculum damnum irreparabile sequatur".

[2]) Cap. 1.

[3]) Can. 1672: „§ 1. Qui ostenderit super aliqua re ab alio detentata jus se habere sibique damnum imminere nisi res ipsa custodienda tradatur, jus habet obtinendi a judice ejusdem rei sequestrationem. § 2. In similibus rerum adjunctis obtinere potest

for actions *ex novi operis* [1]) *nuntiatione et damno infecto* [2]) and for the *exceptio spolii* [3]). The maxim *ut lite pendente nihil innovatur* still prevails [4]).

§ 20. (*b*) *Modern legislations.*

1. German law [5]).

The principal provisions [6]) of German law with respect to interim remedies [7]) are placed, with questionable propriety, in book 8 [8]) of the code of civil procedure, as section 5, entitled „*Arrest und einstweilige Verfügung*" [9]). The law is unfortunate in its terminology, uniting the unlike and separating the similar [10]).

Four different types of remedy are to be distinguished [11]):

(1) *Arrest*, provided in § 916 for securing the execution (*Siche-*

---

ut juris exercitium alicui inhibeatur. § 3. Sequestratio rei et inhibitio juris a judice decerni potest ex officio, instante praesertim promotore justitiae aut defensore vinculi, quotiens bonum publicum id postulare videatur." Can. 1673: „§ 1. Ad crediti quoque securitatem sequestratio rei admittitur, dummodo de creditoris jure liquido constet et servata norma de qua in can. 1923, § 1. § 2. Sequestratio extenditur etiam ad res debitoris quae depositi causa aut quolibet alio titulo apud alias personas reperiantur." Can. 1674: „Sequestratio rei et suspensio exercitii juris decerni nullatenus possunt, si damnum quod timetur possit aliter reparari et idonea cautio de eo reparando offeratur."

[1]) Can. 1676. [2]) Can. 1678. [3]) Can. 1698—9. [4]) Can. 1725 (5).

[5]) For the practice of the German Staatsgerichtshof see §§ 39—42 *infra*.

[6]) Besides these there are other cases governed by specific texts, such as ZPO § 627 as to cases of marital litigation; § 672, depriving a person of civil capacity by reason of inability to handle his own affairs; BGB § 885, 889, entry in land register; § 1716, illegitimate child; § 489, dispute over defective animals; Unl Wettb G of 7 June 1909 § 25, Kunst Urh G of 9 January 1907 § 45, Litt Urh G of 22 May 1910, as to patent and copyright; Bauforderungen G of 1 June 1909 § 23. For a list of these cases see Stern 12—13; Goldschmidt, Zivilprozessrecht 327. In general *Gefährdung* is presumed from the nature of the claim, and jeopardy need not be proved.

[7]) ZPO §§ 916—945. The most important articles follow:

§ 916: Der Arrest findet zur Sicherung der Zwangsvollstreckung in das bewegliche oder unbewegliche Vermögen wegen einer Geldforderung oder wegen eines Anspruches statt, welcher in eine Geldforderung übergehen kann....

§ 935. Einstweilige Verfügungen in Beziehung auf den Streitgegenstand sind zulässig, wenn zu besorgen ist, dass durch eine Veränderung des bestehenden Zustandes die Verwirklichung des Rechtes einer Partei vereitelt oder wesentlich erschwert werden könnte.

§ 940. Einstweilige Verfügungen sind auch zum Zwecke der Regelung eines einstweiligen Zustandes in bezug auf ein streitiges Rechtsverhältnis zulässig, sofern diese Regelung, insbesondere bei dauernden Rechtsverhältnissen zur Abwendung wesentlicher Nachteile oder zur Verhinderung drohender Gewalt oder aus anderen Gründen nötig erscheint.

[8]) Dealing with forcible execution (*Zwangsvollstreckung*).

[9]) The draft of the ministry of justice bore the rubric „Von der Sicherung der Vollstreckung". Stern 8.

[10]) Schmidt 583—4; Wach in 15 Krit. Viert. 372 ff.

[11]) Cf. Goldschmidt, Zivilprozessrecht 319.

rung der Zwangsvollstreckung) of a money claim, or a claim that may be transformed into a money claim [1]).

(2) *Einstweilige Verfügung* under § 935, with respect to the subject matter of the litigation, when it is to be feared that by change in the existing situation the realization of the right of a party will be rendered impossible or essentially more difficult.

(3) *Einstweilige Verfügung* under § 940, to regulate a situation for the time being with respect to a controverted legal relation, insofar as such regulation, especially in case of continuing relationships, seems necessary for warding off substantial injury or impending violence.

(4) Practice under § 940, which goes so far as to amount to virtual satisfaction of the litigated claim, and hence constitutes a new type of summary procedure. This occurs in case of claims for alimentation or support [2]).

The transition between (3) and (4) is seen in cases of controverted legal relationship with periodically recurring duty to pay, such as that of husband and wife. When the payee is in need and the provisional payment serves to ward off distress and injury, the situation seems like (3), since it regulates the controverted relationship temporarily. Yet so far as those instalments go, it is really satisfaction [3]). When the duty is one calling for a single performance (*einmalige Leistung*), the *einstweilige Verfügung* seems plainly to be a summary measure of satisfaction rather than of security [4]).

Note that (1) and (2) protect from the same peril (danger that judgment may not be executed) a different sort of claim, *Arrest*

[1]) Real arrest, or attachment of property, takes place when it is to be feared that otherwise execution of the judgment would be made impossible or essentially more difficult. § 917. Personal arrest is only permissible when necessary to ensure jeopardized execution on property. § 918. It may consist in restriction of personal liberty (such as depriving of passport, etc.) § 933.

[2]) Goldschmidt, Zivilprozessrecht 319, 328; Kleinfeller 946; Neuner in 1 Judicium (1929) 256—260.

[3]) Roth 48.

[4]) *Einstweilige Verfügung* was denied where it would amount to anticipated execution for an instalment (*Abschlagzahlung*). RGZ 15 : 377, § 100, 13 November 1885, distinguishing RGZ 9 : 334, § 97, 30 March 1883, which held only that *einstweilige Verfügung* might involve *Pfändung* and utilize all the resources of execution procedure (see p. 20—21 *supra*); and in fact by way of dictum questioned whether the employer was bound to support plaintiff. RGZ 4 : 400, § 97, 20 May 1881, furnishes a typical case of (3), where a railroad company was forbidden to decide the controversy in its own favor and build a line over plaintiff's land. Danger of resort to force in defense of disputed possession calls for interim regulation. Cf. p. 40 *supra*.

being for money claim, *einstweilige Verfügung* for specific performance, (*Individualleistung*); while (2) and (3) protect the same sort of claim from a different sort of peril [1]).

At common law, and in procedural legislation prior to the ZPO, a different terminology was used. Protection against impossibility of executing the judgment, whether for money claim or otherwise, was called *Arrest.* At the same time there were *Provisorien,* or *einstweilige Verfügungen* to preserve the status quo and public security [2]). As we shall see later, in Austrian law the term *einstweilige Verfügung* covers all these measures, though a distinction between money claims and others is made.

(3) comes from the *possessorium summarissimum* mentioned above [3]), while (4) is derived from the *Mandatsverfahren,* or procedure beginning with an order to the defendant, which gave rise to various modes of summary procedure [4]).

§ 21. The applicant must make a showing that his claim and the ground of jeopardy are probable [5]). In case those requirements are not fulfilled, the order can nevertheless be made if applicant gives security. Even if they are demonstrated, the court may require security [6]).

If the court acts without previous oral hearing of the defendant, its decision is rendered in the form of an order (*Beschluss*) [7]) against which the defendant may make opposition (*Widerspruch*) [8]). After opposition, as in case of previous hearing [9]), the decision is by final judgment (*Endurteil*), in which the court may confirm, modify, or revoke its previous order in whole or part, or make such decision depend on security being given [10]).

Revocation may be requested by reason of changed circumstances, or tender of security [11]). Since, unlike *Arrest, einstweilige Verfügung* is designed to protect specific performance rather than a claim for money, it can be revoked upon tender of security only under exceptional circumstances [12]).

[1]) Oertmann 307, and note 2 *infra.*

[2]) Schmidt 589; Wach in 15 Krit. Viert. 372 ff.; Hannover Processordnung of 1 May 1848, §§ 186—194, Arrestprocess; §§ 205—8, einstweilige Verfügung; § 209, Sequestration. [3]) P. 40 *supra.*

[4]) Goldschmidt, Zivilprozessrecht 319; Stern 10; Seuffert 644; Schmidt 583—4.

[5]) „Der Anspruch und der Arrestgrund sind glaubhaft zu machen". § 920.

[6]) § 921. [7]) § 922.

[8]) Opposition does not suspend execution of the order. § 924.

[9]) § 922. [10]) § 925. [11]) § 927. [12]) § 939.

Except where otherwise provided, the procedure for *Arrest* and *einstweilige Verfügung* is the same [1]). For *Arrest* both the court having jurisdiction of the principal proceeding and that of the situs of the property to be affected by the order are competent [2]); for *einstweilige Verfügung* the latter court has jurisdiction only in cases of emergency [3]). Likewise only in urgent cases may *einstweilige Verfügung* be granted without previous oral hearing [4]). Both *Arrest* and *einstweilige Verfügung* may be ordered by the president of the tribunal in urgent cases [5]).

Arrest creates a lien or right of priority (*Pfandrecht*) [6]). *Einstweilige Verfügung* may consist in any measures appropriate for attaining its purpose, prescribed by the court in its discretion. Such measures may include sequestration, an injunction ordering or forbidding action, especially alienation or encumbrance of real estate [7]).

If the order granting *Arrest* or *einstweilige Verfügung* was unjustified *ab initio*, or is revoked for want of timely prosecution of proceedings, within the period fixed by the court for institution of the principal complaint or for justification of an *einstweilige Verfügung* obtained without hearing, the applicant must make good the damage resulting from execution of the measure, or from the fact that security was given to prevent execution or to obtain revocation of the measure [8]).

§ 22. 2. Austrian law [9]).

Einstweilige Verfügung in Austrian law is treated in the law of 27 May 1896 on procedure with a view to execution and security, part 2, section 2, §§ 378—402 [10]). Although the term *Arrest*

1) § 936. 2) § 919. 3) § 942. 4) § 937.
5) § 944. 6) § 930. 7) § 938. 8) § 945.

9) Austrian law applies in various parts of the succession states arising from the disintegration of the Austro-Hungarian dual monarchy. A unified code of civil procedure is in preparation in Czechoslovakia, which will not modify the provisions of interest here.

10) In addition to the general principles there contained there are a number of specific provisions in other laws. For an account of 16 such instances, see 2 Neumann 1200—1226. See also Krainz-Pfaff-Ehrenzweig, System des österreichischen allgemeinen Privatrechts, 1925, §§ 154, 182 III, 201 II, 227 III, 323 III, 432, 463.

Most important of these are ABGB §§ 340—343, ZPO § 456, 458, with respect to building controversies (*Baustreitigkeiten*); ABGB 347 dealing with provisional determination of possession in *Besitzklagen*; ABGB § 932(*a*) disputes over defective animals; law of 3 April 1906, § 21, forbidding payment of disputed check; law of 26 September 1923 on unfair competition, § 24; Kais V 12 Oct. 1914, § 9 interruption of a civil proceeding pending criminal proceedings for usury; ABGB § 1101, landlord may retain objects on is not used as in German law, distinction is nevertheless made between *einstweilige Verfügungen* for securing money claims, and those for securing other claims [1].

1. For securing money claims. Except when execution [2] or other security [3] is available, *einstweilige Verfügung* may be ordered when it is probable that otherwise the opponent of the endangered party will prevent or substantially hinder collection of the amount by acts withdrawing his property from satisfaction of the claim, or when the judgment would have to be executed abroad [4].

Measures permissible include safe-keeping and administration of tangible movables, prohibition of their alienation or encumbrance, and garnishment [5]. No other measures are permissible in case of a money claim [6].

2. For securing other claims. *Einstweilige Verfügung* is available when it is to be feared that otherwise the judicial pursuit or realization of the claim in question would be rendered nugatory or substantially more difficult, especially by change of the existing situation (necessity of executing the judgment abroad being regarded as such a difficulty), or when such measures seem necessary for warding off impending violence or the prevention of impending irreparable damage [7].

---

which he has a lien when it is sought to remove them, and must at once have them inventoried officially; Grundbuchsgesetz of 25 July 1871, § 61 notation of *lis pendens* in the land registry; Anfechtungsordnung § 20, Konkursordnung § 43, in Kais V. 10 December 1914, fraud of creditors and bankruptcy; Urheberrechts G 31 August 1920, § 52, Patent G, BGBl 1925, no. 366, § 105, attachment of objects to prevent future infringement of patent or copyright and preserve evidence; ABGB § 107, separation, § 117 custody of children; § 168, support of illegitimate child for first three months.

[1]) This was not so in the original Klein draft. 19 ZZP 245; Neumann-Ettenreich 25. It was introduced for reasons of anti-capitalistic social policy, discriminating against „mere money claims". Münz 342.

[2]) § 379 (1). [3]) Rintelen 54.

[4]) „wenn wahrscheinlich ist, dass ohne sie der Gegner der gefährdeten Partei durch Beschädigen, Zerstören, Verheimlichen oder Verbringen von Vermögensstücken, durch Veräusserung oder andere Verfügungen über Gegenstände seines Vermögens, insbesondere durch darüber mit dritten Personen getroffene Vereinbarungen die Hereinbringung der Geldforderung vereiteln oder erheblich erschweren würde". § 379 (2).

[5]) § 379 (3).

[6]) Personal arrest is thus excluded. Rintelen 275. Measures relating to real estate are expressly excluded. § 379 (4); 2 Neumann 1179.

[7]) „Zur Sicherung anderer Ansprüche können einstweilige Verfügungen getroffen werden: 1. wenn zu besorgen ist, dass sonst die gerichtliche Verfolgung oder Verwirklichung des fraglichen Anspruches, insbesondere durch eine Veränderung des bestehenden Zustandes, vereitelt oder erheblich erschwert werden würde; als solche Erschwerung ist es anzusehen, wenn das Urteil im Auslande vollstreckt werden müsste; 2. wenn derartige Verfügungen zur Verhütung drohender Gewalt oder zur Abwendung eines drohendeen unwiderbringlichen Schadens nötig erscheinen". § 381.

Examples of appropriate measures for securing non-money claims are safekeeping or administration of movables in the possession of opponent of the endangered party, or of immovables or incorporeal rights, forming the subject matter of litigation; orders or prohibitions directed to the opponent of the threatened party designed to maintain the condition of such property or the existing status quo; prohibition of alienation or encumbrance of real estate in litigation; prohibition directed to third parties under obligation to opponent of endangered party with respect to the matter in litigation; authorization that the threatened party retain possession of property of opponent held by him until decision; order to husband to support his wife and children in his own or a separate dwelling [1]).

Personal arrest consists in confinement in a public place of detention or in a private dwelling [2]). It is permissible only when there is danger that realization of the right of the threatened party will be prevented by the flight of his opponent [3]). The classical case for personal arrest is to ensure communication of a trade secret. Both claim and danger (*Anspruch* and *Arrestgrund*) must be shown, as the prejudice arising from personal arrest cannot be made good in money damages [4]). But the necessary requirements may be present *before* the beginning of proceedings [5]).

Before the institution of proceedings, as well as during pendency of litigious or execution procedure, the court, on request, may order *einstweilige Verfügungen*. That the applicant's claim is conditional or not yet due does not preclude such measures [6]).

The competent court is that in which the principal proceeding is pending; if proceedings have not yet been begun, the court having jurisdiction of actions against the opponent of the endangered party; if no such forum exists in Austria, then the court

---

1) § 382.

2) It can not consist in other restrictions of personal liberty. Muck 30.

3) „dass durch seine Flucht die Verwirklichung des Rechtes der gefährdeten Partei vereitelt würde". § 386. Cf. the broader terms of § 381 (1). It is *execution* which must be endangered, and the degree of peril must amount to danger that that execution will be *impossible*. Mere difficulty, especially difficulty in conduct of the case (*Erschwerung der Prozessführung*) is not enough. That personal arrest is prohibited in cases involving money claims has already been noted. See note 6, p. 46 *supra*.

4) § 390 (1). Muck 15; 2 Neumann 1227.

5) 2 Neumann 1228.

6) § 378. In case proceedings are not pending, they must be begun before a date set by the court. § 391 (2).

within whose territory the interim measures are to be executed [1]. If the competent court is collegiate, its president may take the decision in especially urgent cases [2].

The application must indicate the nature and duration of the measures desired, and set forth the details of the claim to be secured [3]. In case the claim [4] is insufficiently substantiated, the court may nevertheless order *einstweilige Verfügung* if the damage resulting therefrom can be made good by money damages, and applicant furnishes security. The court may require security even if applicant's allegations are sufficiently substantiated. When security is required, it must be deposited with the court before execution of the measure may begin [5].

The court has discretion as to whether to require a hearing before granting *einstweilige Verfügung* [6]. Opposition (*Widerspruch*) may be made by a party not heard before the order. Such opposition does not suspend execution [7]. The court may make confirmation, modification or revocation of the ordered measures dependent on giving security [8]. Even after confirmation, the court may subsequently, on request, order restriction or revocation of the *einstweilige Verfügung* if the claim which it was granted to secure ceases to exist, or circumstances change, or sufficient security is given, or execution of the measure has been carried out in wider scope than necessary for security [9].

The court's decision takes the form of an order (*Beschluss*) both in the original proceeding (*Anordnung*) [10], and in that following oral hearing in case of opposition (*Widerspruch*) [11], or request for revocation (*Antrag auf Aufhebung*) [12].

If applicant loses in the main action, or fails to bring it in due time, or if the application is otherwise shown to be unjustified, his opponent must be compensated for material damage resulting from the *einstweilige Verfügung*. The amount of such damage is determined by order of the court in the same proceeding. If the *einstweilige Verfügung* is obviously obtained maliciously, the court on request imposes a punishment therefor (*Mutwillensstrafe*) in addition to damages [13].

---

1) § 387. 2) § 388. 3) § 389.
4) Security is not a substitute for substantiation of the *causa arresti*. Rintelen 82.
5) § 390. 6) Rintelen 140. 7) § 397.
8) § 398 (2). 9) § 399 (1). 10) § 391 (1).
11) § 398 (1). 12) § 399 (2). 13) § 394.

More than one measure may be ordered to secure the same claim, if necessary. Among measures equally applicable in a given case, that is to be preferred which is most effective to prevent the impending jeopardy; among those equally effective, that which least injures the opponent of the threatened party [1]). Consequently, and in view of the fact that the enumeration of measures in § 382, unlike that in § 379 (3), is not exhaustive, it would seem that in case of a non-money claim it would be possible to secure at the same time an *einstweilige Verfügung* under § 379 for securing damages in the alternative, as well as under § 382 for securing the original claim. A request invoking § 379 would seem to be sufficient evidence that an eventual money claim is involved to justify application of that article. [2])

Likewise the principle that § 382 is only illustrative leads to the conclusion that for security of a non-money claim, prohibition of alienation or encumbrance of *movables* is permissible [3]). Prohibitions directed to third parties not touching the very subject matter of litigation seems to be allowed only under § 381 (2) to ward off violence or harm, and not under § 381 (1) to secure execution [4]).

What of merely preventing the doing of wrongful acts, not connected with specific property? Apart from the principle that § 382 is not exhaustive, it would seem that § 382 (4) and (5) (cf. also § 384 (1)) permit such injunctions. § 938 of the German ZPO is more clear and direct on this point.

§ 23. Various differences between German and Austrian law may be noted:

1. In Germany land is not excluded from *Arrest* for money claims [5]).

---

[1]) § 392. 2 Neumann 1188: „Die anzuwendenden Mittel sollen zur Erreichung des angestrebten Zweckes hinreichen, dürfen aber auch nicht darüber hinausgehen, das Gericht darf, sobald der beabsichtigte Effekt gesichert ist, die Rücksicht auf den Schuldner nicht ausser Acht lassen, insbesondere darf im allgemeinen nicht im Wege einer einstweiligen Verfügung alles das bewilligt werden was die gefährdete Partei erst seinerzeit im Wege der Exekution auf Grund eines ihr günstigen Urteiles erreichen könnte". The last-mentioned limitation does not apply to cases under § 381 (2) for warding off violence or irreparable injury. Ibid. 1164.

[2]) Rintelen 103. Juster 453 is of opinion that cumulation of remedies is impossible. Unlike German law, which allows arrest not only for a money claim but also for one that may be transformed into a money claim, § 379 applies only to a claim already so transformed.

[3]) Rintelen 247. [4]) 2 Neumann 1187. Cf. Rintelen 257. [5]) Stern 81 ff.

2. In Germany *Arrest* creates a lien on the property attached [1].

3. In Germany *Arrest* is always revoked on giving security [2] or paying into court a sum stated in the order [3], while only under exceptional circumstances can *einstweilige Verfügung* be revoked on giving security [4]. In Austria all interim measures may be revoked in the discretion of the court on giving security [5].

4. In Germany *Arrest* requires only the existence of circumstances jeopardizing the possibility of execution. In Austria *Einstweilige Verfügung* for money claims is granted only if such peril results from certain specified acts of the defendant.

5. In Austria personal arrest for a money claim is excluded. In Germany personal arrest is permitted when necessary to ensure execution on the property of the defendant.

6. In Germany personal arrest may consist in limitations on defendant's freedom of movement and personal liberty. (Thus he may be deprived of his passport). In Austria personal arrest must be by detention.

7. In Germany both claim (*Anspruch*) and jeopardy (*Arrestgrund*) if not sufficiently substantiated may be substituted for by giving security; in Austria the danger (*Gefährdung*) must always be shown, and only the claim may be replaced by security.

8. In Germany the decision is given by judgment (*Urteil*), if after hearing; in Austria it is always by order (*Beschluss*).

9. In Germany the *forum rei situs* is competent, in urgent cases, in addition to the *forum litis pendentis*. In Austria, it is competent only when no proceedings are pending and no Austrian court is the natural judge of the defendant according to Austrian private international law.

10. In Germany applicant is responsible only for damage resulting from *execution* of the interim measure, but no restriction to material damage is laid down. In Austria that limitation is made, but the damage may result from the obtaining as well as the execution of the measure.

§ 24. 3. Swiss law [6].

In Switzerland personal arrest is prohibited by the federal con-

---

[1] In Austria a lien is created by incipient execution with a view to security (*Exekutionshandlungen zur Sicherung von Geldforderungen*) treated in EO part 2, section 1, §§ 370—377.

[2] ZPO § 927.

[3] ZPO §§ 923, 934.

[4] ZPO § 939.

[5] EO § 399 (3).

[6] See also § 38 *infra*.

stitution [1]). Real arrest is governed by §§ 271—281 of the federal law on pursuit for debts and bankruptcy. Even when in that law or other federal legislation [2]) provision is made for interim protection, it is left to the legislative autonomy of each canton to establish a competent authority to exercise such jurisdiction [3]). We shall therefore be obliged to deal with the cantonal codes of procedure, as well as the federal law regulating procedure in the federal court [4]).

(*a*) The law on pursuit for debts provides that an unsecured creditor [5]) may apply for arrest (1) when his debtor has no fixed domicile; (2) when the debtor with intention of escaping his obligations conceals his property, flees or prepares to flee; (3) when the debtor is transient and of the class of persons who frequent fairs and markets, if the debt is by its nature one immediately due; (4) when the debtor does not live in Switzerland; (5) when the creditor holds against the debtor a certificate showing that execution against him has been fruitless for lack of property. In cases (1) and (2) the debt need not be yet due; it becomes payable upon demand [6]).

The arrest must be authorized by the competent cantonal authority of the *locus rei sitae* where the property to be attached is situated. The creditor must make out a *prima facie* case both for his claim and the *causa arresti* [7]). He is responsible for damage caused by the arrest and may be required to give security [8]). He

[1]) § 59 (3) „Der Schuldverhaft ist abgeschafft". Ott 38. § 59 (1) provides as a rule of intercantonal conflict of laws that an upright Swiss is not subject to arrest for personal claims outside his own canton. The Bundesgesetz über Schuldbetreibung und Konkurs of 11 April 1889 is not bound by that provision, but respects its principle. Ott 35—37.

[2]) Schurter-Fritzsche 546—7. These instances are enumerated in F. Ott, Rechtsverfolgung, 228—233. There should be mentioned ZGB § 145, in divorce proceedings; § 321, support of illegitimate child; § 551, preservation of absentee's inheritance by affixing seals and inventory; BG betreffend das Urheberrecht an Werken der Literatur und Kunst of 7 December 1922, §§ 52, 53; BG betreffend die Erfindungspatente of 21 June 1907, § 43, copyright and patent cases.

[3]) Fritzsche 379; citations and literature of cantonal procedural laws at 381.

[4]) Cantonal law may authorize precautionary measures (*vorsorgliche Massnahmen*) for the maintenance of the status quo, even if they are mistakenly designated by the term *Arrest*. 3 R.O. nr. 9, 17 Feb. 1877, 47, 51; 18 R.O. nr. 11, 19 March 1892, 46, 50. But what is really *Arrest*, however designated, is forbidden. 17 R.O. nr. 7, 17 Jan. 1891, 34, 38.

[5]) The law uses the terms creditor and debtor, although applicant's claim has not been judicially established. „Nous n'approuvons pas cette terminologie; elle est claire, sans doute, mais inexacte". Bonnard 39. Delictual or tort obligations are included within the protection of the law. Bonnard 95—6.

[6]) § 271. [7]) § 272. [8]) § 273.

participates in subsequent seizures of the property attached, but acquires no other rights of priority [1]).

When the order authorizing arrest has been made by the proper cantonal authority (*Arrestbehörde*), it is executed by the competent federal office for the collection of debts in the locality (*Betreibungsamt*). In order to establish the competence of these authorities, the request for arrest must indicate specific property of the debtor on which attachment is asked. It may add a general prayer for attachment of such other property as is situated with the jurisdiction, sufficient to cover the creditor's claim. Other property than that specified may be offered by the debtor, so far as is consistent with the interest of the creditor. Since the latter is responsible for damages in case the attachment is unjustified, the executing officer should respect his specification, as he may have contented himself with less than the full value of his debt in order not to run the risk of seriously damaging the debtor by attaching other property than what he designated [2]).

A third jurisdiction, this time a cantonal court (*Arrestgericht*), comes into play if the debtor chooses to contest the *causa arresti* [3]) and make the creditor justify the arrest. On giving security, the debtor may be permitted to retain disposition over the property attached [4]). The creditor must bring his action on the principal claim within 10 days if it is not already pending [5]).

(*b*) The federal law of civil procedure prescribes that provisional orders may be made (1) to protect threatened possession; (2) to prevent alteration of the subject matter of the litigation; (3) to ward off impending damage not easily to be made good [6]).

[1]) § 281. [2]) § 273; Bonnard 101, 138—9; Ott 81—3.

[3]) § 279; Bonnard 193. Only the *Arrestgrund*, not the *Anspruch* is considered at this stage of the procedure. It seems, however, that doubt as to the well-foundedness of the claim may be taken into account in the decision as to exacting security of the creditor. Ott 97; Bonnard 197—8 *contra*. Any grounds existing at the time of the arrest, whether then known or not, but no intervening circumstances, may be relied on to uphold the attachment. Ott 96.

[4]) § 277. This does not revoke the attachment, but merely restore's debtor's control over the property attached. Ott 101.

[5]) § 278.

[6]) BG über das Verfahren bei dem Bundesgericht in bürgerlichen Rechtsstreitigkeiten of 22 November 1850, § 199: „Provisorische Verfügungen *a*) zum Schutze eines bedrohten Besitzstandes; *b*) gegen Veränderungen an dem Streitgegenstände; *c*) zur Abwendung eines dem Impetranten drohenden, nicht leicht ersetzbaren Schadens, — werden während des Vorverfahrens durch den Instruktionsrichter, vor der Einleitung oder nach Beendigung des Vorverfahrens aber durch des Bundesgericht und, wenn dasselbe nicht ohnehin versammelt ist, durch den Präsidenten desselben erlassen."

The purpose of such orders is merely to secure existing relations and hence they should go no further than their purpose necessarily requires. Applicant must given security if his opponent may be damaged by reason of the order [1]). The provisional order shall have no influence on the decision of the question at issue and shall not alter the legal position of the parties. The order may be revoked or modified at any time if the danger disappears or circumstances have changed. Orders made by the judge of instruction or the president shall be laid before the full court for confirmation at the first possible occasion without summoning a special session for that purpose [2]).

§ 25. Very similar are the Bern law of 1883 [3]) and the codes of Vaud and Fribourg [4]). The latter proceed to set forth various

---

[1]) § 200: „Die provisorische Verfügung bezweckt bloss die Sicherstellung der bestehenden Verhältnisse und soll daher nicht weiter gehen als ihr Zweck notwendig erheischt.

„Wenn derjenige, gegen den die Verfügung verhängt werden soll, dadurch in Schaden gebracht werden könnte, soll der Impetrant angehalten werden, für den Ersatz des Schadens Sicherheit zu bestellen".

[2]) § 201: „Die provisorische Verfügung soll auf die Entscheidung des Rechtsstreites keinen Einfluss haben und die rechtliche Stellung der Parteien nicht verändern. Sie kann jederzeit aufgehoben oder modifiziert werden, wenn die Gefahr dahingefallen ist oder die Umstände sich geändert haben. Verfügungen des Instruktionsrichters oder des Gerichtspräsidenten sind bei der ersten Gelegenheit dem Gericht zur Bestätigung vorzulegen; doch ist das Gericht zu diesem Behufe nicht ausserordentlich einzuberufen".

[3]) § 306. The present law of 7 July 1918, § 326 reads as follows:

„Der Richter kann auf Gesuch eines beteiligten als vorsorgliche Massnahme eine einstweilige Verfügung treffen, sofern ihm glaubhaft gemacht wird, dass der Erlass einer solchen sich aus einem der folgenden Gründe rechtfertigt: 1. wider wesentliche Veränderungen oder Veräusserungen des Streitgegenstandes nach Einreichung der Klage; 2. zum Schutze eines bedrohten Besitzstandes sowie zur Wiedererlangung eines widerrechtlichen entzogen oder vorenthaltenen Besitzes; 3. zum Schutz von andern als auf Geld- oder Sichherheitsleistung gerichteten, fälligen Rechtsansprüchen, wenn bei nicht sofortiger Erfüllung *a)* ihre Vereitelung oder eine wesentliche Erschwerung ihrer Befriedigung zu befürchten ist , *b)* dem Berechtigten ein erheblicher oder nicht leicht zu ersetzender Schaden oder Nachteil droht".

In introducing the element of ensuring realization of claimant's right, this version resembles the St. Gallen law of 3 May 1900, § 269: „Eine vorläufige oder einstweilige Verfügung kann beim Bezirksammann verlangt werden: 1. Zur Erhaltung des bestehenden Zustandes einer Sache oder eines Rechtsverhältnisses, worüber ein Rechtsstreit bereits anhängig ist; 2. überhaupt zu jeder vorläufigen Anordnung, welche notwendig ist, um einer Partei die Möglichkeit der Rechtsverfolgung zu sichern.

„Der Besitzstand darf durch vorläufige Verfügungen nur insoweit verletzt werden, als es der Zweck derselben notwendig macht.

„Die vorläufigen oder einstweiligen Verfügungen können je nach der Umständen in Amtsbefehlen zum Tun oder Unterlassen oder in Anordnung unparteiischer Verwahrung, Verwaltung und anderer exekutorischer Massnahmen bestehen".

[4]) Vaud, 20 November 1911 § 39; Fribourg, 12 October 1849, § 188. Similar are Neuchatel, in force 1 January 1879, § 109; and Ticino, 24 June 1924, § 390.

measures which, *inter alia*, may be ordered by the judge: total or partial execution of the obligation in litigation if it has the presumption of regular title; restoration of possession to party ejected; surrender of a chattel or immovable wrongly held; provision of aliments; maintenance or re-establishment of the status of premises in litigation; sequestration or putting under seal of the property in dispute [1]). Provisional measures may be ordered even when the courts of the canton do not have jurisdiction of the merits of the case [2]). The parties shall be cited and heard, if possible, before granting relief [3]).

Slightly different is the formula found in the laws of Aargau, Luzern, Unterwalden-ob-dem-Wald, and Zug. It is there laid down that a provisional order is to be made when a party is threatened with damage not easily reparable, which can be prevented only by timely judicial action [4]). The president of the court having jurisdiction of the principal issue is competent; in urgent cases the *forum rei sitae* [5]). The party desiring an order must indicate plainly the desired measure and show (*bescheinigen*) the facts which make it necessary. When the matter is not clear or not very urgent, the president of the court will invite the parties to a hearing before making his order [6]). In urgent cases which do not permit a hearing, the order may be made at once [7]). Se-

[1]) Fribourg § 189: Dans les cas prévus à l'article précédent, le juge peut, entre autres mesures, ordonner suivant sa prudence: *a*) L'exécution totale ou partielle de l'obligation, objet du procès, et de ses accessoires, si l'obligation a la présomption d'un titre régulier; *b*) La réintégration de la partie qui a été violemment privée de la possession d'un meuble ou d'un immeuble; *c*) L'abandon d'un immeuble ou d'un meuble détenu sans droit; *d*) La fourniture d'aliments pendant le procès, dans les cas prévus aux art. 136, 171 et 174 du code civil; *e*) Le maintien en état, ou le rétablissement des lieux litigieux; *f*) Le séquestre, ou la mise sous scellés de l'objet litigieux". Vaud § 40, 41.

[2]) Fribourg § 197: „Les mesures provisoires peuvent être ordonnées lors même que le procès au fond n'est pas du ressort des tribunaux du canton". Vaud § 50; Ticino § 394; Geneva, code of 1819, § 31.

[3]) Vaud § 45. So Geneva, code of 13 October 1920, § 14; Aargau, law of 12 March 1900, § 248, and others, on this point. In Basel-Land the order is as a rule given *ex parte*. Law of 20 February 1905, § 241. In Graubünden there must be a hearing. Law of 3 November 1907, § 61: „Der Präsident des Gerichtes, bei welchem die Streitsache anhängig ist, hat in Fällen von Dringlichkeit auf Verlangen einer Partei und nach Anhörung der andern die erforderlichen vorsorglichen Verfügungen zur Sicherstellung der streitigen Sache, zur Erhaltung ihres Wertes und ihrere Nutzungen, sowie des status quo überhaupt zu erlassen".

[4]) Aargau § 245: „Eine vorsorgliche Verfügung findet statt, wenn einer Partei ein nicht leicht zu ersetzender Schaden bevorsteht, der nur durch eine vorläufige richterliche Anordnung abgewendet werden kann".

[5]) § 246.

[6]) Zug, code of 15 October 1863, § 145.

[7]) Unterwalden-ob-dem-Wald, code of 2 April 1901, § 192.

curity shall be required when necessary to protect defendant against damage [1]. The order must alter the previously existing situation no further than necessary to ward off the danger and shall be effected with the least possible injury to the parties [2]. It has no influence on the decision of the case and works no change in the rights of the actual possessor [3]. As soon as it is made to appear to the president of the court that continuance of the precautionary measures is no longer necessary, he shall revoke them [4].

Another group of cantonal legislations emphasize the element of illegal action or unauthorized self-help against which speedy judicial assistance is required [5]. Thus Basel-Land ordains that a provisional order shall be made in case there is danger that without speedy judicial help a party will suffer through a wrongful act or omission of his opponent substantial injury, such as that occasioned by disadvantageous alteration of a litigated thing (*streitige Sache*). The order may consist in something being commanded or forbidden. The president of the court which has to decide the principal matter is competent to order interim measures [6]. He may hear the parties, though as a rule such orders are made *ex parte* (*auf einseitiges Verlangen*) [7]. Schaffhausen sets up the same requirements. [8] Basel-Stadt establishes the rule that possession may be protected or obtained by command of the

---

[1] § 193.

[2] § 194: „Die Verfügung darf an dem bisherigen Zustand der Sache nicht mehr ändern, als zur Abwendung der Gefahr oder des Schadens notwendig ist und sie soll in der für die Beteiligten möglichst unschädlichen Art getroffen werden".

[3] § 196: „Die vorsorgliche Verfügung soll auf den Entschied der Hauptsache keinen Einfluss haben und in den Rechten des wirklichen Besitzers keine Aenderung wirken".

[4] Aargau § 254: „Sobald dem Gerichtspräsident der Ausweis geleistet wird, dass der Fortbestand der vorsorglichen Verfügung nicht mehr notwendig ist, hat er dieselbe aufzuheben".

[5] A transitional type between these groups is represented by Valais, code of 22 November 1919, § 345: „Outre les cas expressément prévus par la loi, le juge peut ordonner des mesures provisionnelles, lorsqu'il est à craindre que, sans sa prompte intervention, une partie ne subisse un dommage sérieux. Les mesures provisionnelles peuvent consister dans l'ordre ou la défense de faire quelque chose".

[6] Law of 20 February 1905, § 240: „Eine provisorische Verfügung wird in dem Falle erlassen wenn Gefahr vorhanden ist, dass ohne schnelle richterliche Hilfe einer Partei durch eine widerrechtliche Handlung oder Unterlassung des Gegners ein erheblicher Schaden, wie z.B. durch nachteiliger Veränderung einer streitigen Sache, zugefügt würde. Die Verfügung kann darin bestehen, dass etwas untersagt oder angeordnet wird. Für den Erlass einer vorsorglichen Verfügung ist der Präsident desjenigen Gerichts zuständig, das über die Hauptsache abzusprechen hat".

[7] § 241.

[8] Code in force 1 November 1869, § 449.

court in case of illegal self-help or unjustified conduct, and that anyone about to suffer substantial damage from failure to fulfil a legal obligation or from tort or breach of contract may obtain protection [1]). Thürgau prescribes precautionary measures serving to protect the existing status quo against unauthorized self-help or aggressions and disturbances, to maintain or restore possession, and to secure imperiled means of proof [2]). For this purpose the president of the court may, before or after institution of proceedings, make orders with penalty for disobedience, attach movable or immovable property or cause the former to be deposited in court, and take measures to prevent loss of evidence. The existing situation shall not be altered more than necessary to ward off impending harm [3]).

Other cantons stress maintenance of the status quo. Thus in Zürich the *vitium litigiosi* is recognized. Pendency of litigation has the effect that no party may alter the situation of the things in dispute to the disadvantage of the other party or to increase the difficulty of proof. [4]) To preserve the factual situation, the court, in urgent cases the president, orders the necessary measures. These may be made dependent upon furnishing security [5]). Moreover *Befehlsverfahren*, like the mediaeval procedure by mandate, where an order or injunction is issued immediately to defendant, subject to subsequent attack by him, is available: (1) for

---

[1]) Code revised 9 October 1924, § 259: „Der von verbotener Eigenmacht betroffene oder bedrohte Besitzer einer Sache kann zu seinem Schutz beim Richter vorläufige Wiederherstellung seines Besitzes und ein Verbot der Besitzstörung verlangen. Wer einen rechtlichen Anspruch auf Uebertragung von Sachbesitz hat kann beim Richter die vorläufige Besitzeseinweisung verlangen, wenn ihm durch unbegründete Vorenthaltung des Besitzes erheblicher und schwer ersetzbarer Nachteil droht. Wer durch das vertragswidrige Verhalten eines andern oder dadurch, dass ein anderer eine rechtswidrige Handlung vornimmt oder beabsichtigt, oder eine Handlung, zu der er rechtlich verpflichtet ist, unterlässt, einen erheblichen und schwer ersetzbaren Nachteil zu gewärtigen hat, kann beim Richter den Erlass einer ihn schützenden, vorsorglichen Verfügung verlangen."

[2]) Code of 19 October 1926, § 196: „Es liegt in der Aufgabe des Bezirksgerichtspräsidenten, auf Begehren einer Partei und, sofern dessen Berechtigung glaubhaft gemacht ist, diejenigen Verfügungen zu treffen, die dazu dienen; 1. den bestehenden Zustand gegen unerlaubte Selbsthilfe oder eigenmächtige Eingriffe und Störungen zu schützen; 2. den redlichen Besitz, sei er bereits verloren gegangen, oder werde er erst bedroht, aufrechtzuerhalten; 3. gefährdete Beweise sicherzustellen".

[3]) § 197.

[4]) Code of 13 April 1913, § 130. So Bern, § 161; Glarus, as of 31 December 1923 (now replaced by code of 4 May 1930), §§ 44—5; Graubünden § 59; Uri, code of 24 Wintermonat 1852 (now replaced by code of 29 March 1928), § 11; Luzern, law of 28 January 1913, § 102.

[5]) Zürich § 134.

the rapid enforcement of clear right in case of uncontroverted or instantly ascertainable facts, as well as for execution of judgments; (2) for preservation of the factual situation before institution of proceedings (*vorsorgliche Massnahmen*); (3) to maintain the factual situation against wrongful self-help or other unauthorized aggression and disturbance; (4) in proceedings for protection of possession; (5) or recovery of movables [1]). Such orders may consist in; (1) general prohibitions (with threat of penalty for disobedience); (2) prohibitions or orders directed against particular persons; (3) imposition of security; (4) commands depriving the defendant of power to dispose of particular pieces of property [2]). The application must indicate exactly applicant's right and the nature of violation thereof [3]). If the request appears at once to be unfounded, the president refuses it immediately; if it appears indisputably established, he orders at once the appropriate measures. In all other cases he summons the parties to a hearing [4]). If there is peril in delay, he may immediately order appropriate provisional measures [5]). If the action is not yet pending, a time within which suit must be brought is set [6]). If the other party may be damaged, or in any case at the judge's discretion, the order may be made dependent upon furnishing security [7]).

Zürich decisions show that a *vorsorgliche Massnahme* does not consist in provisional or partial execution or satisfaction of the claim asserted in the litigation. Thus a party can not be compelled to perform an act when it is controversial whether a duty to that effect exists. In one case water company R desired to compel company Z to pump water for its customers as well as Z's, as it had done in the past. There was nothing making it impossible for R to supply its customers with water pumped by itself. R's request was refused [8]). In a suit to obtain transfer of patent rights,

---

[1]) § 292: „Das Befehlsverfahren ist zulässig:

1. zur schnellen Handhabung klaren Rechtes bei nicht streitigen oder sofort herstellbaren tatsächlichen Verhältnissen, sowie zur Vollstreckung von Ansprüchen nach rechtskräftiger gerichtlicher Feststellung;

2. zur Aufrechterhaltung des tatsächlichen Zustandes vor Anhängigmachung eines Rechtsstreites (vorsorgliche Massnahmen);

3. zur Erhaltung des tatsächlichen Zustandes gegen versuchte oder drohende unerlaubte Selbsthilfe oder sonstige eigenmächtige Eingriffe und Störungen...."

[2]) § 293. [3]) § 294. [4]) § 295. [5]) § 296. [6]) § 297.

[7]) § 298. Schwyz, law of 3 December 1915, §§ 354—61 is the same as Zürich §§ 292—8.

[8]) ZR, 27 nr. 193, (1928): „Dagegen kann die vorsorgliche Massnahme nicht darin bestehen, dass die Gegenpartei zu einem Tun gezwungen wird, wenn streitig ist, ob eine Verpflichtung zu diesem Tun besteht. Ein derartiger Befehl würde eine vorläu-

transferee may prevent holder of the patent from transferring to a third party or granting licences, but not from manufacturing and selling the article in question. That would be execution [1]). So an injunction against selling goods in a distinctive package can not be had *pendente lite* [2]).

Glarus [3]) and Solothurn [4]) provide, *inter alia*, for judicial regulation of the exercise of contested rights (*Ausübung der streitigen Rechte*). Appenzell-Ausserrhoden has the simplest and most general provision, that the president of the court competent in the matter shall on request take all necessary interim measures *pendente lite* [5]). Geneva, on the other hand, under the influence of French law, enumerates specific cases where interim measures are permissible. We have already seen that among the excellences of the Geneva code of civil procedure of 29 September 1819 was that of putting title II dealing with provisional measures in its logical place [6]). With changes, those provisions remain as titleII, §§ 6—25 in the law of 13 October 1920.

---

fige Vollstreckung des Streitbegehrens bedeuten". Cf. Whiteman v. Fayette Fuel Gas Co., 139 Pa. 492 (1891), and Brussels Cour d'Appel, 9 march 1900, P.B. 1901, 2e. partie, 26.

[1]) Baur 106. But see R.O. 56—II, no. 55, 1 July 1930, 318, 321. [2]) Baur 107.

[3]) § 106: „....finden richterliche Weisungen in folgenden Fällen statt: 4. Wenn einstweilige Verfügungen in Fällen, wo Gefahr im Verzuge ist, notwendig werden, als: *a*) über Deponierung des streitigen Gegenstandes in dritte Hand; *b*) über Gutheissung oder Oeffnung eines vom Zivilgerichtspräsidenten bedingt erteilten Rechtbotes, sowie über einstweilige, durch dringende Umstände nötig werdende Ausübung eines mit Rechtsbot belegten streitigen Rechtes. Die letztere kann bewilligt werden, wenn dem Gegner kein erheblicher Nachteil daraus erwächst oder die verlangende Partei für allfällig entstehenden Schaden genügende Sicherheit leistet".

[4]) Code as of 2 May 1926, § 250: „Diejenige Partei, welche behauptet, auf Widerrechtliche Weise im Besitze oder im Gebrauche ihres Eigentums oder einer Dienstbarkeit gestört oder gefährdet zu werden, hat ihren Gegner vor den Friedensrichter, oder in Fällen wo eine Erscheinung vor dem Friedensrichter nicht vorgeschrieben ist, vor den Amtsgerichtspräsidenten vorzuladen, und ihre Klage in der Hauptsache sowohl als über die Störung aufzubringen. Der betreffende Richter trifft die nötigen Verfügungen über die Ausübung der streitigen Rechte. Ebenso verfügt der Richter, auf Begehren der einen oder andern Partei, über Aufbewahrung, Besorgung oder Veräusserung im Streite liegender Gegenstände und über Verabfolgung notwendiger Lebensbedürfnisse".

[5]) Law of 26 April 1914, § 85: „Der Präsident des in der Sache zuständigen Gerichtes ist berechtigt, auf Antrag einer Partei für die Dauer des Prozesses die allfällig nötigen vorsorglichen Massregeln zu treffen".

[6]) See p. 24 *supra*. The code of 1791 and the code of procedure contained numerous isolated instances of provisional measures. „Nous avons cru devoir les réunir toutes dans un seul titre. Et comme les mesures provisoires précèdent la demande, ou du moins l'instruction et le jugement, nous avons estimé que le titre qui en traitait, devait précéder tout ce qui concernait la forme de la demande, l'instruction et le jugement". Bellot, exposé des motifs du titre II, p. 24.

The full court with summary procedure passes on all provisional demands, except certain specified cases in which the president of the tribunal is competent [1]). These include sequestration of movables, of which ownership is claimed, in the hands of any possessor; suspension of new work; nomination of experts to verify and determine the condition of objects when there is urgence [2]). The president will not make his decisions until he has heard the parties, unless urgent circumstances in his discretion seem opposed to such a course. [3]) Security may be required [4]). The measures must be executed within 20 days, and suit brought within a month if it is not already pending [5]). The measures remain in force so long as the suit is pending, except that on opposition (which does not suspend execution) [6]) they may be confirmed, revoked or modified according to circumstances [7]).

§ 25. 4. Anglo-American law [8]).

In Anglo-American law equity juridiction plays an important part [9]). There must always be a specific ground of invoking such jurisdiction. These grounds have developed historically. A potent instrument of equity is the injunction, a command directed to the defendant with a view to the prevention and restraint of the commission or continuance of acts contrary to law and apt to result in irreparable damage.

In courts of equity it is the regular practice to apply first for a temporary injunction, which after hearing is made permanent if the applicant substantiates his claims. The most important rules governing the issuance of preliminary injunctions may be summarized as follows:

1. Such interlocutory injunctions do not affect the ultimate decision of the case. They are designed merely to preserve the status quo pending decision on the merits [10]).

2. Their issuance rests wholly within the discretion of the

---

[1]) §§ 12, 7. [2]) §§ 8—11. [3]) § 14. [4]) § 16.
[5]) §§ 18, 19. [6]) § 21. [7]) §§ 20, 22. [8]) See also § 38 *infra*.

[9]) In Pennsylvania and Massachusetts equity was introduced by statute, after an attempt to do without that branch of jurisprudence. In New York and other code states equity has been abolished, but in the sense that principles of equity are applied by the ordinary courts in actions at law. Likewise all English courts, not the chancery division alone, are bound by the judicature act to respect the priority of equity rules if conflicting with rules of common law.

[10]) Beach on Injunctions, §§ 109, 112.

court, and unlike a final decree, can never be a matter of right [1]).

3. In exercising its discretion, the court should weigh two factors; the hardship to the parties respectively and the probability of their being ultimately successful [2]).

(*a*) As a rule, it is necessary only for plaintiff to show a probable right and a probable injury [3]).

(*b*) This is especially true where damage to plaintiff would be irreparable, while hardship to defendant is slight [4]).

(*c*) But if the hardship to defendant is great, plaintiff's right must be clear [5]).

(*d*) The injunction should issue as a matter of course if it is clear that plaintiff will win [6]).

(*e*) If it is clear that plaintiff will lose, preliminary relief should be denied [7]).

4. Interlocutory proceedings should not prejudge the issue, but should be so framed that the successful party will not find his victory valueless:

(*a*) Thus plaintiff will usually not be given preliminary relief

---

[1]) N.Y. Printing and Dying Est. v. Fitch, 1 Paige 97 (1830).

[2]) Harriman v. Northern Securites Co., 132 F. 464, at 475—6: „The granting or refusal of a preliminary injunction, whether mandatory or preventive, calls for the exercise of a sound judicial discretion in view of all the circumstances of the case. Regard should be had to the nature of the controversy, the object for which the injunction is sought, and the comparative hardship or convenience to the respective parties involved in the awarding or denying of the injunction. The legitimate object of a preliminary injunction, preventive in its nature, is the preservation of the property or rights in controversy until the decision of the case on a full and final hearing upon the merits, or the dismissal of the bill for want of jurisdiction or other sufficient cause. The injunction is merely provisional. It does not, in a legal sense, finally conclude the rights of the parties, whatever may be its practical operation under exceptional circumstances. In a doubtful case, where the granting of the injunction would, on the assumption that the defendant ultimately will prevail, cause greater detriment to him than would, on the contrary assumption, be suffered by the complainant, through its refusal, the injunction usually should be denied. But where, in a doubtful case, the denial of the injunction would, on the assumption that the complainant ultimately will prevail, result in greater detriment to him than would, on the contrary assumption, be sustained by the defendant through its allowance, the injunction should usually be granted. The balance of convenience or hardship ordinarily is a factor of controlling importance in cases of substantial doubt existing at the time of granting or refusing the preliminary injunction. Such doubt may relate either to the facts or to the law of the case, or to both."

[3]) Ga. v. Brailford, 2 Dall. 402, 405 (1792); Great Western Ry. Co. v. Birmingham & Oxford Jct. Co., 2 Phil. 597, 602—3 (1848); Am. Smelting Co. v. Bunker Hill Co., 248 F. 172 (1918).

[4]) City of Newton v. Levis, 79 F. 715 (1897).

[5]) Amelia Mining Co. v. Tenn, Coal & Iron R. R. Co., 123 F. 810 (1903).

[6]) De Pauw v. Oxley, 122 Wis. 656 (1904); Allington & Curtis Mfg. Co. v. Booth, 78 F. 878 (1897).

[7]) Gillette v. Treganza, 13 Wis. 472 (1861).

if such relief is all he would be entitled to on final hearing [1]).

(*b*) So if denial of injunction would be equivalent to deciding the case in defendant's favor, it will be granted [2]).

5. As a rule courts are unwilling before adjudication to order affirmative action, transfer of possession, or change in the existing status [3]).

(*a*) But the status itself may be one of continuing action [4]).

(*b*) And wrongful alteration of the status pending suit is not permitted. It is the last uncontested status preceding the controversy which is to be maintained by the court [5]).

6. Applicant must give bond, but is not liable beyond the amount of such security for damage to defendant resulting from the injunction. [6])

§ 27. In proceedings in equity, receivers are frequently appointed to preserve and administer property in dispute. Appointment of a receiver is always incident to equitable relief on some other ground. There is no such thing as a proceeding having for its sole object the appointment of a receiver. As a rule the task of a receiver resembles somewhat that of an executor or administrator, consisting in the management of an estate or business until the property can be distributed among the persons entitled. Bankruptcy is the most usual occasion for receivership .If there is no reasonable probability that petitioner will succeed in obtaining ultimate relief, receivers will not be appointed [7]).

Remaindermen and creditors secured on land may have equitable relief to prevent waste. In some jurisdictions a *lis pendens* may be filed with the land registry and prevents transfer of litigated property to a *bona fide* purchaser in derogation of com-

---

[1]) Bachman v. Harrington, 184 N.Y. 458 (1906); Butterick Pub. Co. v. Typographical Union, 100 N.Y.S. 292 (1906); Mackay Tel. Co. v. City of Texarkana, 199 F. 347 (1912). But this is not decisive against granting the injunction. Minneapolis General Electric Co. v. City of Minneapolis, 194 F. 215, 223 (1911).

[2]) Valley Iron Works v. Goodrick, 143 Wis. 436, 445 (1899). But see Winton Motor Carriage Co. v. Curtis Pub. Co., 196 F. 906 (1912).

[3]) Calvert v. State, 34 Neb. 616 (1892). Cf. Swiss R.O. IX, no. 78, 8 December 1883, 491, 496.

[4]) Toledo Ry. Co. v. Penna, Co., 54 F. 730, 740 (1893); Whiteman v. Fayette Fuel Gas Co., 139 Pa. 492 (1891); Strelley v. Pearson, 15 Ch. D. 113 (1880).

[5]) Fredericks v. Huber, 180 Pa. 572 (1897).

[6]) Borchard 839.

[7]) 4 Pomeroy, Equity Jurisprudence, 4 ed. §§ 1482 ff., 1537—9, 1553—4. In Indiana by statute in actions of replevin for property of peculiar value a receiver may be appointed. Ibid. § 1554.

plainant's rights. The writ *ne exeat regno* may be obtained with difficulty as an exceptional equitable remedy to prevent defendant leaving the jurisdiction [1]).

Attachment or arrest is also provided by statute against non-resident or absconding debtors, or where there is fraudulent disposition, removal or concealment or property. This proceeding was unknown at common law, and arose by the custom of London [2]).

In New York, arrest, attachment, injunction, receivers, and deposit in court are treated in chapter VII of the code of civil procedure under the heading of provisional remedies in an action [3]). In Pennsylvania, personal actions commence with writ of summons in all cases where other process is not especially provided, but may sometimes begin with *capias ad respondendum,* or arrest which is revoked on furnishing *cautio judicatum solvi.* Where action is not begun by *capias,* arrest may be sued out subsequently on satisfactory showing that the grounds therefor exist [4]). In Massachusetts, attachment on original writ is permitted of all property liable to levy. The property so attached may be held as security for whatever judgment may be rendered. Arrest on mesne process is also allowed [5]).

§ 28. 5. Italian law [6]).

In the legal systems previously considered, we have noticed the presence of a general principle extending interim protection wherever it is required to protect jeopardized rights from substantial damage. In the legislations which follow, a casuistic method enumerates specific situations in which remedies *pendente lite* are available. As a rule these cases are the same as those in which protection would be called for under a general rule, and the practical effects are not very different.

---

[1]) Chafee, Cases on Equitable relief against Torts, 1924; Ames, Cases on Equity Jurisdiction, 1904.

[2]) Patton, Foreign Attachment in Pennsylvania, 56 UPLR 137, (1908); 3 Am. & Eng. Encyc. of Law, 2 ed. 1877, 183 ff., esp. 195, 201—4.

[3]) 1 Bliss, N.Y. Annotated Code, 6 ed. 1912, N.Y. CPC §§ 549, 635—6, 713, 717. § 719 provides that where cumulation of remedies is not necessary for security, plaintiff may be compelled to elect.

[4]) 1 Purdon's Digest (13 ed. Stewart, 1905) 243 ff.; Act of 13 June 1836, P.L. 672; Act of 12 July 1842, P.L. 339; Act of 24 May 1887, P.L. 197; Act of 6 April 1870, P.L. 960.

[5]) 2 Mass. Gen. Laws (1921) part III, title III, c. 223, §§ 16, 26, 42; c. 224, § 2.

[6]) See Chiovenda 228—232.

In Italy personal arrest is abolished. The principal provisions dealing with our subject are found in CPC book III, title xi, §§ 921—940, dealing with sequestration and danger from new work or old work. As was the case in other systems of law thus far examined, there is a profusion of special texts covering particular cases [1]). Sometimes these references are rather vague and broad.

The judicial authority may order sequestration (1) of a movable or immovable the ownership or possession of which is in controversy between two or more persons; (2) of things offered by a debtor for liberation from his obligation (when creditor refuses to accept payment) [2]). As in French law, this sequestration is called *sequestro giudiziario*, to distinguish it from consensual sequestration under CC § 1870. The same term is applied to the sequestration provided for in CPC § 921. [3]) That article prescribes that in addition to the cases indicated in CC § 1875 the judicial authority may, on request (*domanda*) of the interested party order the sequestration of a movable or immovable, when there is dan-

[1]) For these see besides Chiovenda, Averara 807 ff. Among these may be noted: CC § 1958 (3), landlord may sequester property removed without his consent; CC § 914 holograph will executed unless *provvedimenti conservativi* are ordered in case of contest; CC § 145, alimentation; CC § 935, acts of simple conservation and administration do not constitute acceptance of inheritance; C. Com. § 71, sequestration and sale of article alleged by purchaser not to be up to specifications; C. Com. § 323, suspension of execution of executable title; C. Com. § 727, measures for the security of bankrupt estate; C. Com. § 871, commercial disputes in fairs and markets; C. Com. § 880, sequestration of ships; C. Com. § 153, inspection of books of company and summoning special meeting of stockholders if fraudulent administration is suspected; CPC § 275, judge viewing scene may make *provvedimenti di urgenza*; CPC § 444, questions of possession in a petitory action; CPC § 572, difficulties during execution; CPC § 808, on failure to reconcile spouses; CPC § 839, interdiction of incapable persons to handle their own affairs, appointment of temporary guardian; CC § 221, runaway child; CC § 2085 provides that a debtor after transcription on the land register instituting execution on real property may not alienate, and remains in possession as sequestrator; CC § 1870 deals with sequestration of disputed property by agreement, to be returned after the controversy is terminated to the party declared owner; the law of 31 January 1926 provides that the property of persons deprived of nationality for acts abroad contrary to Italian interests and prestige may be subjected to sequestration, or in graver cases, to confiscation. The decree ordering sequestration determines its duration and the destination of the goods.

[2]) CC § 1875: „Oltre i casi stabiliti dal codice di procedura civile, l'autorità giudiziaria può ordinare il sequestro

1. Di un immobile o di una cosa mobile, la cui proprietà o il cui possesso sia controverso fra due o più persone;

2. Delle cose che un debitore offre per la sua liberazione." This article copies Code Napoleon § 1961.

[3]) CPC § 921: „Oltre i casi indicati nell'art. 1875 del codice civile, l'autorità giudiziario può, sulla domanda della parte interessata, ordinare il sequestro di una cosa mobile, o di un immobile, quando siavi pericolo de laterazione, sottrazione, o deteriorazione."

ger of alteration, subtraction, or deterioration. The name *sequestro conservativo* is applied to the measure instituted by CPC § 924 [1]), which provides that a creditor who has just motives to suspect the flight of his debtor, to fear subtractions, or who is in danger of losing the guaranty of his credit [2]), may demand the sequestration of movable goods belonging to and sums owed to the debtor, if the law does not exempt such from attachment.

Competent for *sequestro conservativo* is the praetor in the place where it is to be executed, as well as the president of the tribunal with jurisdiction over the principal action [3]). If the case is already pending, only the latter is competent unless there is urgence [4]). This provision, though making for increased efficacy of interim protection, is confusing; for is there not urgence in most cases calling for sequestration? The measure is granted by order (*decreto*) on request *ex parte* (*ricorso*) [5]). *Sequestro giudiziario* requires a hearing [6]). Unlike that under CPC § 921, *sequestro giudiziario* under CC § 1875 is not an independent remedy, but is available only when proceedings have already been instituted with respect to ownership or possession [7]). The judge does not act *ex officio* [8]), but has discretion in granting the remedy [9]).

Security may be required to cover damages in case the sequestration is unjust [10]). A penalty up to 1000 lire may also be imposed [11]). The sequestration is revoked on giving security covering the amount of the debt or the value of the object seized [12]). A summary hearing is held to pass on the validity, revocation or

---

[1]) CPC § 924: „Il creditore che abbia giusti motivi de sospettare della fuga del suo debitore, di temere sottrazioni, o sia in pericolo di perdere le garantie del suo credito, può domandare il sequestro dei beni mobili spettanti e delle somme dovute al debitore medesimo, se la legge no ne vieti il pignoramento."

[2]) CC §§ 1948—9 provide that a debtor's property is liable for his personal obligations and is the common guaranty of his creditors.

[3]) CPC § 926. [4]) § 927. [5]) § 925.

[6]) This point is now settled by decision of Cass. Roma, sezioni uniti, 21 December 1922, note Carnelutti in 1 Riv. di dir. pr. civ. (1924) part II, 87—97. Gianzana 61, 63, 65 had upheld the contrary view; on the other hand Mortara, I, 523. CPC § 38 requires hearing for every *domanda*. In CPC § 924 is used the word *domandare*, while CPC § 925 expressly regulates procedure for the *sequestro conservativo*.

[7]) Gianzana 65.

[8]) Gianzana 29; a decision of the court of Rome in 1881 *contra*.

[9]) Gianzana 19. The text uses the word *può*.

[10]) CPC § 928. This is not for execution, but for obtaining the order. It is no fault to execute what the judge orders, 'the fault is in deceiving the judge. Carnelutti, in 2 Riv. di dir. pr. civ. (1925) part II, 185—205, 200, 202.

[11]) CPC § 935.

[12]) § 934.

confirmation of the sequestration. If the court is competent, the demand in the principal matter may be introduced at the same time [1]).

Sequestration, *nuntiatio novi operis* and *actio damni infecti* being treated specifically in the new Italian legislation [2]), it is generally considered that the *inhibizione de non faciendo* of the Sardinian codes has disappeared [3]). That type of injunction had in practice covered merely the three matters now given individual attention by the legislator.

§ 29. 6. Spanish law.

The Ley de enjuiciamiento civil of 3 February 1881, book II, title xiv, §§ 1397—1428, de los embargos preventivos y del aseguramiento de los bienes litigiosos, and title xx, §§ 1631—85, de los interdictos, are of chief interest [4]).

Embargo preventivo is a precautionary seizure for which it is necessary: (1) that with the request a document be presented from which results the existence of the debt alleged; (2) that the debtor must be a foreigner not naturalized in Spain, or have no known domicile or property or place of business; or have abandoned such domicile or place of business; or that the debtor is in hiding, or there are reasonable grounds for believing that he will abscond or dissipate his property to the detriment of his creditors [5]). If the document is not one authorizing execution, security will be required, unless the applicant is of known solvency [6]). If defendant gives security or pays the debt, the *embargo* will not take effect [7]). The debt may be either in money or in kind [8]). The *embargo* applies to movables, immovables, and money or government paper (*efectos publicos*) [9]).

The judge shall decree the *embargo* with the speed which the case requires, and it will go into effect without defendant having

[1]) § 931.

[2]) CC §§ 698—9 deal with new work and old work. CPC §§ 82, 93 give jurisdiction to the praetor of the *locus rei sitae*. CPC §§ 938—40 regulate procedure. There is a hearing. Experts may be appointed.

[3]) Thus Gianzana disapproves the decision of the court of Torino of 5 December 1871 which considered inhibition as an imperfect sequestration, and hence admissible wherever the code permits sequestration. Averara 712 approves the decision but recognizes that doctrine is the other way.

[4]) Mention should also be made of title xviii, §§ 1609—17 de los alimentos provisionales, alimentation cases, and Código civil § 68, divorce and separation.

[5]) Ley § 1400. [6]) §§ 1401—2. [7]) § 1405. [8]) § 1399. [9]) § 1409.

been heard [1]). In case of urgency the judge of the *locus rei sitae* is competent [2]). If proceedings are not pending, they must be begun within a short time [3]), under penalty of nullity declared at defendant's request without plaintiff being heard. In this case damages and costs shall be included in the same order. When on final judgment an *embargo* is declared ineffectual for lack of the conditions required by § 1400, damages and costs are also put upon the applicant [4]).

A party presenting documents justifying his right in a suit involving ownership of mines, mountains whose principal value is forests, plantations, or industrial or manufacturing establishments, may request by the judicial channel administration of the property in question [5]).

Where there is a public document, or a private document acknowledged before the proper judicial authority, or a confession made before the proper judicial authority (these being documents authorizing execution), from which clearly appears an obligation to do or not to do, or to deliver certain specified things, the judge may adopt, at the request of the applicant and on his responsibility, the measures which according to circumstances are necessary to assure in every case the effectiveness of the judgment to be rendered in the proceeding. If applicant is not notoriously solvent, security may be required [6]).

Interdicts may be had only to acquire, retain or recover possession; to prevent new work; or prevent damage from a ruinous work [7]). Of these the latter two are measures of interim protection. Possessory actions may or may not be, depending on whether they regulate a situation for the time being in connection with a petitory action based on ownership, or whether they are considered as independent remedies [8]).

§ 30. 7. Latin-American law.

Latin American states likewise stress *embargo preventivo, obra nueva*, and *obra ruinosa*. The emphasis on the presentation of documents which appears in the codes of Spanish-speaking countries is doubtless a reflection of the fact that written proof rather than oral testimony predominates in their procedure. Therefore in

[1]) § 1403. [2]) §§ 63 (12), 1397—8. [3]) §§ 1412, 1411. [4]) § 1413.
[5]) § 1419. [6]) § 1428. [7]) § 1631. [8]) Cf. note 3, p. 6 *supra*.

the absence of a document it would be difficult to establish a *prima facie* case (*glaubhaft machen, bescheinigen*); and thus these legislations in reality do not differ materially in the requirements for interim protection from those we have hitherto investigated.

(*a*) Cuba. Cuban law is quite like Spanish [1]). The fact that a document is not required in cases between merchants [2]), where rapid and informal transactions are the customary practice, confirms the view just advanced with regard to the necessity of demonstrating a probable right in order to obtain interim protection.

(*b*) Costa Rica [3]). To prevent debtor from hiding or removing goods and thus rendering illusory the result of the judgment against him, the creditor may seek *embargo preventivo*. If he does not present an executable title, he must furnish security for damages, and indicate clearly the nature of his claim and its foundation [4]).

(*c*) Chile [5]). Sequestration of movables in action by alleged owner may be granted, if there is reason to believe that the property will be lost or deteriorate in the hands of the possessor [6]). Likewise immovables may be sequestrated [7]). Sequestration is available also against a person having power over property without being possessor [8]). Besides sequestration, plaintiff may at any time request, in order to secure the result of the action, naming of administrators or retention of particular goods or prohibition against celebrating acts or contracts with respect to certain goods [9]).

All these measures are essentially provisional. In consequence they shall cease whenever the peril disappears which they were

---

[1]) Ley de enjuiciamiento civil, §§ 1395—1426, embargo and security of litigious property; §§ 1607—15, provisional alimentation; §§ 1661—73, interdicto de obra nuevo; §§ 1674—83, interdicto de obra ruinosa.

[2]) § 1399.

[3]) Codigo de procedimientos civiles, §§ 713—21, new work; §§ 722—8, old work; §§ 178—86, embargo.

[4]) § 178: „Para impedir que el deudor, ocultando o distrayendo bienes, haga ilusorio el resultodo de un juicio, puede el acreedor pedir embargo preventivo". § 179: „si el acreedor no presenta título ejecutivo, debe garantizar los daños y perjuicios que se originen del embargo y determinar con claridad qué clase de prestación va a exigir del demandado y la causa o título de ella".

[5]) CPC §§ 721—6, new work; §§ 727—32, old work; CC § 168, habitation and aliments of wife pending divorce; § 327, provisional aliments; CPC, book II, title iv, §§ 280—92, de las medidas precautorias.

[6]) CC § 901. [7]) §§ 902, 2251. [8]) CPC § 281. [9]) § 280.

designed to avoid, or when sufficient security is offered [1]. Likewise they are limited to an amount of property necessary to satisfy the judgment, and plaintiff should furnish proofs raising at least grave presumption of the right claimed by him. In case of measures not expressly sanctioned by statute security for damages originating from the measures may be required [2]. In grave and urgent cases, if security is given, even when the required proofs are lacking, measures may be granted for a period not to exceed ten days, within which time such proofs must be presented [3].

(*d*) Argentina [4]. Preventive *embargo* is permitted: (1) If existence of the debt is proved by public document or private act with signature identified by two witnesses, if the debt is over 200 pesos; (2) In case of a bilateral contract, if, in addition, summary proof of performance by plaintiff is given; (3) If the debt is proved by commercial books; (4) If, in case the debt is not yet due, plaintiff shows that debtor is concealing or disposing of his goods, or in any way becoming less responsible for the debt [5]. Security is required unless applicant's solvency is notorious. *Embargo* is also allowed in petitory actions where during proceedings by judicial confession or favorable judgment in court of first instance the existence of facts in support of the claim put forward is made to possess verisimilitude.

If no property of defendant's can be found, an inhibition against his transfer of property to others hangs over his head until plaintiff discovers property which can be subjected to *embargo* [6].

(*e*) Bolivia [7]. In addition to the cases in which sequestration may be had in Italian and French law, it is available when there is danger of deterioration or removal of movables; or husband dissipates wife's dower; or possessor appeals from decision, and there is suspicion of mismanagement of dissipation of fruits pending appeal; or the parties so agree; or there is fear that without sequestration the parties will resort to arms [8]. It should be noted how closely Bolivian law resembles mediaeval law with regard to sequestration [9].

---

[1] § 291. [2] § 288. [3] § 289.

[4] CC § 375, provisional aliments. See Salvador de la Colina, Derecho y legislación procesal, 2 ed. 1916, II, 221—39.

[5] CCP § 452. [6] § 472.

[7] CC § 1320, CPC § 106, sequestration; §§ 560—9, new work; § 610, provisional aliments. [8] § 106. [9] See p. 40 *supra*.

(*f*) Paraguay [1]. *Embargo* is permitted a creditor on the same terms as in Argentina [2]; and also, somewhat as in French law [3], to a landlord or other person having a lien, or to an alleged owner [4]. Except in cases where there is a lien, *embargo* becomes ineffective on giving security. [5] In urgent cases the justice of the peace is competent, who must at once notify the judge of first instance [6]. Likewise inhibition to sell or encumber goods is decreed if they can not be found [7].

(*g*) Uruguay [8]. Sequestration or *embargo preventivo* may be had: against a debtor without known domicile in the republic, or who has absconded; or has concealed or disposed of property, or is about to do so; or against the possessor of movables demanded by the owner if there is reason to suspect deterioration, disposition or concealment [9]. Summary justification, in some cases by documentary proof, and security for damages and costs must be offered. No security is required of a creditor having a lien on the sequestrated objects [10]. The embargo is null if action is not pending or brought within 20 days [11], and is revoked if security is given [12].

(*h*) Ecuador [13]. Sequestration or retention of goods may be ordered, if an executable document or one manifesting the existence of the debt is presented, and it is shown that the debtor's property is in bad condition or insufficient to cover the debt or may be concealed or removed [14]. Real estate is sequestrated only when there is danger of deterioration [15]. Personal arrest of a debtor may be had on summary proof of the debt and the fact that the debtor has no real property or known domicile or is transient. He is notified not to leave without paying, or giving security for satisfaction of a judgment against him [16].

(*i*) Mexico [17]. Measures to prevent escaping suit or eluding

---

[1] CPC §§ 378—97, embargos; title xix, provisional aliments; § 519, new work.
[2] § 378. [3] See p. 72 *infra*.
[4] §§ 380—1. [5] § 388.
[6] § 397. [7] § 396.
[8] CPC §§ 828—42, embargos; §§ 1190—1200, new work; §§ 1201—12, old work.
[9] § 828. [10] § 830.
[11] § 841. [12] § 833.
[13] Codigo de Enjuiciamientos en materia civil, § 785, provisional alimentation; §§ 747—52, new and old work.
[14] §§ 950, 952. [15] § 958. [16] § 965.
[17] §§ 241—62, de las diligencias precautorias.

obligations or judgment may be had, upon showing the grounds and necessity therefor [1]).

(*j*) Guatemala [2]).

Personal arrest or attachment of property is granted where there is fear that the defendant will hide or absent himself, or, in an action *in rem*, conceal or dilapidate the property [3]). Plaintiff must show (*acreditar*) his right and the necessity of the measure requested [4]), must furnish security if he is without a title justifying execution [5]), and is responsible for damages. [6]) Action must be begun within 3 days [7]), before the competent judge, if different from that ordering the interim measure [8]). Defendant may be relieved on giving security [9]).

§ 31. 8. French law.

Sequestration of property in litigation or seized from a debtor is permitted, in terms similar to those of Italian law [10]). The seizure of property in French law is a measure employed for many purposes [11]). Mostly these *saisies* are for execution; and the name varies with the type of property affected. But a number of *saisies* are not for satisfaction, and are called *saisies conservatoires* in French doctrine [12]). We shall discuss the *saisie-contrefaçon, saisie-revendication, saisie-gagerie, saisie-foraine,* the *saisies conservatoires commerciales*, and the *saisie-arrêt*, first stage.

These seizures are regarded as substantive law rights of the party seizing. In all *saisies* a right of the applicant is safeguarded, whether the general right of pledge given a creditor over all his debtor's property [13]), or a lien, or ownership or one of its parts [14]). The party effecting the seizure is considered to be exercising a

---

[1]) §§ 241, 252.

[2]) Codigo de procedimientos civiles, I, tit. ix, parrafo v, de las providencias precautorias, §§ 270—300.

[3]) §§ 270, 274. [4]) § 275. [5]) § 282. [6]) § 287.

[7]) § 296. [8]) § 299. [9]) § 279.

[10]) CC § 1961: „La justice peut ordonner le séquestre: 1. Des meubles saisis sur un débiteur; 2. D'un immeuble ou d'une chose mobilière dont la propriété ou la possession est litigieuse entre deux ou plusieurs personnes; 3. Des choses qu'un débiteur offre pour sa libération".

[11]) Cf. note 3, p. 6 *supra*. [12]) Druart 14.

[13]) By CC §§ 2092—3.

[14]) Druart 24; Bouchon 5: „Toutes les saisies conservatoires ont ce caractère commun, qu'elles garantissent un droit du saisissant sur les biens saisis: soit le droit de gage général de l'art. 2092 c.c., soit un droit de gage spécial, soit le droit de propriété ou un de ses démembrements".

right given him by statute law [1]), and the necessity of obtaining permission of the judge before seizing is a restriction on exercise of that right, just as a married woman requires the consent of her husband for exercising rights of which she has title (*jouissance*) [2]). These measures of interim protection would seem to be cases of judicially regulated self-help rather than judicial action.

The code of civil procedure in §§ 806—811 also consecrates the historical practice of procedure by *référé*, where in all cases of urgency the president of the tribunal may make orders executable at once, which do not prejudice the principal issue [3]).

A source of complication in dealing with French law is the intricate distribution of competence between various judicial authorities exercising separate and independent jurisdiction. Thus it is possible that a particular matter may fall within the competence of: (1) the full court; (2) the president of the tribunal, acting by order on request (*ordonnance sur requête*); (3) the president, acting *sur référé*. This division is duplicated by the existence of separate civil and commercial tribunals. There are also judges of the peace.

Saisie-contrefaçon is a seizure of articles manufactured in violation of patent or copyright [4]). It is regarded by French writers as a pure *mesure d'instruction*, designed to facilitate proof by preserving the evidence of infringement [5]). However, especially in the law as to copyright more so than in that as to patents, it would seem as though a twofold purpose, of preventing continuance of violations as well as preserving evidence, is noticeable.

Saisie-revendication [6]) is in aid of the alleged property right of

---

[1]) Hence only in case of *saisie conservatoire commerciale* under CPC § 417 which expressly so provides, may the judge require applicant to furnish security or show sufficient solvency. Druart 99; Bouchon 68.

[2]) Bouchon 13.

[3]) Mention should be made of other *procédures conservatoires*, such as to get possession of a document, affixing of seals or inventory, etc. See Garsonnet VI, 1 ff.

[4]) Pouillet, Propriété littéraire §§ 644—72; Brevets, §§ 768—86; Law of 19/28 January 1793, § 3: „Les officiers de paix seront tenus de faire confisquer, à la réquisition et au profit des auteurs, compositeurs, peintres ou dessinateurs ou autres, leurs héritiers ou cessionaires, tous les exemplaires des éditions imprimées ou gravées sans la permission formelle et par écrit des auteurs"; Law of 5 July 1844, § 47: „Les propriétaires de brevet pourront, en vertu d'une ordonnance du président du tribunal de première instance, faire procéder par tous huissiers à la désignation et description détaillés, avec ou sans saisie, des objets prétendus contrefaits".

[5]) Druart 23; Bouchon 10; Glasson-Tissier, 2 ed. II, 620 describe the *saisie* of the law of 5 July 1844 as a *mesure d'instruction*.

[6]) „La saisie-revendication est l'action par laquelle une personne qui prétend un

the party seizing [1]). This seizure seems practically the same as sequestration under CC § 1961, except that it does not presuppose the pendency of proceedings.

Saisie-gagerie [2]) permits landlords (1) for rent due and unpaid to seize effects and fruits on the premises; or (2) to seize movables removed from the premises without their consent, in order to preserve their lien given by §§ CC 2102 [3]).

Saisie-foraine allows any creditor, even without a document of title, without previous summons, but with permission of the judge, to seize effects found in the community where he lives which belong to a debtor who does not live there [4]).

Saisie conservatoire commerciale is the procedure by which in commercial matters a seizure of movable effects is authorized. The holder of a bill of exchange protested for non-payment may with permission of the judge resort to this measure against drawers, acceptors and endorsers of the bill [5]). Likewise, in commercial cases requiring celerity, the president of the tribunal may permit such seizure [6]).

Saisie-arrêt, like garnishment, is a proceeding in which a creditor may, by notification to third persons in whose hands are

---

droit de propriété, de possession légale ou de gage sur une chose mobilière possédée par un tiers, met cette chose sous la main de justice jusqu'à ce qu'il ait été statué sur le droit reclamé par le saissisant". Dalloz, Rép. prat. X.

[1]) The right of revendication by the owner of lost or stolen property is granted by CC §§ 2279—80.

[2]) If the things are no longer in the tenant's possession, they must first be pursued by revendication, within a short time after their removal.

[3]) CPC § 819: „Les propriétaires.. peuvent.. faire saisir-gager pour loyers et fermages échus, les effets et fruits étant dans lesdites maisons ou bâtiments ruraux, et sur les terres.. Ils peuvent aussi saisir les meubles qui garnissaient la maison ou la ferme, lorsqu'ils ont été déplacés sans leur consentement; et ils conservent sur eux leur privilège, pourvu qu'ils en aient fait la revendication, conformément à l'article 2102 du Code civil."

[4]) § 822: „Tout créancier, même sans titre, peut, sans commandement préalable, mais avec permission du président du tribunal de première instance et même du juge de paix, faire saisir les effets trouvés en la commune qu'il habite, appartenant à son débiteur forain".

[5]) C. Com. § 172: „Indépendamment des formalités prescrites pour l'exercice de l'action en garantie, le porteur d'une lettre d'échange protestée faute de payement peut, en obtenant la permission du juge, saisir conservatoirement les effets mobiliers des tireurs, accepteurs et endosseurs".

[6]) CPC § 417: „Dans les cas qui requerront célérité, le président du tribunal pourra permettre d'assigner, même de jour à jour et d'heure à heure, et de saisir les effets mobiliers: il pourra, suivant l'exigence des cas, assujettir le demandeur à donner caution, ou à justifier de solvabilité suffisante. Ses ordonnances seront exécutoires nonobstant opposition ou appel".

sums and effects of the debtor, prevent the latter from receiving the same [1]).

§ 32. *Saisie-revendication* may take place only in virtue of an *ordonnance sur requête* issued by the president of the tribunal of first instance [2]). If the person in whose possession the property is found refuses to allow the seizure, the seizure is suspended, except that plaintiff may keep watch at the door to prevent removal of the property, until the matter is brought before the judge *sur référé* [3]). The seizure is made in the same form as the *saisie-exécution*, except that the person against whom it is made may be made custodian of the property [4]). Of course, in case the seizure is upheld, the property is not sold, but is restored to the plaintiff, who is asserting his ownership of the goods in question.

Saisie-gagerie does not require permission of the judge, if one day's notice is given to the defendant [5]). The latter may be made custodian of the goods [6]).

Saisie-foraine requires permission of the judge [7]). The person seizing becomes custodian of the goods if they are in his hands; otherwise a custodian will be designated [8]). *Saisie-arrêt* requires permission of the judge, unless applicant possesses an authentic or private document of title [9]). For *saisie conservatoire commerciale*, permission is required. It is now settled that for this *saisie* the jurisdiction of the president of the commercial tribunal is exclusive [10]). The president weighs against each other the likelihood of plaintiff's claim being justified, and the severe character of the measure requested, the *vraisemblance de la créance* and the *gravité de la mesure sollicitée* [11]).

---

[1]) CPC § 557: „Tout créancier peut.. saisir-arrêter entre les mains d'un tiers les sommes et effets appartenant à son débiteur, ou s'opposer à leur remise".

[2]) § 826. [3]) § 829. [4]) § 830. [5]) § 819.

[6]) § 821. [7]) § 822. [8]) § 823. [9]) §§ 558, 557.

[10]) Since § 417 occurs in title 25 dealing with procedure before the tribunals of commerce, it is evident that „the president of the tribunal" is the president of the commercial tribunal. Nevertheless by virtue of the principle of plenitude of jurisdiction in the civil tribunals as common law courts, while the commercial tribunals are courts of exceptional jurisdiction, the former for a time claimed for their president the power of ordering this *saisie*; and due to the policy of abstention on the part of presidents of the commercial tribunal of the Seine after 1818, the jurisdiction was entirely in the hands of the president of the civil tribunal. The court of Paris however by decision of 9 January 1866 annuled as being given without competence an order of the president of the civil tribunal, and jurisprudence now recognizes the exclusive jurisdiction of the president of the commercial tribunal. Druart 68—74.

[11]) Druart 44—5: „Il doit en un mot se demander si la préjudice que le débiteur pour-

Intangible property falls within the scope of *saisie-arrêt.* Airplanes are treated in a special law [1]). Land can not be seized for interim security. In all *saisies conservatoires,* defendant is not heard before execution of the seizure, as its value lies in surprising him before he can secrete the property and prevent its being taken [2]).

At the outset *saisie-arrêt* is purely conservatory; but it becomes a measure of execution for satisfaction in the course of proceedings, when the *assignation en validité* to test the validity of the seizure is brought [3]). Such notification to and action against the debtor of the party seizing must follow within a week of the *saisie* [4]); otherwise the *saisie* will be null and void. Until notified that such action has been instituted, the person against whom the seizure is directed may make valid payments to his creditor [5]). If the *saisie* is declared valid, the property seized is sold, and the plaintiff satisfied out of the proceeds [6]).

Likewise no sale may be made in virtue of a *saisie-foraine* or *saisie-gagerie* until after their validity has been upheld [7]). *Demande en validité* in case of *saisie-revendication* is likewise envisaged by the code. [8]) No text mentions such a procedure in connection with the *saisie conservatoire commerciale.* Consequently it was disallowed by the Court of Cassation in its decision of 30 November, 1927, but is regarded by writers as being admissible. Nevertheless in practice the procedure followed is to proceed in the commercial court to obtain an executable title, in virtue of which execution for satisfaction takes place, irrespective of the

---

rait éprouver du fait de la saisie, l'emporterait en importance sur la perte que devrait supporter le créancier, au cas où son débiteur détournerait les effets mobiliers".

[1]) Druart 59. §§ 17—8 of the law of 31 May 1924.

[2]) Glasson-Tissier, 2ed. II, 621.

[3]) Ibid. 620. [4]) CPC § 563.

[5]) § 565: „Faute de demande en validité, la saisie ou opposition sera nulle; faute de dénonciation de cette demande au tiers saisi, les payements par lui faits jusqu'à la dénonciation seront valables".

[6]) § 579: „Si la saisie-arrêt est déclarée valable, il sera procédé à la vente et distribution du prix..". The civil tribunal, not the commercial tribunal, is competent for *saisie-arrêt* in commercial matters. Mérignac-Miguel, I, 260—1.

[7]) § 824: „Il ne pourra être procédé à la vente sur les saisies énoncées au présent titre, qu'après qu'elles auront été déclarées valables."

[8]) § 831: „La demande en validité de la saisie sera portée devant le tribunal du domicile de celui sur qui elle est faite; et si elle est connexe à une instance déjà pendante, elle le sera au tribunal saisi de cette instance". It is said that the effect of §§ 824 and 831 is to make *action en validité* mandatory for the *saisies* in question. Bouchon 82; Druart 139.

previous *saisie conservatoire* [1]). An *action en validité* in the commercial *saisie* would involve unusual complications, and the case would pass through at least three separate jurisdictions. The president of the commercial tribunal would order the seizure; the civil tribunal pass on its formal validity; the commercial tribunal give judgment on the merits of the case and decide whether the creditor had a valid claim [2]). In addition, difficulties regarding execution might come before the civil tribunal [3]), or its president acting *sur référé* [4]).

§ 33. In all cases of urgency (or where it is a question of deciding provisionally on difficulties relative to the execution of an executory title) the president may hear the parties at a special audience, or, if celerity is required, at his hotel or on a holiday, and make any orders which do not prejudice the merits of the case [5]).

The restriction that the order must not prejudice the principal issue (*faire grief au principal, faire préjudice au principal*) does not mean that the order may not have irreparable effects and in fact cause damage which cannot be remedied by the final judgment [6]). The president may give other measures than those asked, but can not go beyond what is requested. He is bound by the rule *ne ultra petita* [7]). No relief is given if there is not actual peril to applicant's rights [8]).

The law of 11 March 1924 conferred jurisdiction *en référé* on the president of the commercial tribunal [9]). Prior to that time it would seem that there could be no *référé* procedure in commercial matters. [10]).

---

[1]) Druart 145; Ripert 1016. [2]) Ibid. 142.

[3]) CPC § 442: „Les tribunaux de commerce ne connaîtront pas de l'exécution de leurs jugements". [4]) § 806.

[5]) CPC § 809: „Les ordonnances sur référé ne feront aucun préjudice au principal".

[6]) 2 Mérignac-Miguel 188; 3 Glasson-Tissier, 3 ed. 35. See note 3, p. 23 *supra*.

[7]) 2 Mérignac-Miguel 190.

[8]) Ibid. 27: „Il faut qu'un droit soit menacé". Order to determine state of passengers after a wreck denied when no showing of litigation was made (*rapport litigieux actuel ou éventuel*). Cf. Curet 468, action need not be pending.

[9]) To CPC § 417 the following was added: „Le président du tribunal de commerce ou le juge qui le remplace pourra être saisi par la voie de référé, dans tous les cas d'urgence, à la condition qu'ils rentrent dans la compétence des tribunaux de commerce. Les articles 807 à 811 du Code de procédure civile sont applicables aux référés en matière commerciale".

[10]) Curet 39; 2 Mérignac-Miguel 28—30; 2 Bertin 123—5 contended that „president of the tribunal of first instance" meant in commercial matters president of the commercial tribunal. In practice the president of the civil tribunal did exercise such jurisdiction. De Belleyme 246. But this view did not prevail. 2 Glasson-Tissier 3ed. 63.

An ingenious device invented by President de Belleyme, who brought *référé* jurisdiction to its present advanced state of development [1]), raises interesting and controversial problems. As has been seen, judicial permission is necessary for all *saisies* except *saisie-arrêt* in virtue of a document of title and *saisie-gagerie* after previous notice to the defendant. That permission is given in the *ex parte* procedure called *ordonnance sur requête* [2]). President de Belleyme, distrustful of *ex parte* proceedings, counselled a policy of enlightened resistance [3]), (*résistance éclairée du juge*) in granting such requests, but also, esteeming contradictory debate as essential to justice [4]), devised a means of ensuring contentious consideration of cases in which an *ordonnance sur requête* was sought. This was achieved by inserting in the order a clause permitting reference to the judge afterwards if the defendant chose to contest the *saisie* (*réserve d'en référer*). The controversial question then arises, assuming the legality of this course, as to the nature of the jurisdiction thus exercised by the president. Is it a continuance of the original order, as de Belleyme thought, and hence partaking of its quality, whatever that may be, contentious, gracious, or administrative jurisdiction? Or is it the ordinary *référé* jurisdiction established by CPC §§ 806—11? Or a *tertium quid*? [5]) Would the president have the right to retract his *ordonnance* in any case, even without the clause? [6]) Is termination of the provisional *régime* a definitive decision, and one surpassing the powers of a judge on *référé* under CPC § 809? [7]) At all events it is clear that the order can not be revoked after the *action en*

---

1) M. de Belleyme as prefect of police suppressed mendicants and introduced uniformed policemen. Becoming in 1829 president of the tribunal of the Seine, he organised its work in special chambers. „La juridiction des référés, telle que M. de Belleyme l'a organisée, est une des grandes institutions qui ont légitimement illustré son nom". 2 Bertin 21—4.

2) The exact juridical nature of the *ordonnance sur requête* is controversial. Is it an exercise of voluntary or contentious jurisdiction, (*juridiction gracieuse* or *juridiction contentieuse*), if it is a *juridiction* at all? In general appeal is allowed only in cases of contentious jurisdiction. Without deciding the question, the court of cassation permits appeal on the ground that appeal must be permitted whenever the rights of third parties are endangered. Professor Morel considers these orders as a third type of judicial acts called acts of judicial administration (*actes d'administration judiciare*). 3 Glasson-Tissier, 3ed. 568; Druart 170—6.

3) De Belleyme 135.

4) Ibid. 143: „Un débat contradictoire est le principe d'une bonne justice".

5) 1 Mérignac-Miguel 55—8, 71—2; 1 Bonjean § 121.

6) Mérignac-Miguel 1 : 79, 2 : 396; 2 Glasson-Tissier 3ed. 29.

7) 2 Glasson-Tissier 3ed. 37.

validité has been introduced, for then another jurisdiction is seised of the question, and the president can not oust it. If he revoked the *saisie*, there would be nothing left to pass on in the subsequent proceeding [1]).

§ 34. *Référé* procedure, it is said [2]), if not originating in the *in jus vocatio torto collo* of the Twelve Tables, at least was recognized in the edict of 22 January 1685 on the administration of justice in the Châtelet de Paris. An enumeration of many matters calling for speedy decision was contained in §§ 6, 7, 9 and 13 of the edict of 1685 [3]). The code of civil procedure made a concise provision for all matters of urgency. It was felt impossible to enumerate in detail all urgent cases which might arise, and that the text should be made general. M. Réal in the *exposé des motifs* referred with feeling to the value of this institution, and the illustrious magistrates of the past who each evening surrounded by young men of the law thus put an end to controversies more effectively that at the formal audience earlier in the day [4]). To these must now be added the impressive figure of President de Belleyme. During the world war, in view of legislative restrictions on normal procedure, it became customary to transact practically all judicial business by *référé* [5]). The institution is an expression of French national character, and enables the century-old code of civil procedure to function under modern circumstances [6]).

Likewise the *saisies conservatoires* have their roots in old

---

[1]) Ibid. 30; 2 Mérignac-Miguel 254. Cf. Caroli 269, 271, 276.

[2]) Curet 4.

[3]) 2 Neron-Girard 195—6 gives the text. Also quoted in Bazot 174—5.

[4]) Bertin I, 23; II, 19: „Puissent les présidents des tribunaux se pénétrer de tout le bien qu'ils pourront opérer en faisant ainsi de leur hôtel, par des jugements équitables, un temple de conciliation! Puissent-ils imiter, faire revivre en leurs personnes, et en exerçant ces augustes et paternelles fonctions, ces magistrats célèbres, les Dargonges, les Dufour, les Augran d'Alleray qui, chaque soir, environnés de jeunes légistes, dont ils fécondaient les talents, dont ils éclairaient le zèle, anéantissaient par des jugements provisoires, rendus à leur hôtel, plus de procès qu'ils n'en avaient terminé par de jugements définitifs rendus le même jour, à l'audience du matin".

[5]) 2 Mérignac-Miguel 305: „Le référé devint ainsi, au cours de la guerre, la voie normale et à peu près unique d'agir en justice".

[6]) Klein 323 sees in the jurisdiction of the president of the tribunal apart from that of the full court a survival from monarchical times. A German *Senatspräsident* has no special authority greater than that of the other judges. Likewise the president of the Permanent Court of International Justice, when the Court is not sitting, acts as instrumentality of the Court, in accordance with its rules (§ 30 of Statute of the Court), and not as a separate and independent jurisdiction. Cf. Paul de Vineul in 57 RDILC (1930) 768.

French law, notably in title VIII of the custom of Paris [1]). A very curious provisional measure was the feudal custom whereby the lord might remove doors and windows from their hinges, and tenants replacing them before arrears of rent were acquitted incurred a fine [2]). *Saisie-féodale* permitted a lord to appropriate the fruits of land held of him for want of homage when the heir did not pay transfer duties [3]). *Saisie-censuelle,* for default in payment of *cens* (an ignoble rent instead of rent-service, for which *saisie-féodale* was allowed), was in most French customs purely conservatory [4]). *Saisie-gagerie* existed as a conservatory measure in many feudal customs [5]). *Saisie-foraine,* from which the modern commercial saisie also sprang [6]), goes back to early times [7]). Modern *saisie-arrêt* against intangibles is one form of the ancient *saisie & arrêt* which was contrasted with *saisie & exécution* [8]). So too *saisie-revendication* is not of recent origin [9]).

§ 35. 9. Dutch law [10]).

(*a*) Dutch law is modelled closely on French law, with several

---

[1]) 2 Glasson-Tissier 2ed. 620. [2]) 2 Tambour 66.

[3]) Originally the whole estate definitively reverted to the lord, *dominium utile* and *eminens* being united for want of a mesne tenant. Later it became possible for the heir to get back the estate on making homage. Where the *saisie-féodale* was allowed for non-payment of profits instead of for default of homage, as in Auxerre and Troyes, it had more the character of a *mesure conservatoire.* Martin, I, 271, 316, 319; Tambour II, 341, 343.

[4]) Martin, I, 407; Tambour, II, 350, 361.

[5]) Martin, II, 585—6; Tambour, II, 367, 370.

[6]) Druart 28; Garsonnet, III, 50.

[7]) Martin, II, 546; Ferrière, II, 1286. According to Brodeau II, 580, it was instituted by Louis le Gros in 1134. Personal arrest was suppressed by the ordonnance of Louis XVI in 1786. See also Ordonnance d'Orleans of January 1560, § 144.

[8]) Tambour, II, 379; Ferrière, II, 998, 1292. Pothier, Traité de Procédure civile 469 defines the types of measure current in his time: „Le simple arrêt est un acte judiciaire par lequel un créancier, pour sa sûreté, met sous la main de Justice les choses appartenantes à son débiteur, pour l'empecher d'en disposer, Il est bien différent de la saisie-exécution, et de la saisie-arrêt; car l'exécution se fait à l'effet de vendre les meubles exécutés, et la saisie-arrêt aux fins de faire vuider, au débiteur arrêté, les mains en celles de l'arrestant, au lieu que le simple arrêt se fait seulement pour conserver les choses arrêtés, et empêcher que le débiteur n'en dispose". See also Molinaeus, Comm. in cons. Par., tit. II, gloss. I, in verbo arrest ou brandon.

[9]) 2 Glasson-Tissier, 2ed. 620.

[10]) In addition to treatises in the Bibliography, see Molengraaf, Opmerkingen over het voorstel van wet van den heer Hartogh tot wijziging van het Wetboek van Burgerlijke Rechtsvordering, II, de voorstellen betreffende die middelen tot bewaring van het recht, 14 RM (1895) 95—111; Kruseman, Partielle Herziening van het Wetboek van burgerlijke Rechtsvordering, V, Herziening van de bepalingen omtrent het kort geding voor den President der Rechtsbank, 47 RM (1928) 307—330; Maris, Het conservatoir derden-beslag tegen Schuldenaren, die geene bekende Woonplaats hebben binnen het Rijk, 49 RM (1930) 336—349.

improvements. Thus in the *Wetboek voor burgerlijke regtsvordering* (code of civil procedure) the seizure by the holder of a bill of exchange [1]) is extended to the holder of an order bill [2]). Likewise there is *saisie* in all commercial cases where the creditor makes a summary showing of the validity of his claim and a well-founded fear of disappearance (*verduistering*) of debtor's movable or immovable property [3]). The seizure falls if action is not brought within 3 days [4]); or if on summary hearing the debt or necessity of the attachment appears to be unfounded; or if security is given [5]).

(*b*) Book III, title iv, §§ 721—770*g*, *van middelen tot bewaring van zijn regt,* deals with other conservatory measures. *Beslag tot revindicatie van roerende goederen* (*saisie-revendication*) allows everyone entitled to bring an action in vindication of ownership to attach the property, on previous permission of the judge [6]). Within 8 days the action to declare the seizure valid must be brought [7]).

(*c*) *Inbeslagneming of arrest in handen van den schuldenaar* is a measure not found in French law [8]), similar to the Italian *sequestro conservativo* and German *Arrest.* On summary showing of validity of claim and well-founded fear of disappearance of debtor's movable or immovable property, creditor may request permission to attach movables [9]). The debtor may be heard previously, or subsequently, on rapid procedure (*kort geding*) analogous to the French *référé* [10]). The seizure is invalidated on security being given, or if action is not brought within 8 days [11]).

(*d*) *Arrest onder derden* (*saisie-arrêt*) [12]) as in French law requires a title or permission of the judge [13]). Action to declare validity of the seizure must be brought within 8 days [14]).

(*e*) *Pandbeslag voor huren en pachten* (*saisie-gagerie*), as in French law, requires one day's previous notice to debtor or permission of the judge [15]). It must be validated within 8 days. The rule that no sale may be made until the seizure is declared valid [16]) in Dutch law seems to apply only to this *saisie* [17]). But the re-

[1]) § 303. [2]) § 304. [3]) § 305. [4]) § 309.
[5]) § 310. [6]) §§ 721—2. [7]) § 726.
[8]) Druart 26, 71 notes the desirability of a *saisie* in civil matters corresponding to the *saisie conservatoire* in commercial cases.
[9]) § 727. [10]) §§ 289—97. [11]) § 732.
[12]) §§ 735—757 d. [13]) § 735. [14]) § 738.
[15]) § 758. [16]) See as to French CPC § 824 note 7, p. 74 *supra*. [17]) § 763.

quirement that such an action must be brought is found in all *saisies*, even the commercial ones.

(*f*) *Beslag tegen schuldenaren, die geene bekende woonplaats hebben, en tegen vreemdelingen* (*saisie-foraine*) is likewise found [1]. Without any title or summons to pay, but with permission of the judge, property of debtors having no known domicile (*woonplaats*) in Holland may be attached [2]. Foreigners without settled residence (*vast verblijf*) in Holland may be arrested (*gegijzeld*) on order of the judge for debts due and payable to a Dutch creditor [3]. The attachment and arrest are revoked on giving security[4]. Here again the action must be brought in 8 days [5].

(*g*) *Beslag op onroerend goed* enables real property to be attached in the cases mentioned in §§ 303—5, 727 and 764 (commercial, civil, and foreign *saisie*). In addition to the formalities required by those articles, bringing of action to declare the seizure valid must be recorded within 14 days in a special docket kept for that purpose [6].

(*h*) Sequestration of movable or immovable property with respect to which ownership or possession is contested is provided for in the civil code [7].

(*i*) Provisional alimentation and domicile of wife may also be regulated [8]. In violations of copyright, the Dutch law views the *saisie* as one based on the aggrieved party's right of property, and he may treat the offending publications as his own property or have them destroyed [9].

§ 36. 10. Hungarian law [10].

Hungarian law affords the best example of a purely casuistic treatment of interim protection. The general principle which we have noted in many legislations is absent, and the specific cases provided for in statutes cover less ground than do the similar texts in other legal systems which we have discussed. The Hungarian texts correspond in the main to the special provisions customarily made in other laws.

---

1) §§ 764—770. 2) § 764. 3) § 768. 4) § 769.
5) § 770. 6) § 770c. 7) BWB § 1775. 8) §§ 267—8.
9) Law of 23 September 1912, § 28.
10) Hungarian law continues to apply in certain portions of the territory of other succession states of the Austro-Hungarian dual monarchy.

Thus we find alimentation cases [1]; copyright [2]; unfair competition [3]; interim orders for protection of property pending appointment of curator for incapable persons [4]. Likewise sequestration of movables and immovables ownership or possession of which is disputed is found [5]. *Possessorium summarissimum* and entry of *lis pendens* in the land registry are also available in disputes regarding land [6]. Measures for maintaining the security of mortgagee against depreciation in value of the security is provided by a recent law [7]. Similarly provision is made for preserving the secured debts of certain industrial undertakings which receive loans from a central bank [8]. Personal arrest does not exist.

§ 37. From the preceding study of the principles of procedural law and their manifestation in various legal systems, interesting conclusions within the domain of comparative law might be drawn [9]. Likewise the survey we have made furnishes a practical guide for mixed arbitral tribunals, if the view [10] is accepted that such tribunals should apply the law of the parties to the dispute. But more important is the result of our investigation in view of the fact that „general principles of law recognized by civilized states" constitute a not to be neglected element of the international law applicable by the tribunals of our day. We proceed to a consideration of those elements, and of the rules regarding interim protection which international practice has developed. We now turn our attention to measures *pendente lite* in international law.

---

[1]) 1894: XXXXI, §§ 72, 102. [2]) 1921: LIV, § 28 (7).

[3]) 1923: V, § 11. [4]) 1925: VIII, § 54.

[5]) 1881: IX, §§ 237(*d*)—254. Provisional execution with a view to security, like that in Austria, (see note 1 p. 50 *supra*) is available. 1881: LX, §§ 223—236. A *Pfandrecht* is thus created. No such priority is created by the sequestration of litigious property here referred to.

[6]) 1892: XXVIII, 1911: I, §§ 575—582.

[7]) 1927: XXV, § 33. [8]) 1928: XXI, § 18.

[9]) The idea of comparative law introduced by Saleilles, Conception et Objet de la Science du Droit comparé, (rapport presenté au congrès international de droit comparé, Paris 1900), 15, as a „droit commun de l'humanité civilisée" similar to Anglo-American common law or the customary law of France and Germany prior to codification, stimulated fruitful study in that field. Lévy-Ullmann, de l'Utilité des Etudes comparatives, 1 La revue du droit (Quebec 1923) 390. See also Lambert, Etudes de Droit commun législatif ou de Droit civil comparé, 1903. That international law does not stand to suffer from irreconcilable diversities of national legal doctrine is maintained by Lauterpacht, The so-called Anglo-American and Continental Schools of Thought in International Law, 12 BYB (1931) 31—62.

[10]) Of Colamandrei in Riv. di diritto commerciale, 1922, 337 cited by Rabel 38. But cf. Conn. v. Mass., 282 U.S. 660, 670 (1930).

CHAPTER III

INTERIM PROTECTION IN INTERNATIONAL LAW

§ 38. (a) *International law as part of the law of the land.*

In the absence of specific rules of constitutional law applicable in the premises, controversies between component states of federal unions must be decided by the application of international law as part of the law of the land. For war and self-help are ruled out as methods of settling such inter-state disputes; but this does not mean that there are no restrictions upon the injuries which member states are bound to tolerate [1]), or that the federal court having jurisdiction over such litigations is entitled to exercise legislative functions [2]). In the United States [3]), Switzerland [4]), and Germany [5]) the courts apply international law under the circumstances described.

1. In the United States, the federal Supreme Court has original jurisdiction of suits between States. Such cases are tried under liberal equity practice [6]). It has been decided that interim injunctions may issue in a proper case [7]), but in fact relief *pendente*

---

[1]) Ga. v. Tenn. Copper Co., 206 U.S. 230, 237 (1906).

[2]) Mo. v. Ill., 200 U.S. 496, 519 (1905).

[3]) R. I. v. Mass., 12 Pet. 657, 737 (1838); Kansas v. Colorado, 185 U.S. 125, 146—7 (1902): „Sitting, as it were, as an international, as well as a domestic tribunal, we apply Federal law, State law, and international law, as the exigencies of the particular case may demand; and we are unwilling in this case to proceed on the mere technical admissions made by the demurrer"; Kan. v. Colo., 206 U.S. 46, 97 (1906): „International law is no alien in this tribunal".

[4]) Schindler, The Administration of Justice in the Swiss Federal Court in intercantonal Disputes, 15 AJ (1921) 160; Huber, The intercantonal Law of Switzerland, 3 AJ (1909) 90; Bolle, Das interkantonale Recht, 1907, 32.

[5]) Jerusalem 184.

[6]) R.I. v. Mass., 14 Pet. 210, 257 (1840). In an inter-state suit the burden of making out a clear and convincing case for an injunction is greater than usual; but when that requirement is met, the plaintiff is more likely to be entitled to specific relief. Ga. v. Tenn. Copper Co., 206 U.S. 230, 237 (1906).

[7]) In Mo. v. Ill., 180 U.S. 208, 216 (1900) a temporary injunction *pendente lite* had been prayed for in a suit to prevent pollution of a river by sewage. A demurrer to the

lite is hardly ever granted [1]. Most inter-state litigation deals with long-standing boundary disputes, or regulation of the use of rivers.

2. In Switzerland the federal tribunal has jurisdiction of inter-cantonal disputes, whether involving civil or public law [2]. In addition to a general provision that in the absence of contrary dispositions the rules prescribed by the law regulating procedure before the tribunal in civil cases [3] shall be applied [4], there is a specific article authorizing the president of the court to take provisional measures necessary to preserve the status quo or safeguard jeopardized legal interests [5]. Examination of the decisions however fails to reveal any cases in which this procedure has been invoked in practice.

§ 39. 3. The German *Staatsgerichtshof*, on the other hand, has frequently granted measures of interim protection, but the propriety of its exercise of such a jurisdiction is not so clear [6].

---

bill was overruled; but leave to answer was given, and it does not appear whether an injunction was in fact granted. The Court said: „We do not wish to be understood as holding that, in a case like the present one, where the injuries grow out of the prosecution of a public work authorized by law, a court of equity ought to interpose by way of preliminary or interlocutory injunction, when it is denied by answer that there is any reasonable foundation for the charges contained in the bill. We are dealing with the case of a bill alleging, in explicit terms, that damage and irreparable injury will naturally and necessarily be occasioned by acts of the defendants, and where the defendants have chosen to have their rights disposed of, so far as the present hearing is concerned, upon the assertions of this bill." Ibid. 248.

1) In S.C. v. Ga., 93 U.S. 4, 14 (1876) there appears to have been a „special injunction" *pendente lite*: „There is no nuisance against which an injunction should be granted. The special injunction heretofore ordered is dissolved. The bill of the complainants is dismissed".

2) Bundesgesetz vom 22. März 1893 betreffend die Organisation der Bundesrechtspflege unter Berücksichtigung der durch Bundesgesetz vom 6. Oktober 1911 getroffenen Abänderungen, §§ 18, 175.

3) See p. 52 *supra*.

4) § 22: „Wo dieses Gesetz keine besonderen Bestimmungen über das Verfahren enthält, finden die Vorschriften des Bundesgesetzes über das Verfahren bei dem Bundesgerichte in bürgerlichen Rechtsstreitigkeiten und des Bundesgesetzes über die Bundesstrafrechtspflege Anwendung".

5) § 185: „Der Präsident des Bundesgerichts ist befugt, nach Eingang der Beschwerdeschrift auf Ansuchen einer Partei diejenigen vorsorglichen Verfügungen zu treffen, welche erforderlich sind, um den bestehenden Zustand festzuhalten oder bedrohte rechtliche Interessen einstweilen sicherzustellen".

6) Article 108 of the German constitution of 11 August 1919 provides that a *Staatsgerichtshof* shall be established by law to deal with disputes between the federal government (*Reich*) and provinces (*Länder*), between *Länder inter se*, and constitutional questions arising within a *Land*. The court was created by the law of 9 July 1921. § 23 empowers the court to adopt its own rules (*Geschäftsordnung*). In its *Geschäftsordnung* of 20 September 1921 there is no mention of interim measures. The court's power to order such measures in the absence of a text has been the subject of controversy among writers.

a. In its decision of 10 October 1925 [1]) the court first proclaimed its conclusion that the silence of its rules was no objection to application of principles of civil procedure, notably the ZPO. The court deduced its power to grant interim protection from the fact that its final decisions are not mere expressions of opinion, but are executable by the President of the *Reich*. If parties are subject to the jurisdiction of the court to the extent that a situation corresponding to its final decisions may be established for good by force, it is difficult to see why it is not authorized to regulate the situation for the time being [2]).

Consequently, in the dispute between Lübeck and Mecklenburg-Schwerin over the exercise of fishery rights and maritime police in the bay of Travemund, the court decided that regulation of the situation *pendente lite* should take place on the basis of the last uncontested status quo [3]).

b. In its decision of 12 May 1928 [4]) the court refused relief sought by the „*Wirtschaftsbund*" in Waldeck. Applicant desired an *einstweilige Verfügung* to prevent union between Waldeck and Prussia. The court held that plaintiff was not entitled to sue, as it was not really a political party, and did not manifest the necessary activity in the press, in holding public meetings, putting up candidates at elections, etc. Moreover, there was no substantial injury threatening plaintiff's interests. Since the union complained of could be effected only by means of a federal law (*Reichsgesetz*), nothing that Waldeck might be able to do would achieve the result against which plaintiff sought protection.

c. In its decision of 17 November 1928 [5]) the court held uncon-

---

[1]) 1 Lammers-Simons 212; 111 RGZ, Anhang, 21.

[2]) „Sind die Parteien aber der Gerichtsbarkeit des Staatsgerichtshofs in der Weise unterworfen, dass ein durch dessen Entscheidung angeordneter Zustand für die Dauer zwangsweise herbeigeführt werden kann, so ist es nicht leicht einzusehen, weshalb der Staatsgerichtshof nicht auch an einer vorläufigen Regelung befugt sein soll, wenn sie aus besonderen Gründen erforderlich ist. Einer ausdrücklichen Ermächtigung durch den Gesetzgeber bedürfte es hierzu nicht." As to the soundness of this reasoning, see p. 25 *supra* and p. 104 *infra*.

[3]) „Die hiernach zulässige und erforderliche Regelung des einstweiligen Zustandes hat auf der Grundlage des letzten ruhigen Besitzstandes zu erfolgen". 1 Lammers-Simons 215. It was therefore ordered: „Bis zur Entscheidung in der Hauptsache wird dem Lande Mecklenburg-Schwerin die Ausübung der Fischereihoheit und der Schiffahrtspolizei in der Travemunder Bucht bis zur Linie.... untersagt. Die Ausübung dieser Rechte bis zu der bezeichneten Linie steht so lange allein der freien und Hansestadt Lübeck zu". 1 Lammers-Simons 213.

[4]) 1 Lammers-Simons 411.

[5]) 1 Lammers-Simons 156; 122 RGZ, Anhang, 17.

stitutional the law of 9 April 1927 about distribution to the Southern *Länder* of proceeds from beer tax. This decision created a gap in the relations of the *Reich* and those *Länder*, which required to be filled, lest the finances of both parties come into disorder. An *einstweilige Verfügung* was necessary in order to fill that gap. If Prussia should show that the figures set by the court in its order were not proper, it would be possible to modify them later on [1]).

d. In another interesting case, *Länder* claiming to be entitled to appoint representatives to the board of directors of the German railway system (*Reichsbahn*) applied for an injunction to prevent the *Reich* from filling vacancies pending litigation. The *Reich* contended that it was no longer obliged to recognize rights of the *Länder* to appoint directors, since the Dawes plan had reduced the size of the board.

Instead of granting interim protection immediately, the President decided to refer the case to a plenary sitting of the court. The *Reich* opposed the request for *einstweilige Verfügung*, and urged that the decision *in merito* be rendered without delay. A hearing was set for December 15. On December 14 the Reich appointed its own representatives to the vacant places on the board.

When the court met, it postponed indefinitely consideration of the case in chief, declaring that the *Reich's* action had made it impossible for the court to exercise its constitutional duties. In conformity with the court's order, the President, in a letter which was not published, complained to the President of the *Reich*, demanding suitable guarantees that the court not be hindered in its functioning. The President and the government of the *Reich* took no action, except to declare their great respect for the court and its President while disclaiming any desire to interfere with or disregard decisions of the court. The government had been free to act so long as the court had not in fact made any order tying it down, and the state of negotiations with the Director General of Reparations had made it expedient to name the directors without further delay. Feeling responsible for having brought about the situation, by reason of his refusal to grant the *einstweilige Verfügung* as soon as requested, the President of the court, Dr. Wal-

[1]) Note that this *einstweilige Verfügung* regulates the situation *after* the court's decision, not that *until* the decision. Jahn in 59 J.W. (1930) 1162. Cf. Wis. v. Ill., 278 U. S. 399, 419 (1928).

ter C. Simons, resigned in protest against the conduct of the *Reich*. Subsequently he was made an honorary member of the American Society of International Law [1]).

e. In its decision of 13 July 1929 [2]) the court declined to pass upon the constitutionality of a law not yet promulgated. Consequently, being without jurisdiction in the principal proceeding (*Hauptsache*), it would not by *einstweilige Verfügung* interfere with the promulgation.

The court said that oral hearing was not necessary.

§ 40. *f*. In its decision of 23 October 1929 [3]) the court refused a request for *einstweilige Verfügung* presented by a political party, with a view to setting aside an administrative order forbidding Prussian officials to sign papers for a popular referendum on the Young plan.

From this decision it would follow that if they were forbidden to vote, and the court could not render before the election its final decision upholding their right of suffrage, their constitutional right to vote would be of no value.

The court first pointed out that the previous cases in which *einstweilige Verfügung* had been granted involved controversies between *Länder* or between the *Reich* and *Länder*, not constitutional questions within a *Land*. Therefore it was an open question whether *einstweilige Verfügung* is admissible in cases falling within that branch of the court's jurisdiction.

But the request was refused upon the ground that it involved a decision upon the principal question at issue. Such a decision, the court says, requires observance of the rules of procedure with respect to full hearing of the parties and all their arguments. But the court would then be in a position to pronounce final judgment, and nothing would be gained by making a temporary order. Thus there is never occasion for *einstweilige Verfügung* in such a case [4]).

---

[1]) Simons in 15 ABAJ (1929) 767; Jahn in 59 J.W. (1930) 1163; Giese, in 34 Deutsche Juristen-Zeitung (1929) 130—5; Linz, ibid. 187—202; Glum, in 1 Zt. f. aus. öff. Rt. u. Vrt. (1929) teil 1, 458—475; Teil 2, 711—8.

[2]) 2 Lammers-Simons 98.

[3]) 2 Lammers-Simons 72.

[4]) 2 Lammers-Simons 77—8; „Es liegt deshalb nahe zu fragen, ob denn in Verfassungsstreitigkeiten innerhalb eines Landes Raum für eine Einstweilige Verfügung ist. Eine Stellungnahme zu dieser Frage erübrigt sich im Vorliegenden Falle indessen, da

One writer has remarked that this decision lays down an unusual rule, and perhaps indicates that the court is weakening in its view that it has jurisdiction to order *einstweilige Verfügung* [1]. As has been mentioned, that jurisdiction was questioned by some critics of the court's decisions.

In this connection it should be noticed that the court expressly refers to the fact that failure to observe the ordinary rules can be justified *in a procedure based on no express text but simply derived from general considerations* only to the extent that such procedure is possible without necessitating that the court take a position with respect to the matters under consideration in the main proceeding.

If the court's jurisdiction to grant interim protection at all is doubtful, it will very likely refuse to exercise such jurisdiction where it would amount to deciding the main question in dispute. But the rule laid down by the court in this decision will not commend itself to a tribunal having an undoubted and explicit authority to grant interim protection [2].

---

der Antrag auf Erlass einer einstweiligen Verfügung schon daran scheitert, dass mit ihrem Erlass zugleich über die Hauptsache entschieden werden würde. Das wäre aber mit den für den Staatsgerichtshof geltenden Verfahrensvorschriften unvereinbar.. Dagegen haben die Parteien Anspruch darauf, dass die zu ihrem Schutze gegebenen, eine gründliche Erörterung und erschöpfende Aufklärung der Sache gewährleistenden Vorschriften im Hauptverfahren eingehalten werden. Von ihrer genauen Beobachtung darf, zumal bei der Wichtigkeit der zur Zuständigkeit des Staatsgerichtshofs gehörenden Sachen, ohne Zustimmung der Parteien nicht abgewichen werden. Ihre Nichtanwendung in einem Verfahren über eine einstweilige Verfügung, die auf keine ausdrückliche Bestimmung gestützt, sondern überhaupt nur aus allgemeinen Erwägungen hergeleitet werden kann, lässt sich daher nur insoweit rechtfertigen, als dieses Verfahren sich ohne Stellungnahme zur Hauptsache durchführen lässt. Es würde eine mit den für das Verfahren des Staatsgerichtshofs massgebenden Rechtsvorschriften unvereinbare Beeinträchtigung der beklagten Partei bedeuten, wollte man sie nötigen, eine Entscheidung über den sächlichen Streit entgegenzunehmen, ohne dass sie Gelegenheit gehabt hätte, ihre Einwendungen hierzu dem Gerichte ausführlich darzulegen. Dass eine einstweilige Verfügung nur zeitlich beschränkte Geltung besitzt, kann nicht massgeblich ins Gewicht fallen. Denn die ihr tatsächlich innewohnende erhebliche Bedeutung würde sich auch bei der endgültigen Entscheidung auswirken, sofern die einstweilige Verfügung dieser schon vorgriffe. Eine die Endentscheidung vorwegnehmende vorläufige Anordnung dürfte daher nur unter den vollen Sicherungen des Gesetzes über den Staatsgerichtshof und seiner Geschäftsordnung ergehen. Dann würde aber auch die Hauptentscheidung erlassen werden können. Für eine einstweilige Verfügung von solchen Tragweite ist also niemals Raum. Die einstweiligen Verfügungen, die der Staatsgerichtshof bisher erlassen hat, haben sich stets darauf beschränkt, einen einstweiligen Zustand zu regeln, ohne der Hauptentscheidung irgendwie vorzugreifen". Cf. Phillimore report, p. 104 *infra*.

[1]) Jahn 59 JW (1930) 1161: „Die Ablehnung einer einstweiligen Verfügung nur deswillen, weil damit die den Gegenstand des Hauptprozesses bildende Rechtsfrage entschieden werden müsse, wäre nach der ZPO wohl nicht möglich. Ohne dies wird es in zahlreichen, vielleicht in den meisten Fällen gar nicht abgehen".

[2]) See p. 23 *supra*.

To say that the preliminary decision will in fact influence the final decision is to imply that the judges are not capable of exercising their duties with due discrimination. A better argument would be to say that in fact a final decision contrary to the preliminary order would be worthless.

In the hypothetical case we have put regarding the right to vote, a decision rendered after the election would be of no value to either plaintiff or defendant [1]). If the prohibition were ultimately upheld, but the court had permitted the officials to vote, and their vote had carried the election contrary to the desires of the defendant Prussian government, the final judgment would be of no avail.

But on the other hand, as we have already remarked, a final judgment upholding the plaintiff's right to vote would be equally worthless if the court denied interim protection, as in fact it did in this case.

The question of legislative policy to be decided is whether, in cases where ordinary judicial procedure will be futile as a means of safeguarding the respective rights of the parties, the law will refuse to take action interfering with the status quo produced by the lawless or lawful acts of the parties themselves; or whether it will intervene to maintain the last *uncontested* status quo, or to regulate the situation for the time being according to what *prima facie* appears to be demanded by the *probable* rights of the parties.

The former alternative expresses the normal rule that complete cognition and consideration of the case is required before relief is granted by a judicial tribunal. Under this rule, as has been seen, for all practical purposes, the parties are free to decide the issue themselves; the primitive procedure of self-help prevails.

The latter alternative expresses the conviction that interim protection of endangered rights by summary judicial procedure based on a *prima facie* evaluation or estimate of probabilities is better than no judicial protection at all.

---

[1]) Crosby, International War, its Causes and its Cure, 1919, 41: „It would be possible to fill a volume larger than this with illustrations of a familiar fact — namely, that in many disputes, whether between nations or individuals, *mere delay* will actually constitute a *forfeiture of the claim of one* of the parties; and further, that mere delay is often *believed* to carry with it forfeiture of the claims of *both* parties and consequently, to admit delay beyond that which has usually preceded the failure of diplomatic negotiations, will be considered by one or both parties as a complete yielding of his contentions".

Since interim protection thus amounts, in the contingency we are considering, to a condemnation of the defendant upon a *prima facie* case presented by the plaintiff, justice demands that the plaintiff show not only that the probability of his ultimate victory in the principal proceeding is greater than that of the defendant's, but also that without the interim order he will suffer substantial hardship, greater than that which the order if granted will cause the defendant.

When the law-maker has resolved the question of policy discussed above in favor of instituting interim remedies, the judicial tribunal must weigh in every case the two factors of hardship and likelihood of victory on the part of the plaintiff and defendant respectively, and can not legitimately lighten its task by automatically refusing to do so in cases where its preliminary decision involves the same matters which are at issue in the main proceeding.

Once the legislator has recognized that interim protection shall be extended by the courts, a plaintiff need only show that he stands to suffer great hardship, greater than that of his opponent, and that he is more likely than his opponent to win the case.

Of course protection will be granted more readily if applicant shows that his adversary will not suffer great hardship as a result of the measure requested, or that it is a measure of pure conservation, in the interest of both parties.

The decision of the *Staatsgerichtshof* must therefore be considered as a precedent of value only for tribunals having no express authority to grant interim protection.

§ 41. *g.* In its decision of 18 July 1930 [1]) the court refused a request that the *Reich* be ordered to pay, *pendente lite,* a certain monthly sum as previously (*wie bisher*) toward the cost of police expenditures in Thüringen. The federal minister of interior affairs (*Reichsminister des Innern*) had withheld the usual subvention, on the ground that national socialists were being put into positions on the police force in Thüringen.

The court pointed out that danger of substantial damage was required in order to obtain an *einstweilige Verfügung*; but in the case at bar Thüringen's financial disadvantage was outweighed by

[1]) 129 RGZ, Anhang, 28.

the fact that the payment sought would tend to threaten public security in the *Reich.*

Though recognizing that power to grant *einstweilige Verfügung* should be exercised with prudence, the court reaffirmed its doctrine that absence of express authority in its rules did not preclude its jurisdiction to make such orders. No conclusion is to be drawn from the absence of such procedure in administrative courts, for in those proceedings the status quo may be regulated by extrajudicial administrative action. That possibility is not present in cases coming before the *Staatsgerichtshof*. Moreover the objection that the court interferes with executive action in matters of political importance is unavailing, for it would apply equally to the final judgments of the court [1]).

Likewise the court reasserted its opinion that *einstweilige Verfügung* was not admissible in cases necessitating that the court assume as the basis of its action the correctness of the legal attitude of either party with respect to the matter in issue.

§ 42. Critics of the court's conclusion that it had jurisdiction to grant *einstweilige Verfügung* because its final judgments were executable did not attack the criterion on which that conclusion was based. They assumed the validity of the proposition that executability of final decisions justifies issuance of preliminary orders [2]).

Jahn [3]) contends that the court's opinion, in the ultimate anal-

[1]) „Im Verwaltungsverfahren hat der Staat die Möglichkeit, durch aussergerichtliche Akte der Staatsgewalt in einer die gegenseitige Belange unparteiisch abwägenden Weise den einstweiligen Zustand bis zur Entscheidung der Hauptsache befriedigend zu regeln. Bei den Streitigkeiten, die vor den Staatsgerichtshof gelangen, fehlt es an dieser Möglichkeit.

„Auch das Bedenken schlägt nicht durch, dass eine einstweilige Anordnung des Staatsgerichtshofes in rechtlich unzulässiger Weise in die staatliche Exekutive eingreifen würde, und zwar wenigstens dann, wenn erhebliche politische Interessen auf dem Spiele stehen. Dieser Einwand widerlegt sich schon durch die Erwägung, dass alles was in dieser Beziehung geltend gemacht werden könnte, in gleicher Weise auf endgültige Entscheidungen wie auf vorläufige Anordnungen des Staatsgerichtshofs zutreffen würde.

„Festzuhalten ist jedoch daran, dass eine einstweilige Anordnung des Staatsgerichtshofs die endgültige Entscheidung nicht vorausnehmen darf.... Der Staatsgerichtshof kann daher auch in dem vorliegenden Fall im Verfahren über den Erlass einer einstweiligen Verfügung keine Entscheidung treffen, durch die er sich vörläufig den Rechtsstandpunkt des einen oder des anderen der streitenden Teile zu eigen machen würde." Ibid, at p. 31.

[2]) Schüle 24 ff. shows the unsoundness of that proposition.

[3]) 59 J.W. (1930) 1162: „Immer bleibt es nur eine Meinungsäusserung.... Die Regierung allein hat zu entscheiden, ob sie sich fügen will. Tut sie es nicht, so trägt sie

ysis, is merely advisory. He therefore has difficulty in seeing whence the power to regulate the situation *pendente lite* is derived. Moreover, to determine what interim arrangement is the most appropriate is not a legal question but one of political expediency.

Likewise Heinsheimer [1]) points out that jurisdiction to render a final judgment may, but need not, carry with it jurisdiction to fix the status quo in which the parties must remain *pendente lite*. On the other hand, *express* provision is not necessary in order to authorize such a competence. Heinsheimer concludes in favor of the existence of the *Staatsgerichtshof's* jurisdiction, on the ground that it exercises between the *Länder* a federal judicial power with international law content (*Reichs-Gerichtsbarkeit mit völkerrechtlichem Inhalt*), and that international law in *all* cases of power to adjudge appends power to maintain peaceful possession and prevent incidents disrupting the procedure [2]).

Jerusalem [3]) also regards *einstweilige Verfügung* as predicated upon executability [4]), but considers the view of Heinsheimer as too narrow. According to Heinsheimer's reasoning, the power of the court to grant *einstweilige Verfügung* would be limited to cases between *Länder*, where the rules of international law apply. Jerusalem argues that the treaties in question merely express the

---

die politische Verantwortung, gezwungen werden kann sie nicht.... Hat aber der Spruch des Staatsgerichtshofs nicht die Folge, dass der von ihm für richting gehaltene Zustand nach dem Erlass eintritt, so ist nicht abzusehen, woher seine Befugniss stammen sollte, sogar vorher eine Regelung durch einstweilige Verfügung vorzunehmen. Der Staatsgerichtshof ist gar nicht in der Lage, zu prüfen und zu entscheiden, welche Regelung bis zum endgültigen Urteil die sachgemässe ist. Das ist gar keine juristische Frage, sondern eine Frage der Zweckmässigheit, des politischen Ermessens". Cf. Wetzell 204.

[1]) 55 JW (1926) 378: „Es handelt sich dabei nicht bloss um eine Frage des Verfahrens. Die Rechtsschutzform der einstweiligen Verfügung steht materiell selbständig neben der des entgültigen und einmaligen Urteils. Wer nur zu urteilen hat, hat damit nicht ohne weiteres die Befugnis zu einer vorläufigen Ordnung, die sich vielleicht im Urteil als unzutreffend erwiesen wird. Diese Befugnis *kann* in der „Entscheidungs"-Befugnis enthalten sein, aber sie muss es nicht. Ob sie es ist, kann, wo ausdrückliche Normen fehlen, nur aus der Natur der zur Erörterung stehenden Entscheidungsbefugnis heraus beantwortet werden, da andererseits eine *ausdrückliche* Zulassung vorläufiger Anordnungen ebenfalls nicht erforderlich erscheint".

[2]) „Nun ist völkerrechtlich an zahlreichen Belegen nachweisbar, dass die Befugnis zur Entscheidung immer mit der Befugnis verknüpft ist, die vorläufigen Anordnungen zu treffen, die zur Aufrechterhaltung des friedlichen Besitzstandes bis zur Entscheidung und zur Verhinderung aller die Entscheidung störenden Zwischenfälle erforderlich sind". One fears that perhaps Heinsheimer's optimistic view is the result of hasty generalization from a few treaties, a mode of reasoning deplored by Bruns 2.

[3]) Die Staatsgerichtsbarkeit, 1930, 183—7.

[4]) „Die einstweilige Verfügung setzt begrifflich voraus, dass entsprechende Sicherungsmassregeln tatsächlich getroffen werden". Ibid. 185.

principle that power to make temporary orders pending a controversy is a necessary element in all judicial activity. Hence the court, where it has a free hand in shaping its own procedure, is justified in granting preliminary measures [1]). Such measures are appropriate only in concrete controversies between parties, (*Parteistreitigkeiten*), on the analogy of the ZPO, and not in cases where the court renders an abstract opinion on a general question of law.

But in applying the ZPO by way of analogy, § 935 must be disregarded, Jerusalem contends, because the court does not have power to enforce its own orders [2]). Execution is entrusted to the discretion of the President of the *Reich*. Moreover federal execution as prescribed by § 48 (1) of the constitution is confined to cases where a *Land* does not fulfil a duty. Such duties are created only by the constitution, laws, and final judgments of the *Staatsgerichtshof*. There is no duty to obey interim orders of the court.

§ 940, on the other hand, applies. That article, as we have seen, provides for temporary regulation of the status quo with a view to preventing breach of the peace [3]). An *einstweilige Verfügung* in such a case would create no new duty. The *Reich* and the *Länder* are already bound by a constitutional duty to live together in peace. This duty receives concrete form in the court's order [4]).

§ 43. (b) *Express treaty provisions.*

1. In America.

The republics of the new world, desirous of developing their democratic institutions in peace, without being involved in and preoccupied with the European war system, have ever been par-

[1]) „In Wirklichkeit ist die Befugnis zum Erlass einstweiliger Anordnungen während des schwebenden Rechtsstreits notwendiger Bestandteil jeder Gerichtsbarkeit, und wenn das Statut des Haager Cour de Justice internationale und Schiedsabkommen solche Anordnungen vorsehen, so beweist das lediglich, dass auch im Rahmen der internationalen Gerichtsbarkeit solche Prozessmassnahmen für erforderlich gehalten werden. Daraus ergibt sich aber, dass auch die St. G. soweit ihr bezüglich der Ausgestaltung ihres Prozessrechtes freie Hand gegeben worden ist, grundsätzlich berechtigt ist, solche vorläufigen Massnahmen zu erlassen". Ibid. 184.

[2]) Jerusalem here confuses the *executability* of the judgment (i.e., its obligatory, as contrasted with advisory, character) with the question whether the court pronouncing it, rather than some other organ, has jurisdiction to enforce execution. Cf. p. 26 *supra*.

[3]) Cf. RGZ 4 : 400, § 97, note 4, p. 43 *supra*.

[4]) „Die verfassungsmässige Pflicht zur Aufrechterhaltung des Friedens zwischen den im Reich miteinander verbundenen Staatswesen.... erhält eine konkrete Gestalt". At p. 186. Cf. Schüle 86.

tial to arbitration and pioneers in quest of pacific settlement of international disputes. The Jay treaty of 1783, which embodied England's belated recognition of the independence of the United States, reintroduced arbitration into the modern world [1]. On 28 May, 1902, Argentina and Chile concluded a famous treaty of obligatory arbitration and disarmament [2]. On January 20 of the same year at Corinto a convention of peace and arbitration had been entered into by Costa Rica, El Salvador, Honduras and Nicaragua, providing for obligatory arbitration of every difficulty and question arising between the contracting parties [3]. Article 11 of that convention prescribes:

„The governments of the states in dispute solemnly engage not to execute any act of hostilities, preparations for war, or mobilization of forces, in order not to impede the settlement of the difficulty or question by the means established in the present convention" [4].

Subsequent litigation involving this article illustrates the distinction spoken of above [5] between a remedial norm and a remedial jurisdiction, and the desirability of clearly providing for both, lest a subsidiary dispute arise regarding the provisional measures which the parties are obliged to adopt, when it is not plain that the tribunal has the task of prescribing such measures.

In December 1906 a revolution arose in Honduras, fomented, it was said, by Nicaraguan influence. Honduran troops, pursuing the revolutionists, crossed the boundary into Nicaragua. That state demanded reparation, and war seemed inevitable. Both parties, however, were signatories of the treaty of Corinto mentioned above; and through the efforts of Dr. Luis Anderson, Costa Rican minister of foreign affairs, the matter was referred to arbitration

---

[1]) Contrary to what is generally thought, arbitration had never become obsolete, at least in the Netherlands. van Boetzelar 9—10.

[2]) According to Politis 196 the first obligatory arbitration treaty was signed by Salvador in 1876.

[3]) Article 2, in Martens NRG 2e. sér. 31 : 241.

[4]) „Los gobiernos de los estados en disputa se comprometen solemnemente á no ejecutar acto alguno de hostilidades, aprestos bélicos ó movilación de fuerzas, á fin de no impedir el arreglo de la dificuldad ó cuestión, por los medios establicidos en el presente convenio". Ibid. 245; Documentos 50; Conferenzia de Paz Centro-Americana, Recopilación de los tratados 5. An English translation is given in U.S. For. Rel. (1902) 882.

[5]) P. 9 *supra*; p. 127 *infra*.

under that treaty. The tribunal met at San Salvador on February 1, 1907 [1]).

„The tribunal considered its principal duty was to see to it that the award to be pronounced should be made effective", and on motion of Dr. Anderson resolved to request, through the government of Salvador, „the immediate fulfilment of article 11 of the pact of Corinto, and in consequence that the armed forces which both countries maintain should return to normal conditions". It was notorious that both armies were on a war footing, contrary to the agreement to submit to arbitral settlement of the conflict. Such preparations for war were in violation of article 11 of the treaty. „The tribunal in consequence considers it indispensable" to order „immediate disarmament and disbandment of forces, in order that things may return to the pacific state which the arbitral *compromis* contemplates" [2]).

Honduras indicated its willingness to comply with the order of the tribunal, but Nicaragua refused. President Zelaya regarded disarmament as humiliating, and alleged fresh offenses by Honduras. Salvador and Honduras considered that the failure of Nicaragua to comply with article 11 of the pact of Corinto rendered the entire treaty invalid, and prevented further functioning of the tribunal set up thereunder. The powers of the arbitrators from those two states were accordingly revoked by their governments, and on February 8 the tribunal dissolved [3]).

It was the view of Nicaragua that the tribunal in its order had usurped political powers and refused to exercise the judicial function for which it had been convoked [4]). The meaning of article 11 was clear and required no interpretation [5]). It was an agreement between governments and did not operate to confer any jurisdiction or authority upon the tribunal [6]). Moreover it did not prohibit all mobilization, but merely that which hindered settlement

[1]) Munro 207—8; Moreno 159; WPF, VII, 102—2.

[2]) For proceedings of the tribunal, Memoria 103—9; Documentos 179—190. An extract in English of the order of February 1 is given in WPF, VII, 121.

[3]) On 11 February 1907 President Roosevelt of the United States telegraphed the presidents of Nicaragua and Honduras, expressing the hope „that the tribunal may be reconstituted or a new tribunal provided which will sit under rules fully understood and complied with by both parties to the controversy, so that peace, with all its blessings, may be preserved, not only for Nicaragua and Honduras, but for all the states of America". U.S. For. Rel. (1907) pt. II, p. 616. Cf. the telegram of Briand to Greece and Bulgaria, p. 113 *infra*.

[4]) Documentos V—VI. [5]) Ibid. X. [6]) Ibid. 108—9.

of the dispute by the means prescribed in the treaty [1]). For arbitrators to concern themselves with respect to the execution of their award was a reflection upon the honor of the parties [2]).

Dr. Anderson issued a circular commenting adversely upon the unwillingness of Nicaragua to comply with the request of the tribunal. The Nicaraguan answer and Dr. Anderson's reply followed. Shortly thereafter, pacification having ensued as a result of the good offices of Mexico and the United States [3]), a Central American conference met at Washington in December 1907. Dr. Anderson was president of the conference. At his instance, definite language was inserted into the Convention of 20 December 1907 for the Establishment of a Central American Court of Justice [4]) which made it impossible thereafter for a state to advance the contentions put forward by Nicaragua in opposition to the directions of the tribunal at San Salvador earlier in the year [5]). By article 18 [6]) the Court was given power to fix the situation in which the parties must remain in order that the difficulty may not be aggravated and that things may remain *in statu quo* pending final decision of the case [7]).

This important provision, according to the report of the Nica-

[1]) Ibid. 160. In regard to this point, one is tempted to inquire whether, in case a policeman has power to prevent crimes dangerous to human life, he must refrain from acting until after a death has occurred, in order to be certain that the danger involved was really one jeopardizing life, and hence within his jurisdiction. Cf. note 4, p. 140 *infra*.

[2]) Documentos VII.

[3]) See U.S. For. Rel. (1907) pt. II, 606—635, especially 632—3, where it appears that the complete confidence of all parties in the impartiality of the American *chargé d'affaires*, Philip M. Brown, was a weighty factor in bringing about harmony. WPF, VII, 123.

[4]) As to this court, the first permanent international tribunal, see Politis 139—155, esp. 140—1, 152; Eyma 53—63. The United States had strongly urged at the Hague conference of 1907 the creation of such a tribunal, and took great pains to have the Central American Court established, in order to show that the idea was practicable. But the United States did not bestir itself to obtain a renewal of the Court's life when the convention creating it expired. In the meantime the Court had decided that the Bryan-Chamorro treaty between the United States and Nicaragua infringed rights of other Central American states.

[5]) Conferencia de Paz centroamericana, Actas y Documentos, 65—6, 107.

[6]) It should be noted that article 17 (3) of the Regulations of the Court of 2 December 1911 treats article 18 of the convention as a provision relating to the jurisdiction of the Court. 8 AJ sup. 183. In the Ordinance of procedure of 6 November 1912, article 10 provides that the right to apply for orders under article 18 of the convention can be exercised only in cases brought before the Court in conformity with article 6 of the Ordinance, which requires, *inter alia*, the failure of negotiations between the parties, the existence of war, however, being sufficient evidence of that fact. Ibid 195—6.

[7]) „From the moment in which any suit is instituted against any one or more governments up to that in which a final decision has been pronounced, the court may at

raguan delegates to the foreign minister of Nicaragua, was one of the capital ideas of the conference. They describe it as conferring power to order concentration and reduction of the military forces of the parties, restoration of things to their former state, and temporary suspension of measures likely to cause grave harm. The lack of such a provision in the treaty of Corinto, they remark, led to a memorable incident [1]).

§ 44. On more than one occasion before its unfortunate dissolution the Court made use of its powers under this article. In July 1908 a revolutionary outbreak in Honduras occurred. Guatemala and Salvador were thought to be participating in it. At the suggestion of Costa Rica, the Court itself on July 8 telegraphed to the interested parties, suggesting that they invoke its jurisdiction [2]). Honduras then filed a complaint against Salvador and Guatemala by telegraph. Nicaragua did the same as an interested party [3]).

On July 13 the court issued two interlocutory orders forbidding acts of hostility on all hands, and directing, with minute specifications, that Guatemala and Salvador refrain from conduct advantageous to the revolution in Honduras [4]). Modifications were made in these orders by additional decrees on July 17, July 25, August 1, and October 3 [5]). The final decision, handed down December 19, was criticised on the ground that the judges voted in accordance with their national interest. But there was no doubt that war had been prevented [6]). The revolution in Honduras subsided as soon

the solicitation of any one of the parties fix the situation in which the contending parties must remain, to the end that the difficulty shall not be aggravated and that things shall be conserved in *statu quo* pending a final decision." For Spanish text see also Anales de la corte de Justicia centroamericano, I, (1911), 6.

1) Conferencia Centroamericana de Washington, Delegación de Nicaragua, Managua 1908, XXX—XXXI.

2) Comunicaciones cruzadas, 1—2.

3) Munro 218; WPF, VII, 136—7; 2 AJ 838; Moreno 216.

4) Comunicaciones cruzadas 33—4; Mexico, Boletin oficial de la Secretaria de relaciones exteriores, 26; 223—227. English translation in 2 A.J. 838—841. A French translation is given by Basdevant in 16 RGDIP (1909) 101—102.

5) Sentencia 208; 5 Martens 3e. sér. 331; WPF, VII, xiii.

6) Guggenheim 41 gives the impression that after the Court's orders the parties concluded an arrangement which did away with the danger of hostilities: „mais cinq jours déjà après l'ordonnance du 13 juillet 1908, un *modus vivendi* avait pu être conclu, de sorte que le danger de guerre imminente était écarté". For this statement reference is made to Munro 218, which reads: „These messages were transmitted and answered by telegraph, so that within five days of the Court's first note a *modus vivendi* had been established and the immediate danger of a conflict had been dispelled' The *modus vivendi* in question would thus seem to be nothing other than the status fixed by the Court's orders.

as the interlocutory decree was pronounced. There was no manifestation of any refusal to obey the order of the Court, though the President of Salvador intimated that it was unnecessary [1].

These orders have been criticised as constituting „intervention" or interference in the domestic affairs of the states concerned [2]. But it must be remembered that the Central American States in other treaty articles had undertaken extensive and detailed obligations designed to reduce the danger of revolution in Central America. The content of interim measures necessarily is related to the content of the substantive law in force [3]. States may restrict their „reserved domain" by international agreements [4]. When the question of substantive law to be adjudicated involves application of such agreements, it is *petitio principii* to limit the procedural orders to measures predicated upon general customary law apart from the relevant treaty stipulations [5].

Article 18 was again invoked in the course of litigation occasioned by the Bryan-Chamorro treaty of 5 August 1914 between Nicaragua and the United States [6]. Costa Rica contended that this treaty contravened Nicaraguan obligations toward Costa Rica and asked that the Court so find and consequently pronounce the nullity of the treaty. In addition, Costa Rican counsel in the complaint dated 24 March 1916 prayed for a decree in virtue of article 18: „(*A*) Ordering, with relation to a canal across Nicaraguan territory, and with relation to anything that may interfere generally with the navigation of the waters of that republic, that the *status quo* of the right that existed in Costa Rica prior to the Bryan-Chamorro treaty that gives rise to the action be maintained, and (*B*) Directing that, in view of the urgency of the matter, a

[1]) Munro 219; 2 AJ 841.
[2]) Guggenheim 39, 41.
[3]) See articles 3, 16, 17, of the treaty of peace and amity of 20 December 1907, and article 2 of the supplementary convention. Guggenheim insists upon the influence of provisional measures upon the development of substantive law, but does not seem to concede the influence of substantive law on the content of interim measures.
[4]) Case of the nationality decrees, B no. 4, p. 24.
[5]) The restriction on the power of the Council to take provisional measures for the prevention of war suggested by Rolin-Jacquemyns, (C. 342 M. 100. 1928. IX, 80) that they should not affect matters falling by international law within the reserved domain of states, must be considered as similarly qualified, to avoid begging the question. One might accuse the Huber order in the Sino-Belgian case (see p. 149 *infra*) of prescribing a judicial system for China. But in fact that order fell short of what might have been prescribed, namely, complete continuance in force of the treaty of 1865 pending decision as to its caducity.
[6]) Moreno 239—41.

communication be sent by telegraph to the Most Excellent, the Governments of Nicaragua and the United States, of America, to be followed immediately by confirmation by mail, notifying them with all due formality, of the institution of this action and of the decree prayed for in the preceding paragraph (*A*), if, as I venture to hope, my prayer for such precautionary measure shall be acceded to" [1]).

It was the opinion of the Court „That with reference to the interlocutory petition that accompanies the complaint, the Court can properly decide the point relating to the maintenance of the *status quo* between the Republics of Costa Rica and Nicaragua; but not the point relating to the notification to the United States, because that Government is not a party to this litigation". The Court therefore resolved „That the following precautionary measure (*medida precautoria*) be decreed: The Governments of Costa Rica and Nicaragua are under the obligation to maintain the *status quo* that existed between them prior to the treaty that gave rise to the present controversy" [2]).

Likewise Salvador instituted proceedings with a view to judgment that Nicaragua abstain from carrying out the Bryan-Chamorro treaty (*abstención del cumplimiento*) and prayed that in conformity with article 18 the legal situation be fixed in which Nicaragua should remain with respect to the matter in litigation in order to preserve the status quo prior to the treaty [3]). This

[1]) Complaint of Costa Rica against Nicaragua, tr. Washington 1916, 32. Demanda de la Rèpublica de Costa Rica contra la Nicaragua ante la Corte de Justicia Centroamericana, San José, Costa Rica, Imprenta nacional, 1916, 26: „Apoyado en el artículo XVIII de la Convención generadora de ese Suprema Tribunal, suplico que desde luego se provea por él, para prevenir daños y conflictos, irreparables después acaso, y para mientras se dicta en este expediente el fallo que corresponde:

A) Manteniendo, en lo relativo a canal por territorio nicaragüense, y en lo que se roza en general con la navigación en aguas de aquella Rèpublica, el *status quo* de derecho que allí ha existido con Costa Rica antes del Tratado Bryan-Chamorro que ocasiona esta acción. y

B) Acordando se comunique a los excelentísimos Gobiernos de Nicaragua y los Estados Unitos de América, por telégrafo, dada la urgencia del caso, y a reserva de confirmar en seguida por correo la notificación, con todas las formalidades de rúbrica, el habersen incoado el presente debate, y el auto materia del punto A que antecede, si, como me atrevo a esperlo, se acade a mi instancia tendiente a obtener tal medida precautoria".

[2]) Complaint 40.

[3]) Complaint of Salvador against Nicaragua, tr. Washington 1916, 29; El Golfo 177; Libro Rosado de el Salvador. Demanda del gobierno de el Salvador contra el gobierno de Nicaragua ante la Corte de Justicia centroamericana, San Salvador 1916, 25: „Que se fije la situación jurídica en que debe mantenerse el Gobierno de Nicaragua en la materia que es objecto de esta demanda, a efecto de que las cosas litigadas se hallaban ante de la celebración y ratificación del referido tratado Bryan-Chamorro". Cf. the

request was granted by the Court on 6 September 1916, there being nothing said here with respect to the United States [1]).

§. 45. Article 11 of the treaty of Corinto and article 18 of the convention for the establishment of a Central American Court of Justice have been fruitful precedents. Provisions concerning interdiction of military activity and empowering the tribunal to preserve the status quo pending the course of a dispute are persistent features in American thinking and practice.

Both types of provisions mentioned found their way into the Treaties for the Advancement of Peace negotiated by Secretary of State Bryan on behalf of the United States [2]). In article 4 of the treaties with Guatemala, Panama, Nicaragua, Salvador and Persia was contained the following provision [3]): „Pending the investigation and report of the International Commission, the High Contracting Parties agree not to increase their military and naval programs, unless danger from a third power should compel such increase, in which case the party feeling itself menaced shall confidentially communicate the fact in writing to the other Contracting Party, whereupon the latter shall also be released from its obligation to maintain its military and naval *status quo*".

Article 4 of the treaties with China, France and Sweden contains this language [4]): „In case the cause of the dispute should

Belgian-Chinese case, where continuance in force of a treaty rather than its non-application, was sought as an interim measure. P. 148 *infra*.

1) El Golfo 189; 6 Anales (1917) 9:

„Tercero: Fíjase el estado en que deben permanecer las Altas Partes hasta el momento en que se pronuncie sentencia definitiva, en la misma situación que mantenían en el golfo de Fonseca antes de la celebración del Tratado que motiva la demanda."

2) Practical rather than theoretical considerations have dictated the formulation of the two principles mentioned. Theoretically pacific settlement of a particular dispute need not be interrupted by war between the parties (over some other question); or, indeed, the outbreak of war may initiate procedure for pacific settlement. Cf. note 6, p. 95 *supra* and article 11 of the Covenant *A fortiori* preparation for war and mobilization need not be inconsistent with such settlement. But in fact the dangers are notorious. (See p. 123 *infra*). Similarly, in theory, parties might well be capable of themselves agreeing upon the proper provisional measures without resorting to the court. Yet we have seen the difficulties which in practice arose under such an incomplete system of interim protection. Nevertheless there are grave practical difficulties in restricting preparation for war. It is difficult to determine, in the absence of an agreed peace-time level of armament, what constitutes preparation for war. A peaceful and unprepared state might be at a disadvantage. Relations with third states enter in: Thus if France had a dispute with Bolivia, it would not be allowed to increase its armaments, no matter what Germany did. 1 D. H. Miller, Drafting, 5, 392—3. See p. 122 *infra*.

3) Deleted by the United States Senate. See Scott, Treaties for the Advancement of Peace, 1920, xlii; P. M. Brown, La Conciliation internationale, 1925, 88.

4) Which served as the basis for article 41 of the statute of the Permanent Court of International Justice. See § 67 *infra*.

consist of certain acts already committed or about to be committed, the Commission shall, as soon as possible indicate what measures to preserve the rights of each party ought in its opinion to be taken provisionally and pending the delivery of its report" [1]).

It has been suggested [2]) that the purpose of this provision was to preserve evidence and means of proof. That opinion seems to be without substantiation. Another article covers the matter of obtaining evidence [3]). But what is the purpose of the *mesures conservatoires* of article 4, in view of the fact that the Commission of Inquiry has no power to render a binding judgment, that its recommendations may be treated by the parties as they see fit? Plainly the object of such measures is not to ensure execution of final judgment.

It may be helpful to remember in this connection that Secretary Bryan's purpose was to avoid war, not to institute a new means of settling disputes. The „cooling-off" feature of the procedure laid down in these treaties was uppermost in his mind [4]). He thought that if war could be, on any pretext whatever, staved off during a period of time sufficient for reflection, the wiser and saner elements of the population in both countries would be able to make their influence felt and gain the upper hand over the excitable groups passionately clamoring for war. Consequently it was necessary that war be postponed for the time being, no matter what the nature of the dispute might be, no matter what vital interests or questions of national honor might be at stake. On the other hand, as a sop to the militarists, it was conceded that this prohibition of war should be only temporary, should last only a year (unless the Commission reported sooner). It was not because they impeded the Commission's operation that acts of hostility were forbidden; instead, the Commission's activity was instituted simply as an excuse for putting off resort to force.

But what of vital interests endangered in the meantime? It is

[1]) For text see Scott, Treaties, 17, 37—8, 95; U.S. Treaty Series nos. 619, 609, 607; Malloy 2516, 2589, 2856; 39 St. 1887, 38 St. 1887, 38 St. 1872. English text authentic in all three; Chinese in that with China; French in the others. For comment see Brown, Conciliation 89 and Scott, Sovereign States and Suits 102.

[2]) Guggenheim 46. A better view is that of Professor Philip Marshall Brown, Conciliation 89: „La nation donc qui veut protéger ses nationaux contre des abus excessifs a le droit, suivant cet article, d'insister au moins sur un *modus vivendi* pendant une enquête, afin que la justice ne soit pas méprisée".

[3]) See Article 5(2) of the treaty with Sweden.

[4]) Jessup in WPF, XII, (1929) 671.

no light thing to give up for a year the possibility of self-help by war, without any substitute being provided. Many circumstances might during that time lead to the irreparable loss of valuable rights [1]).

To mitigate the harshness of being deprived of liberty to wage war, article 4 comes into play [2]). Where rights (not proofs or evidence merely) of a party were endangered by wrongs already committed or about to be committed the Commission should indicate what measures ought to be taken. That these suggestions would have great likelihood of being observed lies in the fact that they are recommended by the same trustworthy persons whose final report on the controversy is expected to have weight; and in the fact that war is still possible *after* the report. Public opinion would not be soothed by failure to observe interim measures deemed needful by the Commission in order to protect precious interests from irreparable harm.

It is not unlikely that the drafters of this treaty were familiar with article 18 of the Central American Court convention, and intended article 4 to be the equivalent of that provision, *mutatis mutandis* in order to make it appropriate for a tribunal having no power to give a binding decision. They did not carry over article 18 verbatim, doubtless because they felt that it would be „illogical" and contrary to the non-obligatory character of the Commission's decisions if its interlocutory, but not its final recommendations, should have binding force [3]).

§ 46. Likewise both types of provision are found in the Treaty to Avoid or Prevent Conflicts between the American States, signed by sixteen states represented at the Fifth Pan-American Conference at Santiago 3 May 1923. Article I provides: „The High Contracting Parties undertake, in case of disputes, not to begin mobilization or concentration of troops on the frontier of the other Party, nor to engage in any hostile acts or preparations for hostilities, from the time steps are taken to convene the Commission until the said Commission has rendered its report" [4]). Does

[1]) See note 1, p. 88 *supra*.
[2]) Cf. relief from moratorium under the Phillimore plan. p. 104 *infra*.
[3]) Ibid.
[4]) 33 LNTS 36—8.

not this resemble article 11 of the treaty of Corinto, and the thoroughgoing Bryan principle of renouncing war and thought of war during a certain period of time, ideas adopted by the Santiago treaty notwithstanding the practical difficulties involved in prohibiting preparation for war? [1]).

Article V, appendix, ordains: „As soon as the Commission of Inquiry is organized, it shall at the request of any of the Parties to the dispute have the right to fix the status in which the Parties must remain, in order that the situation may not be aggravated and matters may remain in *statu quo* pending the rendering of the report by the Commission" [2]). This is plainly article 18 of the Central American Court convention reappearing. Notwithstanding the fact that the final decisions of the Commission contemplated by the Santiago treaty are not binding [3]) it has the power to make binding interlocutory orders. There is really nothing illogical in such a situation. The power to grant interim protection is not a consequence of the need to ensure execution of final decisions, but of the obligation to refrain from acts of force pending the report [4]).

Both types are found in articles 7 and 15 of the project of pacific settlement prepared by the American Institute of International Law at Havana in 1925 [5]); and in articles 5 and 13 of the project of the International Commission of Jurists which met at Rio in 1927 [6]). The latter type of provision stands alone in the convention between the United States and the Central American Republics for the Establishment of International Commissions of Enquiry, signed 7 February 1923 at Washington, and in the convention of the same date for the Establishment of an International Central American Tribunal. While article 13 of the former convention [7]) is identical with article V, appendix, of the Santiago treaty, article 21 of the latter is somewhat more elaborate:

---

[1]) See note 2, p. 99 *supra*. [2]) 33 LNTS 44. [3]) Ibid. 40, Article 6.

[4]) See p. 100—101 *supra*. What has been said refers to the „logicality" of such a power from the standpoint of legislative policy (*Rechtspolitik*). From a strictly legal standpoint, it is even less „illogical". The action with a view to satisfaction and that with a view to security being separate, (p. 19 *supra*), there is no reason why the judgments in each case need have the same effect. Where provisional measures, such as those taken by the League Council, have as their object preservation of peace, it is quite possible that states should be obliged to conform to such measures, though not to accept the Council as arbiter of the dispute. See p. 104 *infra*.

[5]) 20 AJ sp. sup. 369, 371. [6]) 22 AJ sup. 268, 270.

[7]) U.S. Treaty Series no. 717.

„From the moment when in conformity with the provisions of Article VIII, a complaint has been lodged against one or more of the Contracting Parties, the Tribunal shall have the right to determine, at the request of any of the Parties, the status in which the litigants must remain, to avoid an aggravation of the dispute, and to maintain the case in *statu quo* until the final award is pronounced. For this purpose, the said Tribunal shall have the right, if it should deem it necessary, to make any investigations, to order examination by experts, to conduct personal inspections and to receive any evidence [1])". Unfortunately neither provision was embodied in the treaties of arbitration and conciliation signed at the Pan-American arbitration conference at Washington on 5 January 1929. However, the eighth stipulation of the Protocol of two days earlier between Bolivia and Paraguay shows that the conference, when confronted with the practical task of helping to settle an actual controversy, appreciated the desirability of interim measures [2]).

§ 47. 2. In the League of Nations.

α. Practice under the Covenant.

The Covenant of the League as adopted contains no specific language relating to provisional measures. Preliminary proposals made by American and English writers envisaged an international tribunal having the powers of a court of chancery to issue temporary injunctions [3]). The Phillimore draft convention and

[1]) Conference on Central American Affairs, 309. For drafting see 48, 240, 278. Guggenheim 49 rightly points out the importance of this explicit provision. It might happen that otherwise members of the tribunal or experts might be refused admission to the territory of the state in question, as League of Nations commissions were refused access to Jugoslavia and Turkey. See pp. 110, 113 *infra*.

[2]) 23 AJ sup. 99—100. That stipulation provided: „The Governments of Bolivia and Paraguay bind themselves to suspend all hostilities and to stop all concentration of troops at the points of contact of the military outposts of both countries, until the commission renders its findings; the commission shall be empowered to advise the parties concerning measures designed to prevent a recurrence of hostilities". The last clause would seem to authorize the commission to act as a remedial jurisdiction to prescribe interim measures in the instant case, as well as to make suggestions of legislative character tending to prevent incidents in the future. Cf. a similar provision in the Greek-Bulgarian commission's instructions. Conwell-Evans 157.

[3]) In 1915 President A. Lawrence Lowell wrote (A League to Inforce Peace, WPF Pamphlets, Oct. 1915, V, no. 5, part. I, 14—15): „A second difficulty that will sometimes arise is the rule of conduct to be followed pending the presentation of the case to the international tribunal. The continuance or cessation of the acts complained of may appear to be, and may even be in fact, more important than the final decision. This has been brought to our attention forcibly by the sinking of the *Lusitania*. We

accompanying report [1]), however, which furnished the official starting point for construction of the Covenant, in lieu of such a power proposed to substitute a provision permitting the Council under certain circumstances to relieve a state from the general moratorium on war which was the central feature of the Phillimore plan. Three arguments were advanced against accepting the proposals for a power of injunction. In the first place, it was said that if no sanction was to be provided for execution of final decisions, it seemed illogical that interlocutory decisions should be so enforced [2]). Moreover, in view of probable opposition by the defendant state, the interlocutory decision could be pronounced no sooner than the final one [3]). Lastly, it was doubtful whether out-

---

should have no objection to submitting to arbitration the question of the right of submarines to torpedo merchant ships without warning, provided Germany abandoned the practice pending the arbitration; and Germany would probably have no objection to submitting the question to a tribunal on the understanding that the practice was to continue until the decision was rendered, because by that time the war would be over. This difficulty is inherent in every plan for arbitration of international disputes, although more serious in a league whose members bind themselves to prevent by force the outbreak of war. It would be necessary to give the tribunal summary authority to decree a *modus vivendi*, to empower it, like a court of equity, to issue a temporary injunction".

G. Lowes Dickinson, The Choice Before Us, 1917, 177, after proposing that preparation for war and mobilization should be prohibited pending consideration of the dispute by the court or council, says: „A further point arises in connexion with the interval during which the Court is hearing the case or the Council considering it. There must not be, during this interval, a continuance of the act that is the cause of the dispute. This means that the Court or the Council, or both, must have the power of injunction. And if a sanction is to be applied (a point to be discussed presently), there must be a sanction against the breach of the injunction".

Lord Phillimore commented on both suggestions. Peace Handbooks, vol. 25, no. 160, 33, 55, 66. Apparently no attention was paid to the German proposal for a League of Nations, which provided in § 34 (2): „Sowohl der Gerichtshof als das Vermittlungsamt sind befugt, das Streitverhältnis für die Dauer des Verfahrens durch eine vorläufige Verfügung zu regeln". 2 D. H. Miller. Drafting 752—3; English translation in Pollock, The League of Nations, 2ed. 1922, 245: „Both the Tribunal and the Board of Mediation shall be empowered to regulate the dispute for the duration of the proceedings by a temporary enactment."

[1]) D. H. Miller, Drafting, II, 5 for § 12 of draft convention; I, 7—8 for §§ 16 and 17 of report. See annex 1, *infra*.

[2]) The confusion of thought involved here has been pointed out in § 13 *supra*. A tribunal may have jurisdiction to *pronounce* interlocutory decisions, without jurisdiction to *enforce* them. It is not necessary that such decisions have greater binding force than the final decision. (Although on the other hand there is no reason why they may not, if that seems desirable. See p. 102 *supra*. It is also possible that the final judgment may be binding, while the interim orders are not. See p.126 *infra*. Four combinations are possible: both binding; both advisory; interlocutory decision binding, final decision advisory; interlocutory decision advisory, final decision binding).

[3]) This argument assumes that the tribunal will with woeful incompetence adopt rules of procedure failing to distinguish appropriately between summary procedure for urgent interlocutory proceedings and normal procedure in routine matters.

side Anglo-American law injunction procedure was familiar [1]). Nevertheless in practice the League of Nations has found provisional measures indispensable [2]).

§ 48. The first occasion was during the Polish-Lithuanian dispute over Vilna [3]). That city had been ceded to Lithuania by the Bolsheviks when they were forced to retreat by the Poles, whose eastern frontier was not settled [4]). The advancing Poles, coming into contact with the Lithuanians, appealed to the League to prevent hostilities between the two states, thus leaving Poland free to devote its entire attention to the Bolsheviks.

On 20 September 1920 the Council resolved to propose to the parties that they accept for the time being the Curzon line, and offered to appoint a commission to ensure on the spot strict observance of the agreement [5]).

Not until October 4, however, did the Commission arrive on the spot. On October 7 it arranged a line of demarcation to go into effect October 10. On the 9th, a few hours before the *régime* was to go into effect, the Polish general Zeligowski, calling himself a rebel, crossed the line and seized Vilna. His „rebellious" conduct was officially disavowed by the Polish government, though he was afterwards made *citoyen d'honneur* for his services [6]).

Having signed a victorious peace with Russia on October 12 at Riga, Poland no longer required the „benevolent intervention" of the League against Lithuania, and sought to withdraw the question from consideration by the Council, which at last began to give its attention to the matter on October 26. But the Council did not countenance that brazen proposal [7]). It did not, however, follow

[1]) Although the guarded form of statement made in the Phillimore report forestalls contesting its accuracy, one may say, after our survey of interim protection in various legal systems in chapter II, that the conclusion drawn from their statement by the Committee does not compel assent.

[2]) Cf. p. 103 *supra*, where the Pan-American arbitration conference, though neglecting to provide for interim protection in the draft convention it was convoked to frame, resorted to such provisions when faced with the practical problem of dealing with the conflict between Bolivia and Paraguay which happened to come to the fore during its sitting.

[3]) Conwell-Evans 89—100; OJ sp. sup. no. 4, (1920).

[4]) The „Curzon line" had provisionally been laid down by the Supreme Council on 8 December 1919.

[5]) OJ (1920) sp. sup. no. 4, 59, text at 65.

[6]) Conwell-Evans 94.

[7]) Conwell-Evans 99; OJ, *supra*, 134, 136.

the practical suggestions of the Secretary-General [1]) that Poland be required to isolate the „rebel" forces and shut off their communications [2]). The Council made no further effort to reestablish the status quo, but on the basis of the *fait accompli* and the Polish disclaimer took up the task of trying to decide the ultimate destiny of the territory by plebiscite [3]), in spite of Lithuania's contention that it must first fulfil the more urgent duty of stopping hostilities [4]).

Subsequently, doubting whether the parties really desired an honest plebiscite, the Council proposed that they begin negotiations at Brussels, pending which Poland should reduce the army of General Zeligowski and see that it was not reinforced, and Lithuania in turn should reduce its troops and furnish food for the population of the territory in question, to be distributed under the control of the League commission. No elections or change of administration should take place pending this *régime* [5]).

Poland rejecting the conditions of this provisional measure, M. Hymans, president of the Council, who very patiently did a great deal of work in connection with this dispute, proposed that negotiations open at Brussels April 18 for the purpose of „endeavoring to arrive at a preliminary agreement between the two governments for the settlement of the temporary conditions in the disputed territory, pending a final agreement to solve all territorial, military, economic, etc. difficulties outstanding between the two countries" [6]).

The Council then proposed that negotiations go on at Brussels; Polish and Lithuanian forces being reduced, under the control of the Council's military commission. This proposal was refused by both parties [7]).

The Council found itself obliged to declare that the rejection by both parties of the proposed settlement put an end to the procedure of conciliation under article 15 of the Covenant. Neverthe-

[1]) OJ, *supra*, 25.

[2]) The commission without difficulty could have examined trains from Warsaw to Vilna thus preventing transportation of victuals and munitions, or at least obtaining proof of Polish complicity in the rebel *coup*. Conwell-Evans 111.

[3]) Resolution of 28 October 1920, OJ, *supra*, 143.

[4]) OJ, *supra*, 136.

[5]) OJ (1921) 181—2, resolution of 3 March 1921.

[6]) OJ (1921) 276.

[7]) OJ (1921) 784—5; 879, 880.

less it recognised that its duty to prevent war continued, and took note of the engagement of the parties to abstain from all acts of hostility. It decided to withdraw its commission, recommending that the parties place their interests in the hands of friendly powers whose representatives should supervise the measures of pacification recommended by the resolution. A provisional line of demarcation should replace the neutral zones which the commission had instituted, one on each side of the Curzon line at Suvalki, the other at Vilna [1]).

Poland acquiesced in elimination of the neutral zones, but Lithuania refused. The Council therefore by resolution of 17 May 1922 [2]) decided that the zones should be continued for military purposes, but that for civil administration a provisional line should be laid down. To this end it resolved to send a commission to the spot.

Lithuania pointed out that the neutral zones had been instituted by the military commission as a consequence of the *coup d'état* of General Zeligowski, which had prevented application of the line agreed to in the Suwalki convention. With his departure, there was nothing to prevent restoration of the status quo in accordance with the line established by treaty and violated by that general.

Nevertheless the Council made no attempt to re-establish the status quo as of the time prior to the seizure of Vilna, but laid down a line indicating the spheres which each state should have the right to administer provisionally, pending final decision, without prejudice to the right of either party as to ultimate determination of the frontier [3]).

It should be noticed that here a provisional *régime* was needed *pendente lite* not only for the sake of preventing hostilities, but in order to afford civil administration of the territory in question. Like the care of lost property, in the interest of whom it may

[1]) OJ (1922) 99—100.

[2]) OJ (1922) 549—550. The zones were unpoliced, and had become a happy hunting-ground for lawless folk. OJ (1923) 487.

[3]) OJ (1923) 238, resolution of 3 February 1923. Lithuania objected to abolition of the neutral zones, but the Council was unanimous. Ibid. 239. Lithuania sought to submit to the Court a question as to the propriety of the Council's resolution. Apart from the doubtful wisdom of such a procedure in general, the Council felt that its resolution was undoubtedly proper, and the Lithuanian question had only academic value after definite frontiers had been fixed by the Council of Ambassadors. OJ (1923) 586.

concern, temporary administration by someone as *negotiorum gestor* was necessary, no matter who should ultimately be recognized as owner [1]).

This entire dispute would have been avoided if the principal allied powers had exercised promptly their right to lay down the frontier of Poland. Some excuse for the dilatory and inefficient handling of the affair by the Council is to be found in the fact that the League of Nations was then in its infancy, barely six months old. Arrangements lay for the most part in the hands of French nationals, at a time when France was interested in Polish success. Indeed, there was no unified will to peace on the part of the great powers. No effort at all had been made to stop the war between Poland and Russia. Article 11 of the Covenant was not invoked in that conflict [2]).

§ 49. Another instance is presented by the Albanian frontier litigation [3]). In 1913 the Council of Ambassadors of the six great powers laid down frontiers for Albania (which were not, however, completely delimited by the commission on the spot before the war broke out), declared its independence, and gave it a government consisting of a German prince and an international (Dutch) gendarmerie. These disappeared during the war [4]).

As Monseigneur Fan Noli, Albanian delegate, declared before the Assembly: „We had frontiers before the war; frontiers established by international treaties. Those treaties were signed by Great Powers, and yet, after a war fought for freedom and for the rights of small nationalities, we found ourselves without frontiers. This is a matter which only the jurists of the Great Powers can explain [5]). But.... we have no frontiers and, therefore, there is no violation of frontiers. Consequently, everyone of our neighbors considers himself authorized to invade our territory" [6]).

Having been admitted to the League in this amorphous condition, Albania appealed to the Council to determine its frontiers and protect them from violation by the Serbs. On 25 June 1921

---

1) See p. 21 *supra*.
2) Conwell-Evans 100.
3) Conwell-Evans 43—6, 63—9, 105—7.
4) Lord Balfour in OJ (1921) 1094.
5) The explanation given is that Albanian neutrality, abandoned by its entry into the war on the allied side, was a condition of those frontiers.
6) 2d Assembly 670.

the Council resolved not to take up the matter, since the Council of Ambassadors was entrusted with the task of laying down the frontiers, and urged that body to announce its desision as soon as possible. „Pending the solution.... the Council recommends the three parties, in conformity with the Covenant, strictly to abstain from any act calculated to interfere with the procedure in course"[1]).

Greek and Serb representatives accepted this resolution. Albania appealed to the Assembly [2]). Meanwhile, Serb attacks continuing, Albania appealed to the Council under article 11 to take steps to avoid further bloodshed and to safeguard the maintenance of peace. „The result of these two procedures is", said Lord Balfour, „that the Assembly has been requested by Albania to deal with the determination of the Albanian frontiers, and the Council has been asked to prevent these frontiers from being violated by the action of the Serbs. The two subjects are evidently intimately connected, and it seems absurd to send one of them to the Assembly and the other to the Council. I suggest, therefore, that as the Assembly has been requested to deal with the determination of the frontiers, they should also be asked to deal with the violation of frontiers" [3]). This suggestion was adopted. The decision, it is said, reflected little credit on the Council [4]).

How can non-existent frontiers be violated? But there can be fighting without frontiers. The Assembly thus had before it two distinct questions [5]). It urged Albania to accept the decision of the Conference of Ambassadors as to frontiers, and urged that body to hasten its decision [6]). As the Assembly might be called upon to take action to safeguard effectually the peace of nations under article 11, or issue a report on the dispute under article 15, and for this purpose would require information, it decided that a commission should be sent to Albania to report on execution of the decision of the Council of Ambassadors when given, and on any disturbances on or near the frontiers of Albania [7]).

---

[1]) OJ (1920) 725; („s'abstenir rigoureusement de tout acte qui pourrait troubler la marche de la procédure").

[2]) OJ (1921) 482. [3]) OJ (1921) 1094. [4]) Conwell-Evans 66.

[5]) As Lord Robert Cecil pointed out in the sixth committee. 2d Assembly 6th Comm. 549.

[6]) Resolution of 2 October 1921; 2d Assembly 674—5; OJ (1921) sp. sup. no. 6, 35—6.

[7]) „The Assembly.... requests the Council to appoint a Commission of three im-

Greek [1]) and French [2]) representatives had felt that the body having jurisdiction to decide a question should see to its execution, and that even *mesures conservatoires* were not within the competence of another body.

Dispute then arose as to whether the commission should be sent immediately, or not until the Council of Ambassadors fixed the frontiers. Senator Scialoja declared that „Italy's interests in the Adriatic are perfectly in agreement with those of Albania, and that we are anxious for the independence of Albania according to the rules of international justice". Nevertheless he thought the commission should not be sent until after the decision of the Council of Ambassadors had been given [3]). Lord Robert Cecil reminded the Assembly that the task of the commission was not limited to reporting on execution of that decision [4]).

The Council on October 6 when it appointed the commission decided that it should take no action until the frontiers were fixed. The Serbs, no doubt encouraged by this display of hesitation, invaded Albania, spreading ruin and devastation as they advanced [5]). As soon as the Council of Ambassadors had come to a decision, Mr. Lloyd George dispatched a vigorous telegram to the Secretary general requesting a meeting of the Council [6]). Serbian objections to the expressions used in that message do not seem to be justified [7]). On 19 November 1921 the Council adopted a resolution instructing the commission *sent to Albania* (the Serb representative was explicit in calling attention to the fact that the commission's sphere of activity was so limited) [8]) to keep the Council informed of the retirement of both Serb and Albanian

---

partial persons, to proceed immediately to Albania, and to report fully on the execution of the decision of the Principal Allied and Associated Powers, as soon as it is given and on any disturbances which may occur on or near the frontiers of Albania. The Commission shall have power to appoint observers or other officials, being impartial persons, to enable it to discharge its functions".

1) 2d Assembly 666; 2d Assembly, 6th comm. 546.

2) 2d Assembly, 6th comm. 551.

3) 2d Assembly 663. Subsequently another Italian representative brought up the same point in the Council. It was decided that the commission should be sent at once, but that it should do nothing until the decision was given. Conwell-Evans 68.

4) 2d Assembly 673. 5) Conwell-Evans 68. 6) OJ (1921) 1194.

7) Although as a rule it is doubtless more expedient to appeal to both parties to a dispute in identical terms. Cf. Briand's telegram to Greece and Bulgaria, p. 113 *infra*.

8) Admission to Serbian territory was denied when the commission proposed to enter for the purpose of inquiring whether the Serbs had any complaints to make against the Albanians, although the Serbs in Geneva were continually lodging such complaints, OJ (1922) 98, 149, 156, 260, 267.

troops from the provisional zones of demarcation laid down by the Council of Ambassadors [1]), to satisfy themselves that no outside assistance was given to movements disturbing the internal peace of Albania, and to propose measures to end present disturbances and prevent their recurrence [2]).

Subsequently Albania applied to the League to be supplied with economic and other counsellors, in order to further the development of the country, and by resolution of 13 May, 1922 the Council decided to continue one member of the commission on the spot until those advisers arrived [3]).

It thus appears that the task of the commission was a heterogeneous one. Its activity was not restricted to the application of interim measures. There was confusion of issues throughout the entire handling of this dispute [4]).

§ 50. The principle that parties to a dispute referred to judicial settlement are bound not to anticipate the result of the decision [5]) was applied by analogy when the Council by its resolution of 17 May 1922, after proposing that discussions as to the legality of Polish expropriation of certain farmers of German origin continue between the Polish government and the League of Nations, concluded: „The Council earnestly requests the Polish Government to postpone, until the Council has had an opportunity of taking a decision upon the matter, any administrative or judicial measures likely to affect the normal position of persons of German origin engaged in agricultural work who are Polish subjects, or whose status as Polish subjects is dependent upon the decision taken with regard to the questions of interpretation raised in the report" [6]). Poland declared its desire not to evacuate the farmers during the winter, but pointed out that lengthy or indefinite postponement was undesirable for the economic situation, as the farmers in danger of expulsion did not take proper care of the land. As a compromise, certain classes of persons were left unmolested until the next session of the Council [7]).

---

1) The Council of Ambassadors on 18 November 1921, in the interest of peace and to give the delimitation commission charged with the task of tracing the frontier on the spot complete liberty of action by creating a zone free from troops of either party, had laid down such a zone, which Serbia accepted, protesting against the British „ultimatum" (i.e., the telegram to the League).

2) OJ (1921) 1192—3. 3) OJ (1922) 535. 4) Conwell-Evans 105.

5) See note 8, p. 167 *infra*. 6) OJ (1922) 555. 7) OJ (1922) 918.

Likewise on 23 April 1923 the president of the Council, when agreement could not be reached between Hungary and Roumania in their controversy over expropriation of Hungarian optants under the Roumanian agrarian laws, proposed that the question be postponed until a further meeting of the Council, the Roumanian government being invited in the meantime to suspend any action which might prejudice the definitive solution of the affair [1]. The Hungarian representative attached great weight to that provision, but it was not acceptable to the Roumanian spokesman [2]. The Council finally confined itself to urging the parties to come to an accord.

§ 51. The British dispute with Turkey over the frontier of Iraq furnishes another example of resort to provisional measures by the Council. The two governments had undertaken by article 3 of the treaty of Lausanne of 24 July 1923 that no military or other movements should take place which might modify in any way the present status of the disputed territories. When the frontier dispute was referred to the Council, the latter took note of the declarations of the British and Turkish representatives reaffirming their intention to maintain the status quo [3].

Disagreements and mutual recriminations arose concerning the performance of the undertaking, due to divergent ideas of the areas which each party was entitled to administer until the final decision. The Council at its Brussels meeting on 29 October 1924 delimited a provisional boundary [4]. On 24 September 1925 the Council decided to appoint a commission „to keep the Council informed of the situation in the locality of the provisional line fixed at Brussels on October 29, 1924" [5].

[1] OJ (1923) 609: „4. Le Conseil invite le Gouvernement roumain à surseoir à toute action et à suspendre toute procédure qui pourraient porter préjudice à la solution définitive de cette affaire".

[2] Ibid. 610. M. Titulesco's objection to the paragraph follows logically from his position with respect to the entire dispute. He had pointed out the great public interest involved; it was the *constitution* of Roumania which violated international law, if there was a violation. If Roumanian peasants got the idea that the land now in their possession might be taken away from them by an arbitration commission, it might result in war. The *continuance* of the controversy as an open question hanging fire was the menace to peace. If the Council intended to do anything about the affair, let it make its decision at once and not postpone consideration of the question. Ibid. 609. Consequently, interim measures, which would have no purpose if one accepted the hypothesis that there was no dispute with respect to which the Council might later on have to make a decision, were equally objectionable.

[3] OJ (1924) 1360. [4] OJ (1924) 1659—62. [5] OJ (1925) 1383—6.

Here too the commission had a multiple function. It was charged with the duty of investigating past events as well as preventing future disturbances. Thus it also met with the fate of not being allowed to enter the territory north of the Brussels line, the part administered by Turkey [1]).

§ 52. The most striking instance of resort to provisional measures by the Council is afforded by the Greco-Bulgar dispute in the fall of 1925 [2]). At a frontier post on a lonely hilltop a Greek soldier was shot by a Bulgarian sentry. Around his body, which fell on Bulgarian soil, there raged a struggle like that of old about the body of Patrocles. The Greeks advanced into Bulgaria. That state appealed to the League of Nations, and without resistance yielded its outposts to the invader. Within an hour after learning by telephone of Bulgaria's request, M. Briand, President of the Council, telegraphed from Paris to both parties in identical terms, reminding them of their obligations under article 12 of the Covenant „not to resort to war, and of the grave consequences which the Covenant lays down for breaches thereof", and exhorting them to give immediate instructions that „pending the consideration of the dispute by the Council, not only no further military movements shall be undertaken, but the troops shall at once retire behind their respective frontiers" [3]).

The Council met on 26 October 1925 at Paris, M. Unden of Sweden arriving by airplane. It immediately approved the initiative taken by M. Briand, and proceeded to consider the twofold task which his *exposé* of the situation revealed: to fix the responsibility for the incident, and, of more immediate urgency, to see that hostilities at once ceased [4]).

The President asked the representatives of Greece and Bulgaria what had been done to comply with his invitation to cease fire. M. Marfoff, for Bulgaria, thanked the Council for its prompt action, and began to submit a statement in regard to the incident.

---

[1]) Conwell-Evans 108—10; C. 400. M. 147. 1925. VII, contains the report of the commission discussed by the Council on 3 September 1925. OJ (1925) 130 ff.

[2]) Conwell-Evans 36—8, 47—53, 101—5, 155—60; OJ (1925) 1696—1718. For an amusing and vigorous account of this affair see Jeremiah Smith Jr., The Preservation of Peace, Phi Beta Kappa address at Harvard June 24, 1927, published by Richard W. Hale Esq. of Boston, Mass. pp. 7—9.

[3]) OJ (1925) 1696—7.

[4]) Ibid. 1698.

Whereupon „The President, interrupting the representative of Bulgaria, pointed out that a statement of the facts would come at a later stage. For the moment, the Council was asking the representatives of Greece and Bulgaria to reply to a simple question. The Bulgarian and Greek governments had been invited, before anything further was done, to cease hostilities and to withdraw their troops behind their respective frontiers. He wished to know what response this invitation had received" [1]).

Not being satisfied that military operations had ceased, the Council requested that the two governments notify it within twenty-four hours that unconditional orders to withdraw have been given, and within sixty hours that all troops have been withdrawn. The governments of Great Britain, France and Italy were requested to direct their military *attachés* at Belgrade and Athens to assist and report upon execution of the request of the Council. Withdrawal took place without incident [2]).

Later a commission was appointed to make a full inquiry and ascertain the facts necessary to enable responsibility to be fixed and indemnities to be determined [3]). The commission was headed by Sir Horace Rumbold, British ambassador to Spain, and contained French and Italian generals as well as Dutch and Swedish representatives holding high posts of responsibility in civil life.

In this affair the technique and execution of the League were excellent. The great powers, fresh from Locarno, were in harmony. Sir Austen Chamberlain declared that it would be an affront to civilization if war could break out under such circumstances in spite of the League's peace machinery. The Council distinguished clearly between the preliminary function of taking provisional measures to restore peace and the task of investigating the merits of the case. For the first it resorted to a commission of military experts, located in the neighborhood, to whom every facility was offered by the governments concerned. [4]) For the latter a commission of high distinction contributed the varied skill of their several professions to the delicate task [5]).

---

[1]) Ibid.

[2]) „The frontier posts were drawn back on each side of the hilltops which constituted the frontier, and a few Swedish gendarmes watched over peace in the Balkans". Shotwell, War and its Renunciation in the Pact of Paris, 1929, 212.

[3]) OJ (1925) 1712.

[4]) Conwell-Evans 103.

[5]) Ibid. 156, 143. Not only is the procedure employed by the Council in this case with respect to provisional measures to be commended, but the conclusions of sub-

§ 53. An important report submitted to the Council on June 15, 1927 [1]) enumerates a series of conservatory measures suitable for the Council to take in handling disputes. This report grew out of the Brouckère report in 1926 which brought to the fore the possibilities of article 11 in the task of preventing war, rather than relying on the sanctions of article 16 to punish the aggressor afterward. It was approved by a committee of the Council on March 15, 1927, by the 8th Assembly [2]) and by the Council on December 6, 1927 [3]). It was explicitly stated in the report itself as well as in the Assembly and Council that the measures suggested formed a valuable guide based on past practice, but in no wise were to be understood as restricting the liberty of the Council in the light of future experience and the exigencies of new situations [4]).

The report distinguishes cases under paragraph 1 of article 11, where there is war or threat of war, and under paragraph 2, where circumstances threatening to disturb peace and good understanding are concerned. Where there is no acute threat or war, „if there is a doubt as to the facts of the dispute, a League Commission may be sent to the *locus in quo* to ascertain what has actually happened or is likely to happen. It is understood that such a commission cannot go to the territory of either party to the dispute without the consent of the State to which that territory belongs". This sort of commission is like the committee of a leg-

---

stantive law derived from the final report are equally important, and establish that mere intention to refrain from war does not exempt from responsibility a state which invades another if it „defends" itself with more than reasonable force. (Verdross, Règles, 484—5, OJ (1926) 173, 202.). This incident is practically on all fours with the previous Corfu incident, in which the Council did not emerge so handsomely, due to the fact that Lord Robert Cecil's courageous efforts were not supported by the French delegate. „But at a time when France was occupying the Ruhr as a pledge to obtain satisfaction from Germany respecting reparations — an action whose validity, according to the British Law Officers of the Crown, was doubtful — it was scarcely conceivable that a similar action by Italy to obtain satisfaction from Greece would have been effectively condemned by the representative of France on the Council of the League". Conwell-Evans 81. Greece had the misfortune of coming out on the short end of the deal in both affairs. It should be noted that in the Corfu affair the Council on 1 September 1903 adopted a resolution expressing „the confident hope that in the meantime the two states concerned will commit no act which might aggravate the situation". OJ (1923) 1282. M. Politis had demanded restoration of the status quo prior to the bombardment and occupation of Corfu as the first step to be taken. Ibid. 1281.

[1]) C. 169. 1927. IX, OJ (1927) 832—3.

[2]) 26 September 1927, Actes 177.

[3]) OJ (1928) 125.

[4]) So too the report dealt only with article 11, without touching the powers of the Council under other articles of the Covenant.

islative assembly holding hearings in order to obtain information enabling it to better fulfil its function [1]). No real remedy *pendente lite* is involved here. The Council may make up its mind on the basis of whatever evidence it has, and its conclusions have the same value whatever procedure may have been used in reaching them [2]).

On the other hand, where there is an imminent threat of war the Council acts not merely to inform itself but to preserve or restore peace. In this case its action, designed to safeguard rights of parties to the due process of pacific settlement, affords a real remedy *pendente lite*. Where there is an imminent threat of war, „even before the Council meets, it is desirable that the Acting President should send telegraphic appeals to the parties to the dispute to refrain forthwith from any hostile acts". When it convenes, „the Council may take steps to see that the *status quo ante* is not disturbed in such manner as to aggravate or extend the dispute and thus to compromise the pacific settlement therof. For this purpose it may indicate to the parties any movements of troops, mobilization operations and other similar measures from which it recommends them to abstain. Similar measures of an industrial, economic or financial nature may also be recommended". Reference is made to the fact that in certain cases the Council had established neutral zones. In case the recommendations of the Council are disregarded, diplomatic pressure, naval or air demonstrations, or „other measures of a more serious character" may ensue. „The very general terms of article 11 allow any action which does not imply recourse to war against the recalcitrant state" [3]).

In order to satisfy itself of the way in which recommended

---

[1]) Lord Robert Cecil stressed this purpose in connection with the Albanian commission. p. 109 *supra*.

[2]) OJ (1926) 172.

[3]) If article 16 permits war as a sanction, it is hard to see why article 11 does not, if it should be „deemed wise and effectual to safeguard the peace of nations". So van Vollenhoven 206. Of course in practice we know that „wars to end war" are not so successful that one would wish for their repetition. The fact that article 11 imposes on the League a duty to prevent the war of sanction as well, i.e. to restore peace as soon as possible by whatever means it can, (Kunz 94) does not militate against the construction contended for here. Note that the sanctions of article 11 are not really sanctions, but new measures, more efficacious to safeguard peace. Kunz 142. It should also be observed that even if the limitation on the Council's action proposed by Rolin-Jaequemyns were accepted, (C. 342. M. 100. 1928. IX, 80) that *mesures conservatoires* should not be taken to preserve rights for which compensation in money is adequate, the limitation would hardly ever apply to the Council's action, since it acts not to preserve rights as such but to preserve peace, and it is difficult to assess in cash the blessings of peace.

measures are carried out, the report goes on, and to keep itself informed of the course of events, the Council may send to the *locus in quo* representatives chosen from lists of suitable experts kept by the Secretary General, or have recourse to diplomatic personages stationed in the neighborhood representing states not parties to the dispute.

§ 54. The Szent-Gotthard incident of January 1, 1928 brought another kind of provisional measure to the fore. Austrian customs officials found that a railroad car already handed over to the Hungarian authorities contained not machine parts but machine gun parts, and demanded return of the car to Austria. Hungarian officials refused and in compliance with the treaty of Trianon rendered the war material unfit for use and proceeded to sell it at auction, since no one claimed it, in accordance with international railroad regulations. Meanwhile a demand had been made by Czechoslovakia, Roumania, and Serbia for investigation of the incident by the Council in accordance with the system of surveillance established in the peace treaties to ensure disarmament of the defeated states. After waiting till the last moment before the sale, M. Cheng-Loh, acting President of the Council, Chinese minister to Paris, having consulted M. Briand and other members of the Council in that capital, telegraphed to the Secretary General: „Kindly telegraph the Hungarian Government that since the Council has received a request from the Czechoslovak, Roumanian and Serbian governments, I, having learned from the press that the Hungarian government is about to sell the articles to which the request refers, consider that it would be prudent to suspend this action as the matter is shortly to be considered by the Council" [1]).

Hungary replied that it was impossible to stop the sale, which was required to take place according to the railroad regulations, and pointed out that the peace treaty providing for the right of investigation did not institute provisional measures. Nevertheless out of courtesy for the person of the president of the Council it would request the purchasers to leave the material in the station [2]).

---

1) OJ (1928) 548.

2) Ibid. Cheng-Loh considered his telegram not as an injunction but as friendly Counsel. Ibid. 388.

„It would, of course, be an abuse of the Covenant to use the wide powers of the Council under Article XI to carry out measures deemed necessary by certain of the Allies against their ex-enemies" [1]). In a case of investigation the Council must conform strictly to the treaties providing for the exercise of such an exceptional procedure. To this extent therefore the Hungarian contention was well founded.

But as the Secretary General pointed out at the Council meeting [2]), in case of war of threat of war under article 11 the report already approved by the Assembly and Council gives the President powers to take provisional measures. The dispositions of that report were not touched, but it became necessary to establish a procedure in other cases. Sir Austen Chamberlain pointed out that it was hardly a satisfactory arrangement that the President should consult the members of the Council resident in the city where he happened to be. He should act on his own responsibility or else consult all members by telegraph [3]).

The difficulty was solved by establishing a rule that when a question is submitted to the Council for its examination, the parties should take whatever steps are necessary and useful to prevent anything occurring on their respective territories which might prejudice the examination or settlement of the question by the Council; and providing that when a matter is submitted to the Council the Secretary General shall immediately call the attention of the parties to that rule and request them to reply without delay stating what steps have been taken [4]).

The action of the Secretary General is felt to be more automatic and impartial than that of the President.

It should be noted that this procedure applies only to the interim before a meeting of the Council. Any member of the League may request a special meeting under article 11 (1) if there is war or threat of war. In that case the President of the Council would act.

It would seem desirable to establish a rule providing for such automatic notice by the Secretary General in all cases, including those where there is war or threat of war. Likewise it would seem that the system established for other cases does not prevent the

[1]) Conwell-Evans 192.
[2]) OJ (1928) 390, 7 March 1928.
[3]) Ibid. 389.
[4]) Ibid. 909—10.

President from also addressing a recommendation to the parties if he sees fit. Where there is war or threat of war, the President, as an organ of the League, is bound to do what he can to prevent war, irrespective of whether any state has requested a special meeting of the Council to deal with the emergency [1]).

§ 55. Without any appeal by a Member state the Council on 15 December 1928 telegraphed to the governments of Bolivia and Paraguay recommending „that the parties will carefully abstain from any act which may aggravate the situation and render a peaceful settlement more difficult.... The Council wishes to emphasize the fact that in its experience it is most important to confine all military measures of a defensive character to those which can not be regarded as aggressive against the other country, and which can not involve the danger of the armed forces coming into contact, as this would lead to an aggravation of the situation, rendering more difficult the efforts at present being made for the maintenance of peace" [2]).

§ 56. In connection with his proposal to refer the question of the legality of the proposed German-Austrian customs union to the Permanent Court of International Justice for its advisory opinion, Mr. Henderson said: „I desire again to ask M. Schober the following question: Does our Austrian colleague agree that, until the Council has taken a decision on the advisory opinion of the Court, no further progress should be made towards the establishment of the proposed regime?"

[1]) Kunz 34; van Vollenhoven 215. On principle, although it expresses the normal rule, the statement of Conwell-Evans 42 is not to be supported: „Only in the event of a threat of war may the President intervene before the Council meets, but he will not exercise this initiative unless the dispute has been properly referred to the Council by a State Member in pursuance of Article XI".

His opinion is shared by Rappard, The Geneva Experiment, 1931, 29, and, apparently, by Sir John Fischer Williams in BYB (1931) 222. Nevertheless such a restrictive interpretation, seems unsupported by the text of the Covenant.

Article 11 (1), first sentence, makes war or threat of war a matter of concern to the *League* (hence including the acting President of the Council) which shall take action to safeguard peace. Kunz 34. The second sentence, enabling any Member to demand a special meeting, is merely a means of giving effect to the principle laid down previously. When the Covenant was drafted, there were no rules regarding how meetings should be called; article 4 (3) simply prescribed that the Council might meet from time to time as occasion might require, at least once a year. A threat of war should not be allowed to hang over until an annual meeting; hence article 11 (2), second sentence, was necessary.

[2]) OJ (1928) 72.

Herr Schober replied: „During my speech I twice had occasion to declare that I unreservedly accepted Mr. Henderson's suggestions. I can therefore certainly give him the assurance which he requires in regard to the period before the Council shall have taken its decision" [1]).

§ 57. During the conflict between Japan and China commencing in the fall of 1931, repeated requests to refrain from hostilities and actions aggravating the situation were addressed to the parties by the Council [2]). In this affair the League's action was marked by hesitation and weakness. But perhaps it simply recognized that after all the only guarantee of lasting peace is an honest desire for peace, and the only way to prevent a nation from fighting is in one way or another to make it think that it does not want to fight. One way of producing that conviction is to point out that war will be futile, as other nations are resolved to oppose the war-maker, and are able to defeat it. But there are other ways, and if effective, they are certainly more desirable.

§ 58. It will have been noticed that article 11 is the basis of most provisional measures in the League's practice. That article merely authorizes action which is wise and effectual to safeguard peace. It is a simple police jurisdiction which the Council exercises.

Of course a police jurisdiction may also be divided into stages, aiming at a provisional or a definitive pacification. One may handcuff the culprit before imprisoning him. But measures to preserve peace may also be provisional in another sense. This is the case where pacification is not only an end in itself, but is the necessary prerequisite and condition precedent of effectual exercise of a judicial jurisdiction.

As a rule the League has more to do than simply to prevent fighting [3]). After the combatants are separated, responsibility for

[1]) OJ (1931) 1071, 18 May 1931.

[2]) See the resolutions of 30 September, 24 October, 30 October, and 7 November 1931, of 2 January 1932, as well as various telegrams by the President of the Council, 8 Bulletin of International News 253, 280; 15 Europe Nouvelle 26.

[3]) Conwell-Evans 35: „Measures aiming at a cessation of hostilities do not usually complete the duties of the Council in regard to such disputes. It has usually to suggest a solution of the questions at issue which led to hostilities, or to determine which was the aggressor or to fix the amount of reparations due to the aggrieved Party".

the unlawful outbreak of hostilities may have to be determined; or the dispute which led to that disturbance of peace may have to be settled on its merits [1]).

The League may have the duty of furnishing interim protection in this sense even when another body is charged with the task of deciding the controversy *in merito* [2]). In such a case, where the League acts not only to preserve peace *simpliciter*, but also to prevent war which impedes pacific settlement, contrary to international obligations, it is possible that the other tribunal may also have jurisdiction to extend interim protection; but the League's pressure will doubtless be the most effective instrument available for enforcing the tribunal's order to refrain from hostile acts endangering litigated rights [3]).

It should be observed that in addition to measures for the preservation of peace for the time being, the League has resorted to measures for the temporary administration of the *res* in controversy [4]), and measures for the preservation of evidence [5]).

§ 59. β. Miscellaneous provisions designed to reinforce the Covenant.

One of the main occupations of League gatherings is the elaboration of draft international conventions, some of which are signed and few ratified [6]). Naturally a number of these have dealt with the maintenance of peace, (one of the primary purposes of the

---

[1]) The distinction between these three questions, which may often fall to the same body to decide, but need not, is clearly brought out in the protocol of 3 January 1929 between Bolivia and Paraguay. See Dumbauld, in 18 Geo. LJ 88, 90.

[2]) As in the Albanian frontiers case, where the Council of Ambassadors had jurisdiction to decide the controverted issues.

[3]) Consequently, article 41 of the Statute of the Permanent Court of International Justice provides that notice of interim measures indicated shall be given to the Council. If such measures should contain a prohibition of acts of force with respect to the subject matter of the litigation, the Council would have a concurrent power *ex officio* to order measures of identical content under article 11. Judge van Eysinga pointed out that the Permanent Court of International Justice might have occasion to cooperate with the Council. D no. 2, 2d add. 196.

[4]) As in the Polish-Lithuanian dispute, p. 107 *supra*.

[5]) In the Szent-Gotthard incident, Scialoja described the sort of measures in question as „to preserve material examination of which may be useful in forming a final judgment". OJ (1928) 392.

[6]) A. 10. 1930. V, report of the committee appointed to consider the question of ratification and signature of conventions concluded under the auspices of the League of Nations. In May 1930, 26 out of 39 conventions were in force, 552 signatures had been ratified, while 553 had not. A. 6 (*a*). 1931. V Annex lists ratifications up to 3 September 1931.

League), by strengthening the means provided in the Covenant.

At first there was widespread interest in proposals designed to „put teeth in the Covenant", to organize military sanctions smacking of the French idea to create an international army. The Geneva Protocol of 1924 was a scheme to „close the gaps in the Covenant" and supply a thoroughgoing and sanctioned structure of obligatory pacific settlement for international controversies. Article 7 provided that during the course of a dispute the parties will not increase their armaments, or take any measures of mobilization, or in general, any action of a nature likely to extend the dispute or make it more acute. In case of infraction, the Council shall decide upon the measures to be taken [1]).

Violation of such measures, or refusal to accept an armistice enjoined by the Council, is to be deemed aggression. The sole object of these measures to be taken by the Council is to facilitate the pacific settlement of disputes and they shall in no way prejudge the actual settlement.

Such measures must not include war, since their purpose is to prevent the outbreak of war pending pacific solution of disputes. Whether economic or other sanctions are permissible has been doubted. Raising a loan, evacuation of territory, demobilization, destruction of excess armaments or the creation of neutralized zones under the supervision of League agents are considered appropriate measures [2]).

Interdiction of increase of armaments during a dispute has been criticised on the ground that it would give to aggressive states an advantage over peaceful adversaries unprepared for war [3]). On the other hand it has been observed that where war is abandoned completely (as proposed in the protocol), and not merely during a „cooling-off period" (as in the Covenant and Bryan treaties), the privilege of preparing for war during the course of the dispute would be of no benefit [4]). But the dangers

[1]) Approved by resolution of the fifth Assembly of 1 October 1924, OJ sp. sup. no. 23, 225; text of article 7 at 500; comment by M. Beneš at 492, in report of first and third committees also published as A. 135 (1). 1924. IX.

[2]) Williams, The League, the Protocol and the Empire, 1925, 74; D. H. Miller, The Geneva Protocol, 1925, 72; Salvador de Madariaga, Disarmament, 1929, 185; Baker, The Geneva Protocol, 1925, 94, 95, 98; Sir John Fischer Williams, The Geneva Protocol, 3 J. Brit. Inst. Int. Aff. (1924) 300—1.

[3]) The Protocol of Geneva, Despatches exchanged between the British and Dominion Governments, 17. See note 2, p. 99 *supra*.

[4]) Baker, The Geneva Protocol, 1925, 210.

arising from mobilization and rivalry in armaments are notorious [1]).

Mention should likewise be made of the general convention for improving the means of preventing war approved by the twelfth Assembly and signed by Austria, Colombia, Spain and Greece. France and Germany announced the intention of signing later [2]).

This convention was elaborated by a special committee [3]) on the basis of the model treaty for strengthening the means of preventing war approved by the Assembly of 20 September 1928 [4]). The suggestion was of German origin [5]). The object of the proposed procedure is to invest decisions of the Council as to provisional measures with obligatory force by an agreement in advance to accept them and carry them out [6]). Originally the scheme also sought to facilitate proceedings by stipulating that the Council might decide by majority vote [7]).

The convention is open to several criticisms. (1) It applies only in threat of war, not where there is „war". Although the euphemistic usage prevalent which permits hostilities and invasions of territory without the existence of war would permit the convention to have great practical value, it might also permit a state to argue that it was not bound to obey the Council's measures if it was „obliged to make *war* in self-defence". Yet that is the very time when measures for the prevention of war are most necessary. The Council's duty under article 11 continues during as well as before war [8]). Why should not the scope of the convention be equally broad? (2) No supervision of non-military measures is provided [9]). The restrictions regarding the military measures

[1]) See 19 AJ (1925) 81, note (24); Naval War College, Int. Law Documents, 1917, 100. Gralinski 99 laments as regrettable and dangerous the omission from the Covenant of any restriction on the augmentation of forces. Such augmentation should be interdicted in general but above all during a judicial procedure which implies pacific solution for the difficulty. Increase of armaments pending the pacific procedure does not accord with the desire of the parties to reach a friendly settlement of their differences; it creates an atmosphere of hostility and tension; above all, it may compromise the peaceful procedure.

[2]) 11 Resumé mensuel des travaux de la S. d. N. (Sept. 1931) 324—5, text 405 ff.

[3]) Meeting at Geneva 11—15 May 1931, A. 14. 1931. VII, text at 50—2.

[4]) OJ (1928) sp. sup. no. 63, 58—9.

[5]) Report of Committee on Arbitration and Security, C. 342. M. 100. 1928. IX, 71—8. [6]) Ibid. 76. [7]) Ibid. 75. [8]) Kunz 94.

[9]) The distinction into non-military measures „relating to the substance of the dispute" and military measures is not particularly happy or clear. What is included within the first group? The distinction was made in order to limit the military measures. Of course the Council could not order the sinking of the British navy or the razing

which the parties are obliged by the convention to accept might give rise to the impression that similar restrictions hold with respect to non-obligatory measures prescribed by the Council in virtue of its broad powers under article 11 [1]).

Similarly the convention for financial assistance to states victims of agression approved by the eleventh Assembly [2]) provides that such assistance shall be conditioned upon compliance by the applicant with provisional measure laid down by the Council. The beneficiary must also submit the dispute to such mode of pacific settlement as is prescribed by the Council.

Provisional measures for restoring interrupted freedom of transit *pendente lite* are envisaged in various conventions [3]); and the statute of the Bank of International Settlements [4]) and the Hague reparations agreement with Germany of 20 January

---

of French fortresses, as a measure which the parties might reasonably be *obliged* in advance to accept. It will be noticed that certain military measures permitted relate to restrictions upon a state's action *within* its own territory. Of course withdrawal behind its own lines is the first thing the Council would order.

[1]) Kunz 108 is of course in error when he says that measures under article 11 are binding on the parties as signatories of the Covenant which gives the Council power to take such measures. Review by (Sir) J(ohn) F(ischer) W(illiams) in BYB (1931) 222.

[2]) On 29 September 1930. 11 Ass. (1930) 142. The convention was signed by 28 states. Ibid. 192. Text of article 2 at p. 503. See also Sir John Fischer Williams, La Convention pour l'Assistance financière aux Etats victimes d'Agression, 34 Rec. 1930-IV, 81—147.

[3]) Article 15 of the preparatory documents of the first general conference on Communications and Transit, dealing with disputes, reads: „These disputes shall in cases of urgency be accorded an accelerated procedure, the Permanent Communications and Transit Committee and the Permanent Court of International Justice having the power without prejudice to the final opinion and judgment on the basic cause of dispute, of pronouncing a provisional opinion and judgment to the extent of prescribing any provisional measures designed in particular to restore the facilities for freedom of transit which existed before the act or occurrence which gave rise to the dispute". These documents were drafted on June 11, 1920 by the provisional communications and transit committee, immediately before the committee met to draw up the Statute of the Court, June 16—July 24, 1920.

In article 13 of the Statute on Freedom of Transit, Barcelona April 20, 1921, it is provided „In urgent cases, a preliminary opinion may recommend temporary measures intended, in particular, to restore the facilities for freedom of transit which existed before the act or occurrence which gave rise to the dispute". 7 LNTS 30—1; similar are the terms of article 22 of the statute on the *régime* of natural waterways of the same date, 7 LNTS 62—3; and article 21 of the statute on the international *régime* of maritime ports of 9 December 1925, 58 LNTS 308—9.

[4]) Article 56 (3): „Before giving a final decision and without prejudice to the questions at issue, the president of the Tribunal, or, if he is unable to act in any case, a member of the Tribunal to be designated by him forthwith, may, on the request of the first party applying therefor, order any appropriate provisional measures in order to safeguard the respective rights of the parties". 24 AJ supp. 340.

1930 [1]) authorize interlocutory measures to prevent violations of the rights of the parties. Projects on double taxation prepared by League experts contemplate the possibility of relief from fiscal measures of disputed legality upon order of the Permanent Court of International Justice under article 41 [2]). M. Guerrero's codification project with respect to responsibility of states provided for commissions of inquiry having power to order measures for safeguarding the rights of parties concerned until the report is submitted [3]).

§ 60. 3. Post-war European arbitration treaties.

The peace machinery of the Covenant has been supplemented by numerous treaties of arbitration, conciliation and judicial settlement [4]). Switzerland, after becoming a member of the League, took the lead in concluding such treaties [5]). Many of these instruments contain provisions regarding interim measures. The earliest to do so is that entered into by Switzerland with Germany at Bern on 3 December 1921, before the latter state had become a member of the League of Nations. Article 18 of this treaty was significant and influential [6]).

The parties there agreed, after first stipulating that the arbitral

[1]) Article 15 (4): „Before and without prejudice to a final decision, the chairman of the Tribunal, or, if he is not available in any case, any other member appointed by him, shall be entitled, on the request of any party who makes the application, to make any interlocutory order with a view to preventing any violation of the rights of the parties". 24 AJ supp. 268.

[2]) These projects (C. 562 M. 178. 1928. II) provide for reference of disputes in the first instance to a technical organ designated by the League, and go on: „La procédure ouverte devant l'organisme visé ci-dessus, ou l'avis formulé par lui, n'entraînera en aucun cas la suspension de la mesure qui fait l'objet du litige; il en sera de même dans le cas d'une instance devant la Cour permanente de Justice internationale, à moins que celle-ci n'en décide autrement aux termes de l'article 41 de son Statut." (Article 14 of conv. Ia on direct taxes, article 6 of convention on succession). See Niboyet, Les doubles Impositions au point de vue juridique, 31 Rec. 1930 I, 32—33. Similar is article 8 of the convention of 8 November 1927 on the abolition of import and export prohibitions and restrictions. 25 AJ Sup. 124—5. Would a provision such as the above, if no reservation as to article 41 of the Court Statute were made, be a supplementary rule of procedure admissible under rule 32? See p. 162 *infra*.

[3]) C. 196. M. 70. 1927. V, 103.

[4]) For these see Habicht and Systematic Survey. Great impetus was given to the negotiation of such treaties by the resolution of the third Assembly of 22 September 1922. Records of the third Assembly, part. I, 200.

[5]) The Swiss scheme was inspired by the Bryan treaties. Bericht des Schweizerischen Bundesrates an die Bundesversammlung betreffend internationale Schiedsverträge vom 11. Dezember 1919, printed in Société des Nations, 1920, 220—3.

[6]) LNTS 12 : 277.

award should be fulfilled by the parties in good faith [1]: (1) To refrain, so far as possible, during the procedure of arbitration or conciliation, from any measure which could react prejudicially upon the execution of the arbitral award or the acceptance of the proposals of the conciliation commission. (2) To refrain from any act of self-help by force [2]) until the time which the conciliation commission has appointed for the acceptance of its proposals. (3) That the arbitral tribunal, upon the request of a party, can order precautionary measures (*vorsorgliche Massnahmen*) insofar as they can be carried out by the parties through their administrative machinery; likewise the conciliation commission may make proposals for the same purpose [3]).

It will be noticed that this article would be improved by omission of the weakening words „as far as possible [4])" and „so far as they can be carried out by the parties through their administrative machinery" [5]). The addition of an explicit agreement to accept and apply the measures would strengthen the article, although apparently the orders of the tribunal (as distinguished from the proposals of the conciliation commission) are binding [6]). With respect to the latter the „logical" [7]) solution has been adopt-

---

[1]) This juxtaposition is evidence for the contention that interim protection, like execution of the award, is a consequence of submission to arbitral procedure required by good faith and good sense. See p. 182 *infra*.

[2]) „gewaltsame Selbsthilfe". Note the „howler" („acts of a legal nature") in the English version in the League of Nations treaty series. Habicht does not correct this slip.

[3]) The tribunal's power is expressed by the word „anordnen"; the commission's by „Vorschläge machen".

[4]) The insertion of such words in article 2 of the Hague Convention of Pacific Settlement of 1907 requiring mediation before resort to war deprived that provision of practical value.

[5]) „auf dem Verwaltungswege". This expression has no meaning in international law, and no uniform meaning in different systems of internal law. Guggenheim 68—70. It probably means „without conflicting with national legislation or judicial decision having force of *res judicata*". See note 1, p. 147 *infra*. The desire is to avoid necessity of legislative modification or disregard of the sanctity of a court decision. If the government may initiate judicial proceedings, as criminal prosecution, request for postponement or dismissal made as *amicus curiae*, proceeding to take testimony, etc. in accordance with local law, it must do so. What of exercise of pardoning power? If by national law there can be no temporary reprieve, but only definitive pardon, must a government resort to it to comply with temporary order of the international tribunal?

[6]) See note 3 *supra*. In the German-Swedish treaty „bezeichnen" is used instead of „anordnen" and the words „die zum Schutz der Rechte dieser Partei" are added, making the formula closely resemble article 41 of the Court Statute. Hence here the interim orders are not binding. See p. 168 *infra*.

[7]) See pp. 101, 102, 104 *supra*. This view overlooks the fact that the function of interim measures is to furnish protection against the harm due to *delay* entailed in rendering

ed, that if the final decision is not obligatory, neither is the interim order.

Article 18 has been reproduced with variations of wording in subsequent German treaties [1]. A formula most frequently found, in connection with various modes of pacific settlement [2], is clause (1) alone, either as it stands or with the words „as possible" omitted. This abbreviated formula lends itself to complications in that subsidiary disputes regarding the proper provisional measures may arise [3]. In content it hardly goes beyond the common law obligation implied in the very act of invoking procedure for pacific settlement [4]. Nevertheless it is of value in that it embodies a clear and express statement of obligation in an instrument likely to be brought to the attention of the parties during the dispute and capable of founding a forum, if there is in force between the parties a not uncommon stipulation that disputes over interpretation and application of treaties are among those for which obligatory jurisdiction of an international tribunal is accepted [5].

Clauses (1) and (3) become separate articles in the treaties of Pacific Settlement concluded between Sweden, Norway, Finland and Denmark [6]. They are combined into a convenient short for-

---

a final decision. In a treaty of obligatory conciliation, though the findings of the commission are not compulsory, the *delay is compulsory*, and at the end of conciliation proceedings the party rejecting the proposals will not be in the same position as if it could reject immediately the proposal to conciliate. As a remedy against prejudice caused by the change in circumstances made possible by compulsory *resort* to conciliation, it is quite „logical" to provide for obligatory jurisdiction to grant interim protection. The prejudice which may result to rights of parties pending a procedure does not in the slightest depend upon the legal nature of the formal pronouncement with which that procedure terminates. Rolin-Jaequemyns notes a tendency to entrust conciliation commissions with power to make binding interim orders. C. 342 M. 100. 1928. IX, 80.

[1]) Nowhere else has clause (2) been followed, although it would seem to be of practical value, and resembles somewhat the non-mobilization provisions common in American treaties. See §§ 45 and 46 *supra*.

[2]) Pacific settlement (arbitration and adjudication) LNTS 49 : 371—3; conciliation, arbitration and judicial settlement, 55 : 100—1; arbitration and conciliation, 48 : 392; conciliation and judicial settlement, 33 : 98; conciliation, 34 : 182 or judicial settlement alone, 33 : 418, 43 : 396.

[3]) See § 43 *supra*.

[4]) See p. 182 *infra*. It should be noted that the absence of such a provision in the Swiss treaty with France does not authorize conduct of the sort expressly forbidden in the treaties with other countries. Schindler in 52 RDILC (1925) 859.

[5]) The advantage mentioned by Guggenheim 67, (that a new dispute arises in which damages might be sought for violation of the norm regarding interim protection) is not confined to cases where there is an express treaty. In the case of an implied norm, however, there is not so likely to be a tribunal having jurisdiction to deal with the dispute.

[6]) Articles 5 and 9; LNTS 49 : 371—2.

mula in several Belgian treaties. „During the course of proceedings of conciliation, judicial settlement or arbitration the Contracting Parties shall abstain from all measures likely to exert any influence on the acceptance of the proposals of the Conciliation Commission, or the execution of the judgment of the Permanent Court of International Justice, or the award of the Arbitral tribunal. For this purpose, the Conciliation Commission, the Court of Justice and the Arbitral Tribunal shall, if necessary, lay down the provisional measures (*mesures provisionnelles*) to be adopted" [1]).

According to this wording, acts having any influence on the acceptance or execution of the decision, not merely those having a „prejudicial repercussion" thereon, are interdicted [2]). Power to lay down provisional measures is conferred without distinction upon each of the three bodies to which disputes are to be referred under the treaty.

Likewise clauses (1) and (3) recur in article 19 of the Locarno arbitration conventions of 16 October 1925, the most thoroughgoing formula to be found with respect to interim protection:

„In any case, and particularly if the question on which the parties differ arises out of acts already committed or on the point of commission, the Conciliation Commission, or, if the latter has not been notified thereof, the arbitral tribunal or the Permanent Court of International Justice, acting in accordance with Article 41 of its Statute, shall lay down (*indiqueront*) within the shortest possible time the provisional measures (*mesures provisoires*) to be adopted. It shall similarly be the duty of the Council of the League of Nations, if the question is brought before it, to ensure that suitable provisional measures are taken. The German and French Governments undertake respectively to accept such measures, to abstain from all measures likely (*susceptible*) to have a repercussion prejudicial to the execution of the decision or to the arrangements proposed by the Conciliation Commission or by the Council of the League of Nations, and, in general, to abstain from any sort of action whatsoever which may aggravate or extend the dispute" [3]).

[1]) Article 21 of Swiss-Belgian treaty, LNTS 68 : 54.

[2]) There would seem to be no difference in meaning between this article and the usual wording.

[3]) LNTS 54: 312, 324, 336, 350.

It will be noticed that the opening words of this article borrow language from the Bryan treaties, and amplify it to escape an ambiguity which the framers of article 41 of the Statute of the Permanent Court of International Justice dealt with by omitting instead of adding words [1]).

This article imports from article 7 of the Geneva protocol [2]) an interdiction of any action tending to aggravate or extend the dispute. It refers specifically to article 41 of the Statute of the Permanent Court of International Justice, which governs the indication of provisional measures by that tribunal [3]). It provides for the indication of such measures not only by the Court, but also by the arbitral tribunal, the conciliation commission, or the Council of the League of Nations, as the case may be. Most important of all, it contains the obligation to accept such measures as binding.

Several Swedish treaties [4]) make use of a formula in substance equivalent to the Locarno article, but with the order of the undertakings reversed. Another slight difference is that only the Court, or the Court and Council, or the Court and arbitral tribunal are mentioned as having authority to indicate measures which the parties agree to accept.

Article 33 of the General Act for the Pacific Settlement of Disputes adopted by the Ninth Assembly [5]) follows the order of the Locarno article but divides it into three numbered paragraphs, which make a distinction between the powers of the Court or arbitral tribunal [6]) and those of the conciliation commission [7]). Action by the Council of the League of Nations is not mentioned.

§ 61. 4. Mixed Arbitral tribunals.

Of post-war arbitration treaties, the most important from a practical standpoint were the agreements constituting the Mixed

[1]) See note 4, p. 145 *infra*. [2]) See p. 122 *supra*.

[3]) Does the use of the expression „*shall* indicate" deprive the Court of discretion under article 41? Even if this were a new rule of procedure for the Court under rule 32, it does not in content differ from what is ordained by article 41. See p. 162 *infra*.

[4]) LNTS 48 : 182; 61 : 202.

[5]) 26 September 1928, OJ (1928) sp. sup. no. 63, 24. See also pp. 31, 36, 39, 44—5, 50, 56.

[6]) „indiquera, dans le plus bref delai possible, quelles mesures provisoires doivent être prises. Les parties en litige seront tenues de s'y conformer".

[7]) „pourra recommander aux parties les mesures provisoires qu'elle estimera utiles". As to the wisdom of such a distinction we have already spoken. See pp. 102, 104, 126 *supra*.

Arbitral Tribunals which were constituted pursuant to the treaties of peace to settle claims between allied governments or nationals and defeated governments or nationals [1]). These tribunals were not hypothetical commissions of conciliation [2]), but presented an example of compulsory arbitration not as a Utopian wish but as a practical necessity.

It was provided that „Each Mixed Arbitral Tribunal will settle its own procedure" subject to the proviso that „The Tribunal may adopt such rules as shall be in accordance with justice and equity" [3]) Most of the tribunals adopted rules providing for interim measures [4]). The Anglo-German rules [5]) were silent on the subject, but that tribunal in practice decided that it had power to award an interim injunction, and exercised that power [6]). The Anglo-Austrian rules [7]), following the Austrian procedure in providing for a preliminary hearing [8]), empowered the tribunal at that hearing to give directions necessary for the further progress and final determination of all questions at issue, in particular, *inter alia*, as to the preservation and interim custody of the subject matter of the dispute.

The Franco-German, German-Belgian, German-Czech and German-Italian rules vary slightly in form, but establish the following provisions commonly copied in Mixed Arbitral Tribunal rules [9]): (1) In addition to provisional measures expressly provided for in the treaties of peace, the tribunal (in case of emergency the president) may order (*peut ordonner*) any conservatory or provisional measure which seems equitable and necessary to guarantee

---

1) As to these tribunals see Mendelssohn-Bartholdy in Der Zivilprozess; Gidel-Barrault, Le Traité de Paix avec l'Allemagne du 28 juin 1919 et les Intérêts privés, 1921; Isay, Die privaten Rechte und Interessen im Friedensvertrag, 3ed. 1923; Zitelmann, Die gemischten Schiedsgerichtshöfe. Aufgaben und Hoffnungen, 29 Niemeyers Zt. f. int. Rt. (1921) 248—262. They arose by agreement between the parties, not directly out of the peace treaties, for some states did not set up a tribunal as they might have done. Rundstein, L'Arbitrage international en Matière privée, 23 Rec. 1928-III, 391.

2) As to the questionable utility of an enormous number of inactive or non-existent commissions of this sort, see Sir John Fischer Williams, in 10 Int. Aff. (1931) 335.

3) Treaty of Versailles, article 304*d* and annex 2.

4) The rules were influenced by the procedure of various states. Widely followed were the rules of the Franco-German tribunal, drafted under the influence of its Swiss president Mercier, in which the 1911 code of civil procedure of the canton of Vaud was drawn upon. The German-Italian rules were colored by a draft of Professor Chiovenda, which took account of Austrian and Swiss codes. The Anglo-German rules were based on a comparison of the procedure of those two states. Rabel 13.

5) 1 TAM 109—118. 6) 1 TAM 857. 7) §§ 60—62, 1 TAM 632.

8) See Austrian ZPO §§ 239—242. 9) See annex 3 *infra*.

the rights of the parties. (2) The order may be made at any time, even before the institution of proceedings. In that case suit must be brought as soon as possible. (3) The party affected should be heard if possible. If not, reconsideration of the decision may be requested, but such request does not suspend the measures unless the president or tribunal so orders, in which case security may be required of the party opposing the measures. (4) Third parties prejudiced may make opposition, which does not suspend the measures, unless the tribunal or president so orders. (5) Applicant may be required to give security or make a deposit to cover damages resulting from the measures. (6) The decision determines the scope and conditions of the measures. It has the same binding force (*force exécutoire*) as a sentence of the tribunal. The agent of the government in question may be required to see to its execution even before it is notified to the party concerned, in which case notification should be made within a week or so thereafter. (7) The German-Italian rules add that the measure must consist in sequestration or administration or custody of property in dispute [1]).

Further rules regarding the nature and requirements of interim measures may be deduced from consideration of relevant decisions made by the tribunals.

§ 62. 1. [2]) Sequestration of paintings deposited with defendant in Berlin was ordered, and the German agent required to indicate the proper sheriff in Berlin to execute the order. It appearing that the defendant had sold the paintings, the order was modified to the effect that they should be sequestrated in the hands of the purchaser [3]).

2 [4]). Defendant was named sequestrator of the property in dispute when it would have been harmful to interfere with the normal administration of the property. Defendant was ordered to exercise due and reasonable care in administration (*bon père de famille*).

---

[1]) This limitation is approved by Rabel, in JW (1922) 343 as excluding fantastic demands. „Mit der Einschränkung soll phantastischen Anträgen vorgebeugt werden". The verbose form of the rules reflects the Italian ministerial practice of setting forth details. Ibid. 341.

[2]) Franco-German, 4th section, 21 July 1920, 1 TAM 10.

[3]) Cf. case 18, § 63 *infra*.

[4]) Franco-German, 3d section, 30 October 1920, 1 TAM 12.

3 [1]). Defendants were forbidden to obtain satisfaction on a seizure ordered by the court of Aix-la-Chapelle. The seizure ordered by the German court was revoked by the tribunal [2]).

4 [3]). Defendant company was ordered to keep the railroad cars in ligitation from deterioration. In order not to interfere with normal administration of its business, only those cars which would be harmed by usage need be kept out of circulation. A neutral expert was named to examine the cars and supervise their operation. Plaintiff, being notoriously solvent, was not required to give security.

5 [4]). Seizure of real and personal property had been requested. The tribunal found seizure of the real estate to be sufficient, and did not order sequestration of the merchandise, which would have interfered with defendant's business. No security was required.

6 [5]). Company W was forbidden to vote an increase in its capitalization. Plaintiff owned company A, whose asserted ownership of company W was to be decided *in merito* in the pending action. If plaintiff wins, it would have a right to vote on the increase of capitalization.

7 [6]). Seizure of one of three pieces of real estate was considered sufficient to secure the pecuniary claim of plaintiff.

8 [7]). The city of Sofia had taken over the enterprise of plaintiff electricity company. It was agreed that it should be returned, and only the modality was in question. Since the city might not be able to pay or borrow a large sum at once on condemnation, and since plaintiff would require capital at once on beginning operations, it was in defendant's own interest to have income not required for operation set aside for plaintiff's security. But only one-fourth of the gross receipts, instead of two-thirds, as asked by plaintiff, was set apart for that purpose, in accordance with the principle that the prejudice caused by the measure ought not to be out of proportion to the benefit obtained therefrom by plain-

---

1) German-Belgian, 16 March 1921, 1 TAM 82.

2) 8 April 1921, 1 TAM 84. The tribunals had by article 305 of the peace treaty power to replace parties in the position they were in before decisions of German courts contrary to the provisions of the treaty. See note 8, p. 133 *infra*.

3) German-Belgian, 8 April 1921, 1 TAM 85.

4) French-Bulgarian, 22 February 1922, 1 TAM 937.

5) French-German, 3d section, 8 April 1922, 2 TAM 56.

6) French-Bulgarian, 26 July 1922, 2 TAM 338.

7) Belgian-Bulgarian, 6 January-26 February 1923, 2 TAM 924.

tiff [1]. The tribunal also decided that a high degree of utility was equivalent to the necessity requisite for interim measures [2].

9 [3]. Plaintiff tramway company, having asked for payment of damages, and in the alternative for restitution of its property, was not interested in administration of the property, but only in ultimate payment of the amount due. This utility does not amount to the necessity required by the rules. Later on protection may be given if needed.

10 [4]. Since the property had become dilapidated during its administration by the city, it was not advisable that it be administered by plaintiff company as sequestrator until determination of the conditions on which it should be taken over by plaintiff. The city requested that a neutral person be named, but did not suggest the name of any such person who would be qualified. The tribunal therefore named Col. Enaux, a person of unquestionable competence, familiar with the Bulgarian language [5].

11 [6]. Pending suit brought by Alsatian against Austrian company, latter's nationality became Czechoslovak by agreement between Austria and Czechoslovakia. This was not a voluntary change of nationality on defendant's part in order to escape liability. Indeed the judgment of the tribunal is executable in Czechoslovakia. There is no need for ordering measures of protection.

§ 63. A number of interesting cases against the Polish government, arising out of Polish land expropriation laws, were decided by the German-Polish tribunal.

12 [7]. Plaintiff, alleging that he had acquired Polish nationality and hence was protected from liquidation [8], asked the tri-

---

[1] „Un principe qui, pour n'être pas inscrit dans le réglement, n'en est pas moins digne de considération et en vertu duquel le préjudice causé par la mesure conservatoire ne doit pas être hors de proportion avec le profit que peut en retirer le requérant" Ibid. 926—7.

[2] Ibid. 927.

[3] Belgian-Bulgarian, 10 February 1923, 2 TAM 928.

[4] Belgian-Bulgarian, 24 July 1923, 3 TAM 593.

[5] The practical difficulty of finding suitable persons to carry out measures ordered by the tribunal is also referred to by the German-Polish tribunal in case 12, § 63 *infra*.

[6] French-Austrian, 26 March 1923, 3 TAM 160.

[7] German-Polish, 21 May 1923, 3 TAM 596.

[8] Treaty of Versailles, article 297*b*: „Subject to any contrary stipulations which may be provided for in the present treaty, the Allied and Associated Powers reserve the right to retain and liquidate all property, rights and interests belonging at the date of the coming into force of the present Treaty to German nationals, or companies con-

bunal to order suspension of liquidation, forbid disposition of the property by defendant, and appoint experts to determine the value of the property.

The tribunal pointed out that a consideration of its jurisdiction in the main matter was of importance for its decision on the question of interim measures, in the sense that it was important to know the nature of the judgment which the tribunal would be called upon to render. If it had jurisdiction to grant specific restitution of property wrongfully liquidated, it would be much more natural to grant plaintiff's request for *mesures conservatoires* than if it could only award an indemnity in money [1]).

The tribunal then decided that it had no jurisdiction under article 297*b* of the treaty of Versailles, the article which forbade liquidation of property of persons acquiring Polish nationality.

Proceeding to consider its jurisdiction under article 306, permitting it to determine the reparation due to a party aggrieved by the judgment of a competent tribunal not in conformity with the stipulations of the treaty, it held that in view of certain provisions of Polish law there was reason to think that the Polish expropriation board's decisions might be considered judgments of a competent tribunal. The question of jurisdiction was reserved for consideration in connection with the merits of the case; but a negative answer to the question of jurisdiction did not impose itself at once. In order to grant interim measures it is sufficient that lack of jurisdiction does not appear immediately [2]).

Likewise the tribunal held that interim protection was not precluded by the fact that, at the moment, plaintiff would lose his case on the merits, by reason of the availability of a dilatory plea

---

trolled by them, within their territories, colonies, possessions and protectorates, including territories ceded to them by the present Treaty.... German nationals who acquire *ipso facto* the nationality of an Allied or Associated Power in accordance with the provisions of the present Treaty will not be considered as German nationals within the meaning of this paragraph". Article 305: „Whenever a competent tribunal has given or gives a decision in a case covered by Sections III, IV, V or VII and such decision is inconsistent with the provisions of such Sections, the party who is prejudiced by the decision shall be entitled to obtain redress which shall be fixed by the Mixed Arbitral Tribunal („aura droit à une réparation qui sera determinée par le Tribunal arbitral mixte"). At the request of a national of an Allied or Associated Power, the redress may, whenever possible, be effected by the Mixed Arbitral Tribunal directing the replacement of the parties in the position occupied by them before the judgment was given by the German court".

[1]) 3 TAM 599—600.

[2]) Ibid. 607.

to the effect that the expropriation was not yet completed. It was theoretically possible that the competent Polish authority might find in favor of plaintiff's claim to Polish nationality, and suspend the liquidation [1].

Nevertheless, the tribunal concluded that it had no power to order suspension of the liquidation. That measure had been demanded in virtue of article 297*b*. But the tribunal did not have jurisdiction under that article. Its jurisdiction could be based only upon article 305. But that article empowered it only with respect to *German* tribunals to replace the parties in the same situation where they were before the judgement rendered. To suspend liquidation would be to interfere with execution of the decisions of a Polish tribunal. No power to do that was given by article 305 [2].

Similarly the tribunal concluded that there was no occasion to appoint experts to determine the value of the property. It was difficult to find neutral experts as to the value of property in that part of Poland. Natives of Danzig were impeached by Poland as pro-German. Moreover opinions as to the value of the property were not what the judge of the indemnity would need. Rather would a description of the physical condition of the property be important. There was no evidence that such an inventory would not be forthcoming as part of the documentation of the Polish expropriation proceedings. If later on it should appear that no report on these points had been made, it would be proper to take measures appropriate to guarantee plaintiff's means of proof. So too Polish solvency was not in doubt. There was no need to require that security be given [3].

13 [4]. In a subsequent application for measures of protection in the same case, after the liquidation had been completed, the tribunal made a more careful analysis of article 305 of the treaty of Versailles, reaching the correct conclusion that if reparation which it had the power to determine included restitution *in specie* of particular property, instead of merely money damages, then it would have power to order such interim measures are were nec-

[1] Ibid. 607—8.
[2] Ibid. 608.
[3] Ibid. 610.
[4] 30 July 1924, 9 TAM 321.

essary to ensure execution of the judgment ordaining such restitution [1]).

From the use of the words „reparation" and „indemnity" in various parts on the treaty, the tribunal decides that article 305 does not refer simply to money damages. Consequently Poland was ordered not to dispose of the property liquidated, lest thereby a judgment for restitution might be rendered vain.

In a dictum the tribunal mentioned two possible interpretations of the second sentence of article 305, referring to German courts. That provision might mean that decisions of German tribunals were to be nullified, or treated as non-existent. This would be a grave infringement of Germany's sovereignty. On the other hand it might mean that though the German judgment was valid, its *effects* were to be annihilated by putting the parties in the same situation as if it had not been rendered [2]).

14 [3]). So too when plaintiff asked that defendant be prohibited from taking any measure modifying the material and juridical situation of the parties in law or fact, notably by taking from plaintiff ownership and enjoyment of his property, the tribunal ordered only that the state refrain from alienation of the expropriated realty. It was pointed out that the state is not prevented from taking the property itself, but only from disposing of it to third parties. There is thus no interference with its sovereignty by suspension of liquidation. That operation is completed with the transfer of property to the state.

---

[1]) Ibid. 322—3: „L'art. 305 prévoit que la partie qui aura subi un préjudice aura droit à une réparation qui sera déterminée par le T.A.M. Si cette réparation n'est autre que le versement d'une somme d'argent, la mesure conservatoire requise est superflue, la solvabilité de l'Etat polonais n'étant pas mise en doute. Il en est autrement si par réparation on peut entendre ici l'obligation de restituer son bien au propriétaire injustement liquidé en sa qualité d'ancien Allemand devenu de plein droit polonais en vertu du traité de Versailles. Il convient alors d'interdire au défendeur de rendre vaine la condemnation qui le ménace en aliénant la chose qu'il devra peut-être restituer, et en se mettant ainsi par avance dans l'impossibilité de satisfaire à la décision du Tribunal".

[2]) In other words the tribunal's authority would not be that of an appellate jurisdiction, to reform the German judgment, but an independent praetorian or equity jurisdiction disregarding it. The practical difference, with respect to the extent of encroachment on German sovereignty, is hard to see. The same distinction might have been applied to Polish liquidation: the tribunal need not have directly forbidden liquidation, but could have ordered that liquidation proceedings, however legal under Polish law, should have no effect from the standpoint of international law, and that Poland should take such steps, legislative or administrative, as might be necessary to enable it to fulfil its international obligations *in specie*.

[3]) 4 March 1925, 6 TAM 326.

15. Similar orders were made in other cases [1]). The reasons which had motivated the tribunal's previous decisions that liquidation should not be suspended were there made known [2]). The *ratio decidendi* was that the tribunal considered deprivation of possession as an injury for which compensation could be made in money. Interim measures ordered by the Tribunal under article 305 are admissible only for the purpose of preventing acts rendering impossible restitution *in specie* in case the tribunal should determine such reparation to be proper.

16 [3]). In 21 cases similar to these decided May 4 and March 4 the tribunal ordered that if Poland transfered to third parties personal rights of possession of the land which it had been forbidden to alienate, it must insert in the contracts a clause providing that possession will be given up immediately in case the tribunal should order restitution to the owner.

17 [4]). In 31 cases the measures ordered on March 4, May 4 and July 9 were revoked, because of a decision by the tribunal that it had no jurisdiction in cases where plaintiff claims to have acquired Polish nationality *ipso jure* by the peace treaty, and hence by article 297 *b* to be immune against liquidation [5]).

18 [6]). Plaintiff alleged that Poland disposed of property in spite of tribunal's order, and he fears expulsion. Relief was denied, the tribunal declaring that Poland, if no longer owner, can not expel plaintiff. Expulsion is to be feared only from the new owner, who is not a party to the case, and not subject to orders of the tribunal [7]). If Poland remains owner, the tribunal can not prevent dispossession of plaintiff, as its power to order interim measures in the case is based upon its right to ensure possible reparation *in specie* under article 305. Possibility of such restitution is not precluded by plaintiff's being deprived of possession [8]).

---

[1]) 4 March 1925, 6 TAM 328; 4 May 1925, 6 TAM 329.

[2]) In the decision of May 4, Ibid. 330.

[3]) 9 July 1925, 6 TAM 332.

[4]) 5 December 1925, 6 TAM 348.

[5]) 2 December 1925, 6 TAM 334. It was pointed out that the provision in question was inserted in the treaty of Versailles at the request of the Serb-Croat-Slovene delegation for the purpose of insuring that former German nationals who became nationals of states in the allied camp should not be subjected to liquidation. If England expropriated an Alsatian who had become French, the question would fall within the jurisdiction of the Polish-German mixed arbitral tribunal, according to the thesis put forward by the Germans claiming to be Polish.

[6]) 3 July 1926, 6 TAM 331.

[7]) Cf. cases 1 and 6, § 62 *supra*.

[8]) Cf. case 20, § 64 *infra*.

19 [1]). Plaintiff had been deprived of possession and enjoyment of his property, but it was not in evidence that the liquidation had been completed. Destitute, plaintiff sought maintenance. After making a notable pronouncement regarding the nature of interim protection [2]), the tribunal declared that the necessitous state of the plaintiff was not sufficent ground for condemning the defendant, but that the latter must be debtor of the former. Until liquidation is complete, Poland owes plaintiff nothing. Nevertheless the tribunal held that deprivation of possession and enjoyment was liquidation *pro tanto*, and granted relief [3]).

§ 64. 20 [4]). Plaintiff company applied for interim protection because Roumanian government refused to promise not to alter the status quo pending proceedings. Tribunal ordered that it abstain from all measures changing the legal or factual situation, notably alienation of the property taken from plaintiff. It was pointed out that defendant was not harmed by these measures,

[1]) 29 July 1924, 5 TAM 457.

[2]) See p. 20 *supra*. There seems to be no foundation for the statement of Guggenheim 30 that the tribunal's hesitation to grant plaintiff's request for support except insofar as it corresponded with already effected deprivation of possession was due to desire to avoid „une atteinte sérieuse à la souveraineté de l'Etat". The reason would seem to be rather unwillingness to condemn a defendant who owed nothing simply by reason of plaintiff's necessitous condition. „Le besoin d'un demandeur ne suffit pas à justifier la condemnation du défendeur, encore faut-il que le second soit actuellement débiteur du premier. Or, tant que la liquidation n'est pas terminée, l'Etat polonais ne doit rien". 5 TAM 460. It does not appear whether the tribunal was aware of the distinction between a provisional jugdment and a measure of interim protection. See § 13 *supra*.

[3]) A similar application requesting an allowance for support out of plaintiff's property taken by defendant seems to have been made in the case of Natalia Szechenyi before the Czech-Hungarian tribunal. Defendant contended that the measure sought was provisional execution of a purely pecuniary claim, and hence not admissible as a *mesure conservatoire*. See p. 23 *supra*, and p. 149—150 *infra*. The president of the tribunal, apparently feeling that something should be done for the plaintiff, but being unwilling to take the responsibility of granting the relief requested, invited the parties to come to an agreement. No such agreement was made, but the request for interim protection was not further pressed.

The question presented by such cases is interesting. Does a defendant, simply by taking all of plaintiff's property, become liable to support plaintiff? Alimentation cases involving orders against husband or putative father (see p. 43 *supra*) are not analogous. There there is a duty of support. Here there is only a duty to return certain property which has been taken, or to pay damages. Plaintiff's suffering and irreparable hardship *pendente lite* arises only from lack of other property. But is a defendant's obligation altered by the fact that plaintiff has no other means of support? Must a reckless motorist maintain the wife and children of his victim, provided they have no rich relatives? Cf. RGZ 9 : 336, note 4, p. 43 *supra*.

It might be possible to regard an alimentation allowance as a partial restoration of the status quo prior to the facts giving rise to the controversy. P. 187 *infra*.

[4]) Hungarian-Roumanian, 4 July 1925, 5 TAM 951.

whereas, even if notwithstanding alienation it might be possible to restore the property to plaintiff, such procedure would involve delay and other grave inconvenience for plaintiff. The argument advanced by Roumania that the measures asked were an interference with defendant's sovereignty was disregarded as incomprehensible.

21 [1]. Plaintiff alleged that he would receive only 6 million crowns indemnity for his property taken under agrarian law, and would be taxed 12 million under fiscal law. The President had made a temporary order for a short time until hearing by the tribunal [2]. That order expired automatically with the making of a new order by the tribunal. The Czech agent had not asked that it be declared *nulle et non avenue*, though it had not been executed by the Czech government, on the ground that the tribunal had no jurisdiction, and that by reason of danger of revolution public interest permitted no delay in execution of the agrarian law.

Taking note of the new situation created since the president's order by reason of the fact that plaintiff had not been required to pay at once the large sum exacted of him under the fiscal law, and of the declarations of the Czech agent that the government would deal leniently with plaintiff under the law, the tribunal considered that in view of the great public interest involved on the part of defendant state, whereas injury to plaintiff would not be irreparable (in fact he asks in the alternative for an indemnity), there was no need of interim measures.

The tribunal rejected the argument [3] that the tribunal must make sure of its jurisdiction in the principal matter before ordering interim protection. If that contention were true, all that a party need do in order to prevent interim measures from being taken would be to file a plea to the jurisdiction. The tribunal reaffirmed the rule laid down by the German-Polish tribunal [4] that it is sufficient that want of jurisdiction is not manifest. Nevertheless the tribunal recognized that a seriously contested objection to jurisdiction is a consideration to be taken into account by the tribunal as a factor making for prudence in ordering interim measures.

---

[1]) Czech-Hungarian, 31 January 1928, 35 RGDIP (1928) 61.

[2]) Ibid. 75—6.

[3]) Advanced by Professors Jèze and Hobza on behalf of Czechoslovakia. Ibid. 86.

[4]) See cases 12 and 14, § 63 *supra*.

§ 65. The German-Polish tribunal's decisions that it has no power to suspend the procedure of liquidation are severely criticised by Professor Bruns [1]). He declares that those judgments are a particularly naive expression of the unsound doctrine that an international organ must abstain from every interference with the sovereignty of a state. They rest on a complete misconception of the nature of interim protection and of international obligations.

The doctrine for which Professor Bruns contends is undoubtedly sound, that a state's internal law can not be invoked as an excuse for failure to fulfil its international duties; that such duties may prescribe what its internal law must contain [2]); that an international tribunal may have jurisdiction to deal with violations of such international duties, and to fix the reparation therefor, which may consist in restitution of the *status quo ante* [3]); and that in this case, where the tribunal has power to order reparation *in specie*, if its procedure provides for interim protection, it may order cessation of the wrongful act before the injury has occurred against which the measures prescribed are designed to afford protection [4]).

---

[1]) See annex 2 *infra*.

[2]) A state is equally responsible for violations of its international obligations, whether by its constitution or legislation, or by its executive, administrative or judicial organs. Huber 557, 562. Thus article 305 of the treaty of Versailles rather strangely singles out judgments of tribunals for rectification by the Mixed Arbitral Tribunal in case of violations of the treaty provisions. Perhaps the reason is that it is customary for judicial tribunals to have their decisions reversed on appeal to a higher instance, so that it is no great jump to provide for appeal to an international tribunal; whereas nowhere except in states following the principles of American constitutional law is judicial review of legislative and executive action the rule. Public policy suggests prudence in letting one man (the alien umpire of an arbitral tribunal) nullify the most important legislation of a state. See case 21, § 64 *supra*. With article 305 compare point 5 of the agreement of 11—12 February 1871 between the United States and Spain. 2 Malloy 1662—3.

[3]) Restitution is the normal form of reparation, except for money claims. Damages are appropriate only when it is impossible to effect redress *in specie*. Huber 561: „In erster Linie ist das rechtswidrige Urteil zu beseitigen; Schadensersatz tritt erst dann ein, wenn das durch das Urteil zugefügte Unrecht an sich irreparabel ist. Die Gewährung von Schadensersatz wird in der Regel da genügen, wo der von dem Gericht widerrechtlich verlegte Ausspruch in einer Geldforderung bestand". The Swiss-German arbitration treaty in article 10 provides for equitable redress of a different sort in case one state's constitutional law does not permit it to undo the wrong completely by administrative measures. Guggenheim 182.

[4]) Preventive, substitutional, and restitutional redress may form the object of the main proceeding. Interim measures may be had in support of all three types. According to the thesis of Bruns, a legal system admits preventive relief when it admits restitutional redress plus interim measures to secure execution thereof.

But did not the tribunal itself recognize the soundness of this reasoning, and declare that if it had jurisdiction to grant restitution it would be much more natural to order interim measures than if it had only jurisdiction to award damages? [1]) The tribunal's fault rather lies in its extreme technicality in treating the request for interim protection as based entirely upon article 297*b*, as to which the tribunal felt it had no jurisdiction in the main matter, and in failing to consider (until a second application for interim protection was made in the same case) whether it did not have power under article 305 to award reparation *in specie*. Because the second sentence of article 305 expressly authorized restoration of the status quo existing prior to the judgment of a *German* court the tribunal hastily concluded that it had no such power in the case of judgments of Polish courts, without considering whether the first sentence of article 305 did not authorize such measures.

Nevertheless it must be admitted that the tribunal employed language from which it might be surmised that suspension of liquidation was inadmissible as being an interference with the sovereignty of the Polish state [2]). But the expression „sovereignty" is doubtless here used in the sense of „liberty of action" [3]). It is of course begging the question to say that certain action can not be forbidden, because it would interfere with Poland's freedom of action, when the question at issue is whether Poland's international obligations permit such action. Nevertheless it remains true that in fact certain prohibitions would amount to a considerable restriction upon the freedom of action which would be enjoyed apart from the obligations in controversy and orders of the tribunal. And when an order of the tribunal would cause considerable hardship to a party, and especially when it would put the defendant government in the embarrassing position of either having to disregard its own internal legislation or else disobey the tribunal's decree [4]), it is appropriate that the tribunal

---

[1]) See p. 134 *supra*.

[2]) Case 14, § 63 supra; cf. case 13, p. 136 *supra*, and 35 RGDIP (1928) 63.

[3]) See A/B no. 41, 58, 77.

[4]) Huber 555; cf. Hungarian reply to Cheng-Loh's telegram, p. 117 *supra*; case of Czechoslovak agrarian law, no. 21 *supra*; and rule of United States Supreme Court, note 6, p. 82 *supra*. In cases of this sort, the *résistance éclairée du juge*, which President de Belleyme prized, is particularly appropriate.

should be reluctant to make such an order. For it is a fundamental principle governing interim protection that the measures prescribed must go no further than is needed for the purpose of affording plaintiff adequate security, and that the hardship to defendant must be weighed against that of the plaintiff [1]). And apart from metaphysical speculations regarding sovereignty, it is clear that the interests of a state, as spokesman for a multitude of people, may often outweigh the opposing interest of an individual plaintiff [2]).

The principle just mentioned is particularly applicable to the mixed arbitral tribunals, since their rules are worded more narrowly than is usually the case, and require that interim measures must be „necessary" („équitable et *nécessaire*"). Nevertheless absolute necessity is not indispensable; utility may be so great as to amount to necessity [3]). In the *Erdgas* case [4]), the tribunal pointed out that Roumania's interests were not harmed by prohibition of alienation, whereas plaintiff would suffer considerable delay and inconvenience if defendant disposed of the property, even if it were possible ultimately to get it back again. In the Polish liquidation cases, the tribunal seemed to think suspension of liquidation a measure involving too great hardship on the defendant state, while prevention of transfer to third persons was not [5]). If absolute necessity were required, it would be impossible to justify the latter measure, when it would suffice to ordain that alienation must be made subject to a condition subsequent (*condition résolutoire*) to the effect that upon judgment by the tribunal that plaintiff was entitled to the property expropriated, the rights of the new owner acquiring from the Polish state would become null and void. Nevertheless, unless by reason of particular cir-

---

[1]) See pp. 185—186 *infra*. Guggenheim 31—2 states that this principle is generally not considered at all in the decisions of the Mixed Arbitral Tribunals. Apart from the express language of the tribunal in case 8 note 1, p. 133 *supra*, and in case 21 (35 RGDIP (1928) 66), the principle was acted on in cases 2, 4, 5, 20 and the Polish liquidation cases. Guggenheim 31 is consequently erroneous in finding a contradiction between the decisions in cases 20 and 21.

[2]) In a case where both parties are states, discrepancy between the parties due to their representative character tends to disappear.

[3]) Thus the Belgian-Bulgarian tribunal in case 8 found that utility amounting to necessity was present, while in case 9 the contrary was true.

[4]) Case 20, § 64 *supra*.

[5]) As Bruns points out, the latter measure is equally an interference with Poland's „sovereignty".

cumstances, as in the case of the Czechoslovak agrarian law, a law embodies an important public interest, or its terms are mandatory and it is impossible for officials to refrain from enforcing it without illegality, it is difficult to see what harm the state would suffer if execution of the law were suspended *pendente lite*, until its conformity with international law is established. Where certain specific property is in question, it would seem logical to permit the plaintiff to continue in possession and enjoyment when possible, as then it is not necessary to indulge in speculation and conjecture as to the amount of damage he will have suffered if the expropriation is declared to be illegal [1]).

§ 66. It is worthy of note that no specific text authorized the Mixed Arbitral Tribunals to order interim measures; that jurisdiction grew out of the power to adopt rules of procedure in accordance with justice and equity. Even without a provision in its rules, the Anglo-German tribunal granted an interim injunction. No word of protest or disapproval was evoked by exercise of jurisdiction to extend interim protection [2]). It must therefore be taken as settled by international practice and the common consent of states that when an international tribunal has power to regulate its procedure in accordance with justice and equity, it may provide for interim protection. Such jurisdiction is obviously

[1]) After all is is a matter of judgment whether in a given case money damages are adequate. Anglo-American equity jurisdiction is available ordinarily only where damages are inadequate, and many delicate rules are worked out. In particular it should be noted that all cases involving real estate are treated as justifying specific performance; for one piece of land, it is said, is not the same as another. Nevertheless it is possible to say that any injury whatever can be made good by pecuniary compensation. In international law, frequently, even loss of life may be atoned for by an indemnity paid by the delinquent state to that of which the victims were nationals. But that is a mere makeshift, when real redress is impossible. The tribunal should interpret liberally the criterion of adequacy of money damages, in accordance with reasonable expectations under the circumstances. If there is specific property which forms the real subject-matter of dispute, it is inexpedient to conjure up a hypothetical indemnity at the end of a rainbow of procedural delay as an excuse for not preserving the very *res de qua agitur*. The difficulty of determining an equitable equivalent, at best an approximation, is thus avoided.

[2]) Even in the Czechoslovak agrarian law litigation, the jurisdiction of the tribunal to order interim protection as such was not questioned; it was merely argued that such protection should not be given where the tribunal had no jurisdiction in the main matter (*Hauptsache*), and such jurisdiction was contested vigorously with respect to cases touching the agrarian law. Doubtless Guggenheim 31 does not mean to imply the contrary in the statement „....le tribunal devait commencer par établir sa compétence pour les mesures provisoires envisagées", which refers to the argument by Professor Jèze.

just and equitable; it is therefore admissible when the tribunal is given such broad powers of regulating its procedure, notwithstanding the rule that an international tribunal's jurisdiction must be established expressly or by implication and can not be deduced from „general principles of law" [1]).

Another important principle emphasized in the jurisprudence of the Mixed Arbitral Tribunals is that in order to grant interim measures it is not necessary to decide whether the tribunal has jurisdiction in the main proceeding on its merits, but it suffices that *prima facie* there is possibility of a decision in favor of plaintiff and the tribunal's lack of jurisdiction if not manifest.

§ 67. 5. The Permanent Court of International Justice.

α. Texts.

Indication of measures of interim protection (*mesures conservatoires*) by the Permanent Court of International Justice is governed by article 41 of its Statute, supplemented by rule 57 of the Rules of Court, as amended on 21 February 1931 [2]). Whether in this matter the memorandum prepared by the Secretariat of the League of Nations [3]) had any influence on the committee of jurists drafting the Statute does not appear from the minutes of their deliberations. Article 41 originated in a proposal introduced by M. Raoul Fernandes of Brazil [4]), with a view to meet the need for a procedure analogous to the interdict procedure borrowed

1) See p. 181 *infra*, and especially Anzilotti, Corso 3ed. 1928, 108.

2) See annex 4 *infra*.

3) Which reproduced article 18 of the Convention for the Establishment of a Central American Court of Justice, and referred to article 12 of the draft convention attached to the Phillimore Report, and article 34 of the German proposals for the establishment of a league of nations. Documents presented, p. 106—7: „Si la Cour est compétente pour rendre un arrêt relativement à l'objet du différend, peut-elle décréter le status quo, en attendant que la sentence soit rendue?" The English text, probably the original, reads: „Is the Court competent to decree, as regards the subject-matter of the dispute, the fixation of the *status quo* pending its decision?"

4) Article 4 of the Bryan treaty of 13 October 1914 between the United States and Sweden served as the basis of this proposition. Minutes 637. M. Fernandes „wished the provisional measures to be supported by effective penalties, though it should be left to the Court to decide the extent to which the penalties should be imposed in the particular instances.... MM. Root, Adatci, de Lapradelle and Lord Phillimore were opposed to this, as they thought it would be unwise (*imprudente*)". At the proposal of de Lapradelle a second paragraph was added, providing for notification to the Council of the measures indicated. Minutes 588.

from Roman law by modern legislations [1]. Two slight changes in wording were subsequently introduced [2] in order to make clear that measures were to be „indicated" by the Court rather than „suggested" [3], and that not only „acts" but also omissions to act might occasion the indication of such measures [4]. The committee of jurists which met at Geneva 11—19 March 1929 to study the Statute with a view to proposing amendments decided to recommend no change in article 41, since it had been referred to in so many subsequent arbitration treaties [5] that a modification of its terms might produce considerable uncertainty [6].

§ 68. Article 25 of the Statute provides that the Court shall exercise its functions in plenary session except when otherwise expressly provided [7]. Article 30 says that the Court shall determine by Rules the manner in which it shall exercise its functions [8]. Accordingly, the Court provided, in article 57 of its Rules adopted on 24 March 1922, that when the Court is not sitting, indication of interim measures is made by the President; and that refusal to conform to such measures is to be placed on record.

A more elaborate procedure had been contemplated in article 35 of the draft Rules of Court submitted by the League Secretariat [9]. Provision was there made for proposal of measures by the

[1] This procedure affords immediate protection against interference with possession while excluding all controversy based on rights of ownership. Minutes 608.

[2] For text of article 39 of the draft of the Commission of Jurists, see OJ sp. sup. no. 2, 11.

[3] At the suggestion of Dr. Max Huber the subcommittee of the third committee of the First Assembly on 29 November 1920 amended the English text to conform with the French text as found in the Bryan treaties, taking as authentic „indicate" rather than suggest. Documents concerning, 134. It will be noticed that the English text of the second paragraph of article 41 and of former rule 57 escaped correction.

[4] At the suggestion of Ricci-Busatti the third committee on 9 December 1920 deleted the words „If the dispute arises out of acts which have already taken place or are imminent". Documents concerning, 103. Cf. Locarno arbitration treaties which lengthened the formula to achieve the same purpose. P. 129 *supra*.

[5] See § 60 *supra*.

[6] C. 166. M. 66. 1929. V, 63—4.

[7] „Sauf exception expressément prévue, la Cour exerce ses attributions en séance plénière".

[8] „La Cour détermine par un réglement le mode suivant lequel elle exerce ses attributions. Elle régle notamment la procédure sommaire". The English texts are not so clear and explicit as the version we have given: „The full Court shall sit except when it is expressly provided otherwise.... the Court shall frame rules for regulating its procedure. In particular it shall lay down rules for summary procedure". See Minutes 620.

[9] D. no. 2, 62: „Les mesures conservatoires, destinées à sauvegarder les droits respectifs des parties, peuvent être proposées sur la requête de l'une des parties ou sur

Court *ex proprio motu*, and for hearing the party against whom measures were directed, as well as for a rehearing upon complaint by third parties, to be made, apparently, after indication of the measures but before their execution.

The Committee appointed by the Court to draw up a questionnaire embodying the main points to be settled in the Rules of Court included the inquiry: „Is it desirable to provide for a special procedure for suggestions regarding interim measures of protection referred to by article 41 of the Statute, more particularly with a view to safeguarding the interests of third parties?" [1]) The „Committee on Procedure" was of the opinion that „As the Court has no power to enforce decisions with regard to interim measures for preserving the respective rights of the parties, there was no need to prescribe detailed regulations in regard to the method of indicating such measures. The Committee nevertheless recognized that rules for safeguarding the rights of third parties might be desirable" [2]).

When that item of the questionnaire came up for discussion, Lord Finlay explained the opinion of the „Committee on Procedure" [3]). Judge Nyholm desired that refusal to comply with measures suggested by the Court, when it was within the power of

---

l'initiative de la Cour. Avant que ces mesures ne soient proposées, la partie contre laquelle elles sont dirigées, a droit à être entendue. Ces mesures pourront faire l'objet d'un nouvel examen à la demande d'une tierce partie qui affirme que ces mesures, si elles étaient mises à l'exécution, seraient de nature à compromettre ses intérêts légitimes". Notwithstanding the verbal rectification of the text of article 41, (see note 3, p. 145 *supra*) the Secretariat draft preserved the English „suggest" and rendered it in French by „proposer", obviously an ill-chosen word.

[1]) D no. 2, 290.

[2]) Ibid. 302. As was later pointed out by Judge Fromageot, D no. 2, 2d add. 183, see p. 25 *supra*, the reason given by the „Committee on Procedure" would apply equally to all judgments of the Court. Perhaps the thought was that since the Court was not responsible for the execution of the measures, it did not have a moral duty of satisfying its conscience beyond all peradventure, as by means of special safeguards such as the provisions for hearing and rehearing in the Secretariat draft, that no injustice would be produced by its order. Cf. Statute § 53 as to judgment by default.

[3]) Guggenheim 55 erroneously makes Lord Finlay answer, not the questionnaire of the Committee, but a question supposed to have been put by Judge Altamira: „Dans le cas de l'article 41 du Statut, la Cour indique les mesures conservatoires aussitôt connu l'objet de la requête.... Est-il convenable d'accorder aux parties le droit de proposer des incidents et des exceptions?" The first part of the „question" quoted is point I, 3 in Judge Altamira's draft of Rules of Court. D no. 2, 276. The query about incidental proceedings and exceptions is a separate point, having nothing to do with interim measures. It is not separately numbered, because where he was in doubt as to the desirability of a rule, Judge Altamira included in his draft a question rather than a proposed text on the point. Ibid. 275.

a party to do so, should be taken into account in the final judgment [1]). It was understood that when the Court is not sitting, the indication of interim measures should be made by the President [2]).

The Rules of Court were amended on 21 February 1931 in order to give effect so far as possible, in accordance with the wish of the Eleventh Assembly, to the principles enunciated in the amendments of the Statute which by reason of Cuba's failure to ratify had not come into force. The principle that the Court should sit continuously being thus recognized, it was no longer necessary that the President bear the heavy responsibility of indicating interim measures. The whole Court was now available for that purpose at any moment. Consequently rule 57 was replaced by a new text, providing that the Court, *statuant d'urgence*, shall indicate such measures, being summoned without delay if not actually in session when a request is received. It is also expressly provided that the Court may *ex officio* indicate measures in the absence of an application. In no case shall measures be indicated without giving parties an opportunity to be heard. The second paragraph of the old rule is omitted; no reference is made to failure to comply with measures indicated is not mentioned.

§ 69. β. Decisions of the Court.

Two cases have arisen involving the application of article 41. The first related to the denunciation of the treaty of 2 November 1865 between Belgium and China [3]). That instrument in article 46

---

[1]) D. no. 2, 77: „M. Nyholm wished to establish a distinction between cases in which provisional measures had to be taken on the territory of one of the parties and cases in which such measures applied to the territory of a third party In the first case M. Nyholm thought that, in the event of a refusal to comply with the measures suggested by the Court, this fact should be taken into account in the final judgment. Lord Finlay agreed with M. Nyholm. In such a case damages should be stipulated in the judgment". Cf. Nyholm draft rules, D no. 2, 377: „§ 105. If the measures have to be taken upon the territory of the parties to the dispute, it shall be the duty of the respective Governments to carry them out, in so far as their national legislation permits. In case of non-compliance (*non exécution*) with the order, the Court shall attach due legal weight to the fact when deciding the principal question in issue. § 106. If the measures have to be taken upon the territory of a State not concerned in the case, the order shall be forwarded by the President to the Government of the State, with a request for information regarding the action taken in execution of the order". Judge Nyholm thus seems to be responsible for the second paragraph of rule 57, which is couched, however, in terms resembling article 49 of the Statute, regarding refusal to furnish documents or explanations.

[2]) D no. 2, 77.

[3]) For proceedings in this case see A no. 8; C. no. 16-I; Michel de la Grotte in 56 RDILC (1929) 273—5.

provided how modifications might be introduced from time to time by Belgium, but said nothing about denunciation by China. Nevertheless the Chinese government announced that it regarded the treaty as inoperative from 27 October 1926. By presidential mandate of 6 November 1926, declaring that the treaty had ceased to be effective, the Chinese ministry of foreign affairs was ordered to negotiate as speedily as possible a new treaty with Belgium, on the basis of equality. „With regard to the Belgian Legation, Consulates, nationals, products and ships in China, the local authorities are hereby ordered to extend full and due protection to them in accordance with the rules of international law and usage" [1]).

Belgium on 25 November 1926 instituted proceedings under the optional clause, asking the Court to give judgment that China is not entitled to denounce the treaty unilaterally, and to indicate, pending judgment, provisional measures for the protection of rights which may subsequently be recognized as belonging to Belgium or to Belgian nationals. On December 17 the President of the Court fixed the dates for filing documents in the proceedings. On December 20 the Registrar informed the Belgian agents that from the documents so far filed the President was not convinced that provisional measures were required. This decision was subject to reconsideration upon the presentation of further information. [2]) The Belgian case was submitted on 4 January 1927, adducing arguments and evidence in support of the request for interim protection. It was urged that even if compensation might be decreed in the final judgment for revenues from tariffs improperly collected, and perhaps also for wrongful treatment of persons and property, it would involve a long and complicated procedure; while with respect to consular, judicial, and criminal matters the damage would be irreparable. It was therefore asked that the treaty of 1865 be continued in force wherever its non-application would place Belgium in a more unfavorable position that other nations in China. In particular the judicial dispositions and most-favored nation clauses should remain in effect [3]).

On January 8 the President issued an order indicating, subject

---

1) C no. 16-I, 75. 2) Ibid. 305—6. See annex 5, *infra*.

3) Ibid. 23—4. Cf. § 44 *supra*, where suspension of a treaty, rather than its continuance in force, was sought.

to change, that the protection extended pursuant to the Chinese presidential mandate of November 6 should include certain items (modeled in part upon various articles of the treaty of 1865 and in part upon the report of the commission on extraterritoriality in China), respecting the person and property of Belgian nationals in China [1]). After calling to mind that the purpose of interim measures, according to article of 41 of the Statute, is to preserve the respective rights of the parties pending decision, the order proceeds to limit the scope of application of that provision in the case at bar. In the first place, Chinese rights in Belgium under the treaty of 1865 are not endangered, because Belgium regards the treaty as still binding [2]). Nor do Belgian rights in China stand in need of protection, so far as they are based on international common law apart from treaty, because the Chinese government in the aforementioned presidential mandate manifested its intention to accord treatment in conformity with that standard of conduct. Only Belgian rights in China accorded by the treaty of 1865 over and above the normal *régime* of customary law are in issue. But not even all of those rights are entitled to protection *pendente lite*. Insofar as infraction of such rights can be compensated for in money damages, an adequate remedy is provided by the Court's jurisdiction under the optional clause to assess and award damages [3]).

---

[1]) This mode of expression seems to be merely a roundabout way of ordering that China observe the measures enumerated, for clearly more is contemplated than a direction to China to obey international law in general. It would amount to assuming the correctness of China's contention that the treaty of 1865 was no longer in force if Belgium received only the protection due to a friendly state under international law, apart from treaty stipulations. Similarly, to continue the treaty in force *in toto* as requested would amount to assuming the correctness of Belgium's contention on the merits of the case. What the order does is to take steps for preserving *alleged* rights of each party which would, if ultimately upheld, have been the subject of infractions *pendente lite* irremediable by a money indemnity.

[2]) It is submitted that this statement unduly narrows the issue. It is not merely Chinese rights *under the treaty* which must be considered, but also the totality of China's rights in the event that the Chinese contention is found to be correct, namely the right to exercise the powers of sovereignty untrammeled by treaty restrictions. Nevertheless the conclusion is doubtless correct that China will suffer no irreparable injury by continuing for a few months more to act in conformity with certain of the stipulations which had been in force for sixty years, whereas those provisions of the treaty protect Belgian interests unmeasurable in money damages. Cf. case 21, § 63 *supra*; 35 RGDIP (1928) 66.

[3]) De la Grotte in 56 RDILC (1929) 273—4: „L'ordonnance.. pose en principe que les mesures conservatoires dont il s'agit ne peuvent avoir pour objet que la protection d'intérêts qui, sans elles, courraient le risque d'être irrémédiablement compromis; par contre, les intérêts à l'égard desquels la réparation en argent est, le cas échéant, possible, tant matériellement que grâce à l'existence de moyens de recours ap-

But where in exercise of its power to determine the nature and extent of the reparation to be made the Court would find pecuniary compensation inadequate, there is need of interim protection [1]). Consequently only those treaty rights of Belgium in China, violation of which is irreparable by an indemnity in money, fall within the protection of the President's order.

§ 70. The Chinese legation on 15 January 1927 notified the Registrar that the parties had resumed negotiations with a view to concluding a new treaty to replace that of 1865, and had agreed not to proceed with the case pending such negotiations. The Registrar replied at once that proceedings once under way could be suspended only by withdrawal of the case entirely or by extension of the time limits by the Court [2]). Belgium on January 18 requested an extension, which was granted. That a corresponding prolongation of the period during which the interim measures

---

propriés, sont exclus.. Elle donne à entendre qu'il y a lieu d'établir une distinction entre les intérêts qui, s'ils étaient lésés, pourraient faire l'objet d'une réparation à l'aide d'une prestation matérielle quelconque, et ceux qui ne le pourraient pas. Pour les premiers, elle donne encore à entendre que les parties en acceptant la 'juridiction obligatoire' de la Cour aux termes de l'article 36 du Statut, ont accepté d'un commun accord une juridiction compétente pour fixer et allouer, le cas échéant, les prestations dont il s'agit. Dans ces conditions, il n'est nécessaire de protéger par des mesures conservatoires que les intérêts non susceptibles de comporter, en cas de violation, réparation par le versement d'une indemnité".

[1]) It is not clear whether the reference to the optional clause in the order was intended to serve as the reason for denying interim protection in case of rights measurable in money, or as a reason for granting such protection in case of rights not so reparable. Doubtless both views are correct. The first is delineated in the comments of the learned writer quoted in the preceding note; the second is supported by the reasoning of the German-Polish tribunal (see case 13, § 63 *supra*, and annex 2, *infra*) and seems to be the view of Guggenheim 61: „Il convient d'ordonner des mesures provisoires lorsque le dommage susceptible d'être causé par l'attitude d'une des Parties paraît devoir être irreparable. Le fait que les Parties ont reconnu comme obligatoire la juridiction de la Cour permanente de Justice internationale constitue un argument supplémentaire". Guggenheim 68 seems also to adopt the first view, when speaking of „le principe d'après lequel des mesures provisoires doivent être indiquées lorsqu'un droit risque d'être perdu et que la réparation matérielle du préjudice qui s'ensuivra semble problématique".

According as one or the other criterion were accepted as the sole test, different answers would be reached in the following cases: (1) Where the Court has power to determine the amount of pecuniary reparation, but not to give specific relief. Cf. *compromis* in Lotus case, A no. 10, 5. (2) Where the Court has power to grant reparation *in specie*, but not an indemnity; as if an Allied national claims return of property under article 297*f* of the treaty of Versailles, and the question whether it „exists *in specie*" is submitted to the Court (the property having been so changed in form that a question as to its legal identity arises), but the parties reserve for further negotiations the amount of indemnity, if the Court should decide that the property no longer exists.

[2]) C no. 16-I, 317—8.

were applicable was thereby effected was made clear by the Registrar in his letter of January 20 to the Belgian agents [1]). On January 21 the Chinese minister wrote to the Registrar that the parties had agreed to suspend, during their negotiations, all proceedings before the Court, including the interim measures [2]). The Registrar replied on January 25 that since that communication from the Chinese minister was not official, it was not necessary to consider the various possible interpretations of it, and what the attitude of the Court in the light thereof should be [3]). On February 3 the Belgian agents informed the Registrar that the parties had concluded a provisional *régime* covering the matters dealt with in the order, and that consequently the interim measures therein indicated had become pointless. They added that if the President would revoke the order, his decision would please China and thus facilitate negotiations [4]).

The order of February 15, revoking that of January 8 in its entirety and finally, took pains to state that revocation, as well as indication, of interim measures must take place because of purely legal reasons and upon objective grounds, regardless of its repercussion on the course of diplomatic negotiations. On proceeding to examine whether at this stage of the case interim protection is called for, it is found that there are no circumstances making proper continuance of the order of January 8. The reasons which dictated its issuance no longer hold good. The sole purpose of the order had been to safeguard Belgian rights under the treaty of 1865; but since that *régime* had been entirely superseded for the time being by the *modus vivendi* just concluded, infringements of such rights taking place during the life of the new agreement could not be made the basis of an action at law [5]), whatever the tenor of the Court's final judgment might be. Moreover the same conclusion would follow from voluntary renunciation of such rights by Belgium.

Equally effective would be abandonment of the action at law for assertion of these rights. Belgium was entitled to withdraw the

---

[1]) Ibid. 320. [2]) Ibid. 322. [3]) Ibid. 323.

[4]) Ibid. 324—5: „Dès lors les mesures provisoires.. sont devenues sans objet, et si M. le Président voulait bien rapporter ladite ordonnance, sa décision, qui répondrait au désir du Gouvernement chinois, serait ainsi de nature à faciliter les négociations".

[5]) „Nous voudrions ajouter, ou même par la voie diplomatique". De la Grotte in 56 RDILC (1929) 275.

request for interim protection by amending its original conclusions [1]). China had officially never taken any part in the proceedings; the time limit for filing the Chinese counter-case had not expired; the order had been obtained by Belgium for the protection of Belgian interests. There was nothing to prevent its revocation on unilateral application by the same government [2]). Moreover it was declared that China approved the proposed action.

Similarly the order declared that „there are no other circumstances independent of the legal situation created by the parties, resulting either from agreements concluded between them or from unilateral declarations in regard to matters concerning which they may use their discretion, which would point to the indication of measures of protection in the interests of the procedure alone". The meaning of this paragraph is far from clear and a number of deductions from it are legitimate. Perhaps its primary purpose is to call to mind the fact that the Court on its own initiative may indicate interim measures. Consequently the Court would consult its own opinion and probably continue the measures in force if a party simply sought to withdraw a request for interim protection, without definitely renouncing for the time being the rights in question [3]). In this case the final judgment would have to take account of violations of such rights *pendente lite,* and without interim measures might be rendered nugatory or impossible of execution. Likewise the dignity of the Court as well as economy of procedure would forbid repeated indication and revocation of protective measures corresponding to the vicissitudes of diplomatic negotiation. In the case at bar the measures prescribed by the order of January 8 were to continue, unless modified, *pending proceedings* up until final judgment in the case. The provisional *régime* concluded by the parties, on the other hand, was to be effective only *pending negotiations* until a

---

1) The Belgian proposal is really not aimed at amending its pleadings by modifying or abandoning its original conclusions, but at quashing the order. Feller in 25 AJ (1931) 497.

2) It was pointed out that there was no question of an agreement settling the dispute under rule 61 (1) in which both parties would have to take part officially, and which would also raise the question later presented as to whether the Court should record such settlement by means of an order or a judgment. See A no. 18/19, and Paul de Vineuil in 57 RDILC (1930) 768—9.

3) Thus the Belgian declaration that the measures were „without object" (see note 4, p. 151 *supra*) might mean merely that since China had agreed to a *régime* of interim protection (supplanting the *order* rather than the *treaty*) the order was no longer useful.

new treaty was concluded. If therefore there had been a reasonable probability that negotiations would be broken off, and hence the *modus vivendi* terminated, *before* the Court rendered its final decision, it would have been inappropriate to revoke the order. If the necessity for interim protection is to disappear only for a short time, and then be revived, and then perhaps disappear during another provisional *régime*, and then possibly be revived again, the Court will not revoke and reinstate its order every time the parties change their position. Nevertheless, of course, although never formally revoked, the order would have effect only to protect existing rights, not those renounced or hibernating for the moment. Its egis is always commensurate with the rights it is designed to protect, like the trees of Troy which by command of the gods never grew higher than the walls of the city [1]).

§ 71. Article 41 was again invoked in the case concerning the Chorzow factory during the course of protracted litigation and negotiation with respect to German interests in Upper Silesia. The Court having held that expropriations made by Poland were contrary to her international obligations, Germany instituted proceedings to obtain payment of 96 million reichsmarks. Meanwhile, on 15 November 1927, the German government requested the Court to indicate to the Polish government as a provisional measure under article 41 that it must pay the sum of 30 million reichsmarks within one month. Relying on the statement of the Court that „it is a principle of international law that the breach of an engagement involves an obligation to make reparation in an adequate form", Germany contended that only the upper limit of the sum to be awarded was in dispute. Statistics were adduced to show that the date of payment was as important as the amount of compensation. In view of the development of the industry, delay in payment would cause increasing and irreparable injury. The genesis of article 41 was referred to in order to demonstrate that an act, as well as a cessation from action, could be indicated as a measure of interim protection.

On November 21 the Court, as normally composed, without the addition of national judges, decided that effect could not be given to this request. What had been asked for was not a measure of in-

[1]) See Beale, Cases on the Conflict of Laws, 2 Ed. 1928, II, 31;

terim protection but a provisional judgment covering part of the claim pending before the Court. Consequently the application presented by the German government did not fall within the terms of article 41 and rule 57. Under the circumstances there was no reason to invite the Polish government to submit observations[1]).

§ 72. γ. Analysis.

Having surveyed the pertinent texts and decisions, we now proceed to an analytical discussion of how the Court indicates interim measures, what grounds it requires for doing so, what sort of measures are to be indicated, and what their effects are. We shall thus deal in turn with (*A*) Procedure; (*B*) Requirements; (*C*) Nature; and (*D*) Effects of interim measures.

(*A*) Procedure (*Verfahren*).

1. Indication of interim measures is made by the Court in plenary session, and not by the President. If the Court is not is session, it is convened specially whenever there is occasion to consider the question of indicating such measures.

Such is the effect of rule 57 as amended. Formerly that rule provided that if the Court is not in session indication of interim measures is made by the President. The change merits approval. Now that the Court is permanently is session, it is no longer necessary that this responsibility, a heavy one, rest on the President [2]). Added weight is given to the conclusions reached when the full Court is convoked specially, and the parties are heard [3]). Moreover there is no doubt that the new procedure „more closely conforms to the Statute" [4]), although the view that previous practice was not sanctioned by the Statute is not correct [5]).

[1]) A no. 12; de la Grotte in 56 RDILC (1929) 255.

[2]) Anzilotti in D no. 2, 2d add. 182.

[3]) Hurst, Guerrero, van Eysinga, ibid. 183, 184, 196.

[4]) As Professor Manley O. Hudson accurately says. 25 AJ (1931) 434.

[5]) Judges Rolin-Jaequemyns, Rostworowski, Guerrero and Urrutia thought indication of interim protection by the president conflicted with the Statute. D. no. 2, 2d add. 184, 185, 189. So did Signor Scialoja in the committee of jurists for amending the Statute. C. 166. M. 66. 1929. V, 63. Judge Anzilotti considered the practice to be of doubtful legality, but a necessity when the Court was not in continuous session. Ibid. 64; (also in D no. 2, 2d supp. 182). But as M. Raestad and Mr. Root there pointed out, article 41 must be read in connection with article 30 of the Statute. Ibid. The French text is especially clear. See note 8, p. 145 *supra*. The literal interpretation proves too much. It would prevent the Court from delegating to the President by rule 33 the power to make orders fixing the time-limits for filing documents of procedure, as that function is conferred on *the Court* by article 48 of the Statute. Likewise it would prevent interim measures in cases before the special chambers.

The chambers for summary procedure [1]), labor [2]) and transit cases [3]) may indicate interim measures in accordance with the rules for procedure before the full Court [4]). Likewise, to the extent that procedure in requests for advisory opinions is governed by the rules applicable in contentious cases, interim protection is permitted in advisory procedure [5]).

2. The Court may act *ex officio*, or upon application by the parties, or by one of them [6]). The Court can not on its own initiative prescribe measures before the main action has been brought in accordance with article 40 of the Statute, either by notification of the special agreement between the parties or by unilateral application where the Court has compulsory jurisdiction [7]). But on request by the parties, or one of them, it is not necessary that the principal action already be pending [8]). The rights for which interim protection is sought, however, must be actionable at law [9]).

---

[1]) Statute, article 29. [2]) Ibid. article 26. [3]) Ibid. article 27.

[4]) According to rule 67, „the rules for procedure before the full Court shall apply to summary procedure". By analogy, the same principle would apply in the labor and transit chambers. Judge Nyholm's draft rules were explicit. § 101, D no. 2, 177.

[5]) Article 68 of the revised Statute (not yet in force) provides that in advisory procedure the Court shall be guided by the provisions of the Statute for contentious cases to the extent to which it recognizes them to be applicable. But the Court of its own motion has to a certain extent applied its contentious procedure by analogy, notably in rule 71. That rule applies article 31 (national judges) in cases involving an actual controversy submitted for advisory opinion. Cf. also Eastern Carelia case, B no. 5, 29: „La Cour, étant une Cour de Justice, ne peut pas se départir des règles essentielles qui dirigent son activité de tribunal, même lorsqu'elle donne des avis consultatifs".

[6]) New rule 57. Since the President may convene the Court if it is not sitting to submit to it the question of the desirability of interim measures, it follows *a fortiori* that if the Court is in session it may indicate such measures *ex proprio motu* in the absence of an application. Even before rule 57 was amended the Court had power *ex officio* to indicate interim protection. De Bustamante 225. Likewise „the former rules did not speak of applications for the indication of interim protection; but in practice such applications have been made". M. O. Hudson in 25 AJ (1913) 435.

[7]) See p. 27 *supra*.

[8]) Cf. pp. 6, 47, 52, 66, 79. 131 *supra*. Doubtless a period within which the main action must be brought would have to be fixed. Cf. note 7, p. 186 *infra*.

Since the proceeding to obtain interim protection is distinct from that on the merits (§ 11 *supra*), an application for interim protection made by both parties, or by one of them in cases where the Court has compulsory jurisdiction, is itself a fulfilment of the terms of article 40 of the Statute. Moreover subsidiary actions need not be begun as provided in article 40. Anzilotti, La Riconvenzione nella Procedura internazionale, 21 Riv. (1929) 314.

[9]) A no. 8, 10; p. 151 *supra*; cf. Stern 18, Rintelen 33; see p. 186 *infra*. By this is meant not mere potential justiciability (cf. Scott, Sovereign States and Suits, 147; R.I. v. Mass., 12 Pet. 657, 737 (1838), but actually existing jurisdiction in an international tribunal, either by general agreement creating obligatory jurisdiction, or by special *compromis* already concluded in the particular case. Thus if a question has been submitted to a special tribunal and has thus become justiciable, but the tribunal has no

3. Request for indication or revocation of interim measures may be made at any time [1]). Whenever circumstances exist which make such measures proper, they may be indicated, even if a previous request has been denied. The decision is provisional and does not have the effect of *res judicata* in preventing subsequent change of opinion on the part of the Court. Similarly, when circumstances have changed, measures previously indicated need not remain in force [2]).

If separate requests are made at approximately the same time by different parties, economy of procedure would seem to dictate that they be considered at one hearing. If the parties agree in making a common request, even specifying in detail the measures desired, the Court is not bound by such agreement [3]). Parties remain free of course to make whatever agreement they like with regard to regulation of their respective rights *pendente lite* [4]), without invoking the Court under article 41; but if they do apply to the Court, it is the conscience of the Court and not the will of the parties which determines what measures of protection are appropriate. Similarly if one party makes an application, the Court is free to consider what measures are necessary in order to safeguard the rights of the *other* party [5]). For the Court has the power of indicating measures on its own account, and the rule *ne ultra petita* does not operate to substitute the discretion of a

---

jurisdiction to grant interim protection; and at the same time the parties are bound by the obligatory jurisdiction of the Court, it would be possible for the Court to protect *pendente lite* rights actionable before another tribunal, to prevent denial of justice, unless an inconsistent intention on the part of the parties was manifested. Cf. A no. 9, 30, quoted note 3, p. 27 *supra*. Cf. p. 121 *supra*; note 4, p. 165 *infra*.

[1]) It was therefore superfluous in the application made by Denmark instituting proceedings in the Eastern Greenland case to reserve the right to apply for interim protection. See 26 A.J. (1932) 17.

[2]) Statute, article 41 „à titre provisoire"; pp. 148, 149, 151 *supra*. Cf. German ZPO § 927. That a new request may be presented even when facts have not altered, RGZ 33 : 415, 28 June 1894; approved by Stern 57. A decision denying interim protection establishes simply that *at the time of rendering the decision* no interim measures are appropriate. Mortara, Commentario, III, 778. But cf. Caroli 352. As to *res judicata* see Morelli 220—1.

[3]) Fromageot and Guerrero in D no. 2, 2d add. 194—5.

[4]) Provided such agreement does not conflict with a previous order of the Court indicating interim measures necessary for the protection of certain rights, unless at the same time such rights are renounced or the action pending in respect of such rights is abandoned. See p. 152 *supra*.

[5]) The text of article 41 is explicit on the point. Cf. the German-Swedish arbitration treaty, note 6. p. 126 *supra*.

party for that of the Court in determining the nature of protection proper under the circumstances [1].

4. It is therefore not necessary that the application contain an enumeration of the measures desired, though such a course is desirable in order to focus the attention of the Court on matters in need of consideration. Otherwise the Court, on a general survey of the situation, might more readily come to the conclusion that there was no occasion to take action with a view to protection *pendente lite*. In view of the Court's wide powers, it would seem not unwise that the application should conclude, like a bill in equity, with a prayer for such other and further relief as to the Court may seem wise and just [2].

5. Decisions as to interim measures are made by majority vote of the Court as normally constituted [3]. National judges of the parties in question need not be added to the Court when sitting for the purpose of passing on requests for the indication of interim measures [4].

6. An application for the indication of interim measures has priority over all other cases [5]; the decision thereon is treated as

---

[1]) Swiss federal law imposes such a rule because the court's power is based on the presence of property within its jurisdiction. P. 52 *supra*. Ott 68. Another ground for such limitation is the liability of applicant without *culpa* for damages arising from the measures; hence the court can not by going beyond the request increase the extent of that responsibility. Neumann, II, 1244. Cf. Garsonnet-Cézar Bru, VIII, 326, § 3004. It would seem that the Permanent Court of International Justice when ordering measures *ex officio* ought to be more prudent and cautious than when a request has been made, for obviously in the former case no one is responsible for injury if it later appears the measures were not called for.

[2]) Cf. C no. 16-I, 305—6, annex 5 *infra*.

[3]) Fachiri 100; § 55 of the Statute.

[4]) A no. 12, 10. That decision, made before rule 57 was amended, is not affected by the change requiring hearing by the Court; for in that case it was the Court, not the President, which acted, and there was a hearing. The principle laid down is doubtless dictated by the urgent character of applications for interim measures, while designation of national judges implies deliberate procedure in ordinary cases. In any case if the right to designate a national judge should be admitted, that right would be deemed to have been renounced if the judge were not present at the time of hearing, fixed in accordance with the urgency of the case. Cf. rule 4, providing for the contingency where parties entitled to a joint judge do not reach agreement within a time fixed by the Court. According to N.L. Hill, National Judges and the Permanent Court of International Justice, 25 AJ (1931) 679, „It has not been the practice, as a rule, to provide *ad hoc* judges in deliberations which have led to issuance of *orders*". See p. 159 *infra*.

[5]) Nothing is said regarding priority *inter se* of requests for interim protection. Doubtless they are disposed of in chronological order as filed. Nevertheless it would not seem improper that exceptionally urgent matters be considered ahead of less pressing applications earlier received. The question is not likely to arise in practice.

a matter of urgency; if the Court is not in session it is convened without delay [1]).

There is no other text in the Statute or Rules of Court defining what is meant by urgency [2]). Nevertheless it is clear that urgent procedure is not to be confused with summary procedure, as provided for in article 29 of the Statute [3]).

7. Before interim measures are indicated, the parties shall have an opportunity (*possibilité*) to present their observations [4]). It is evident that this provision does not enable a recalcitrant party to sabotage the procedure by neglecting or delaying to present its views, but affords a reasonable opportunity to be heard. In urgent cases the delay involved need never be greater than that necessary for telegraphic instructions from a government to its diplomatic representative at the Hague [5]).

The rule is that „the Court shall only *indicate* measures of protection after giving the parties an opportunity of presenting their observations". It is the *indication*, not the *denial* of interim protection which must be preceded by a hearing [6]). The amendment to rule 57 was so framed as not to conflict with the practice established in the Chorzow case [7]). If it is clear from applicant's request that the application is unfounded, it would be superfluous to insist on hearing the opposing party [8]). Nevertheless the *Pres-*

[1]) New rule 57.

[2]) Thus the request for an advisory opinion regarding the Austro-German customs union was also qualified as „urgent". OJ (1931) 1069. But an application for interim protection, by its very nature, would receive more rapid treatment. Likewise the President considered the case of the Serbian loans as urgent (C no. 16-III, 9); and on 30 January 1931 the Court resolved that it should not be convened between July 1 and October 1 except for urgent cases. E no. 7, 285,

[3]) Summary procedure here is simply a simplified and accelerated mode of deciding the dispute submitted to the Court. Cf. p. 22 *supra*. The argument that interim protection is unnecessary where rapid procedure for settling the case in chief is available, (unsound in itself, see note 2, p. 22 *supra*) is not applicable to summary procedure before the Court, because the two procedures are indisputably distinct, being treated in separate articles of the Statute, and because rule 67 expressly applies to summary procedure the rules governing procedure before the full Court. See note 4, p. 155 *supra*.

[4]) Judge van Eysinga's original proposal was „une équitable faculté de se faire entendre". D no. 2, 2d add. 188. It is plain that nothing more than a fair and reasonable opportunity to be heard is called for.

[5]) This is a fact militating against recourse to national judges. See note 4, p. 157 *supra*.

[6]) Cf. 20 R.O. nr. 52, 19 September 1894, 308, 309.

[7]) § 71 *supra*.

[8]) Only where there are circumstances moving the Court toward possible indication of interim measures *ex officio*, where there is some likelihood that inadvertent admissions on the part of the defendant might reveal circumstances unknown to the applicant which necessitated protection, is there any occasion for proceeding to a hearing under the hypothesis in question.

ident can not avoid the necessity of convoking the Court to pass upon a request [1]).

Undoubtedly the requirement that the parties be heard before indication of interim protection adds to the moral weight of the Court's decision [2]). Nevertheless, as Judge Guerrero wisely pointed out, time might not always permit a hearing [3]). The most usual practice is to provide for a hearing if the matter is not too urgent [4]), urgency due to applicant's lack of diligence in making timely complaint being duly discounted by the court [5]).

8. The Court indicates interim protection by order (*ordonnance*), and not by judgment (*arrêt*) [6]). This is in accordance with the Court's practice to render judgments only in cases where the decision has the effect of *res judicata* [7]). The Statute is not only inconsistent in terminology, but also reveals several startling omissions. It is well known, for instance, that the Statute does not directly empower the Court to give advisory opinions [8]). But neither does it anywhere expressly authorize the Court to render judgments [9]). And according to prevailing doctrine the power to make

---

1) Of course where he does not think that there is reason for indicating interim measures, the President would not exercise his power of convoking the Court to consider the desirability of indicating such measures *ex officio*.

2) See p. 154 *supra*.

3) D no. 2, 2d add. 186.

4) See note 4, p. 184 *infra*. In cases involving bad faith, the utility of interim measures depends upon surprising the adversary intending to confront his opponent with a *fait accompli*. Glasson-Tissier, 2ed. II, 621 (*supra* p. 74); Neumann-Ettenreich 407. While states are supposed always to act in good faith (Politis in C. no. 13-I, 53, 80), since otherwise international law would be a vain thing (Hold-Ferneck, Lehrbuch 200—1), yet cases may exist where the possibility of immediate protection through an impartial agency, and speedy publicity, may help a state to overcome temptations toward bad faith which might otherwise beset it too strongly.

5) Cf. Klein in GZ 1911, nr. 41, 323.

6) Michel de la Grotte in 56 RDILC (1929) 273.

7) Paul de Vineuil in 57 RDILC (1930) 769; A no. 22, 13. Assuming from article 39 of the Statute the identity of „arrêt" and „jugement", and from article 53 that of „adjuger" and „faire droit", one may conclude that a judgment is a definite decision upon a point of law arising in a case, as distinguished from administrative or incidental „décisions" (see article 55) which are simply entered in the minutes of the Court, and not communicated to the parties, as is the practice in case of judgments and orders. Cf. Duguit, Traité de droit constitutionnel, 2 ed. 1923, II, 314, 322.

8) Article 1 of the Statute states that the Court is created in conformity with article 14 of the Covenant, which calls for the creation of a court capable of giving advisory opinions at the request of the Council or Assembly of the League of Nations. Another theory advanced by Jessup is that article 36 gives the Court jurisdiction in all cases provided for by treaties or conventions in force; article 14 of the Covenant is such a provision.

9) Except judgments by default, provided for in article 53. But this power is most plainly implied. (1) Numerous articles specify the form and effects of judgments.

orders conferred by article 48 is merely a direction that in the matters there referred to the Court's action shall take the form of an order [1]; just as its decision to permit revision of a previous judgment must take the form of a judgment [2]. The reticent language of the Statute [3] has not been productive of embarrassment in practice [4].

9. Indication of interim measures is to be made if the Court „considers" („estime") that circumstances so require. It thus ap-

§§ 56—8; 60—1. (2) Article 14 of the Covenant states that the Court shall „hear and determine" („connaîtra": the English text shows that more than a mere forum of discussion to „take cognizance of" questions is meant) such cases as the parties submit to it. (3) Power to give judgment is an essential feature of a court of justice. Cf. A no. 24, 33—4. where Judge Kellogg employs this method of reasoning to demonstrate a limitation of the Court's jurisdiction; it may likewise be used to establish the Court's power to give judgment.

[1]) Article 48 reads: „The Court shall make orders for the conduct of the case, shall decide the form and time in which each party must conclude its arguments, and make all arrangements connected with the taking of evidence". In the Savoy case between France and Switzerland, the parties desired the Court to make known its opinion whether an old treaty between those countries was still in force, and at the same time to set a date within which the parties must conclude a new agreement regulating their relations, failing which the Court in its final judgment should settle all questions at issue between the parties. Endeavoring to give satisfaction to the parties without violating the Statute, the Court issued an order setting the time limit requested, in the motivation of which it let its views regarding the validity of the old treaty appear. Judge Pessôa contended that this „order" went beyond the powers of the Court under article 48 of the statute, and amounted to giving an advisory opinion at the request of the parties. A no. 22, 48—9. His interpretation of article 48 was not shared by the Court, although it was realized that the pronouncement made on that occasion was somewhat of a *tour de force* and an exceptional phenomenon.

[2]) Article 61. Accordingly rule 59 provided that the decision as to intervention under article 62 of the Statute should take the form of a judgment. Influenced doubtless by that rule, the Court in its first judgment (A no. 1) followed a similar practice in taking note of intervention under article 63, which is of right and does not require a decision of the Court permitting it, although it would seem that an order would have been appropriate in the latter case. Where, as in that case, a judgment does not terminate proceedings, it is styled an „interlocutory judgment" („arrêt interlocutoire") in the publications of the Court. Cf. the various types of judgments in internal law. Chiovenda 803; Glasson-Tissier, 2ed. § 478; Italian CPC § 492.

[3]) As compared with other procedural laws. Thus Austrian ZPO: „§ 425. Sofern nach den Bestimmungen dieses Gesetzes nicht ein Urteil zu fällen ist, erfolgen die Entscheidungen, Anordnungen und Verfügungen durch Beschluss.. § 390. Wenn der Rechtsstreit nach den Ergebnissen der durchgeführten Verhandlung und der stattgefundenen Beweisverfahren zur Endentscheidung reif ist, hat das Gericht diese Entscheidung durch Urteil zu fällen (Endurteil).." Cf. Italian CPC §§ 50, 492. Likewise the Central American Court of Justice in article 35 of the Ordinance of Procedure of 6 November 1912 (8 AJ sup. 202) is very detailed: „The resolutions of the court are: 1. Sentences, if they finally decide the question in controversy, or, if upon an incident, they put an end to the litigation by making its prosecution impossible. 2. Decrees (*autos*) if their object is to decide an incidental question. 3. Orders (*providencias*) if they refer to questions of mere procedure".

[4]) For the sake of completeness, a fourth form of official act should be mentioned along with judgments, orders, and advisory opinions: the simple „decisions" envisaged by articles 16, 17, 24, 55. Cf. articles 36, 59, 62, 64. See note 7, p. 159 *supra*.

pears that a *prima facie* showing of probable right and probable injury is all that is required. In view of the need for rapidity and the provisional nature of the order, absolutely convincing proof, such as would be necessary in forming the Court's opinion on final judgment, is not necessary [1]).

The Court's decision must be based on the evidence before it, however, and not upon mere speculation [2]). When a refusal to furnish information [3]) or to carry out provisional measures [4]) is put on record, apparently a presumption arises which takes the place of direct evidence in the sense that it legitimates a conclusion derived from the fact in question by reasonable inference.

The proof submitted may be of any sort which the Court's rules of evidence permit it to receive [5]). In view of the summary nature of the procedure, the rules of evidence should be relaxed rather than made more rigid than usual [6]). Substantial credibility rather than formally impregnable accuracy should be sought. There is no limitation requiring liquid means of proof, excluding any evidence which can not be laid before the Court at the first hearing [7]); the Court may well adjourn, for the purpose of receiving further evidence, though of course the delay for this purpose is not unlimited, and must not be incompatible with the essentially urgent character of interim protection [8]). It is not necessary that proof be exclusively documentary in nature [9]), though that will be the usual manner of bringing information to the attention of the

---

1) Hence the mere fact that weighty evidence exists in favor of the contrary conclusion does not prevent the indication of measures if the preponderance of evidence points toward the desirability of protection. Cf. A no. 9, 32.

2) Judge Anzilotti and the minority in the Austro-German customs union affair, A/B no. 41, 70, 76.

3) Statute, article 49.

4) Old rule 57.

5) The author knows no work on rules of evidence in international tribunals, but understands that Dr. Leo Gross of Vienna is engaged in such a study. The question one thinks of first in this connection is the admissibility of „travaux préparatoires" in interpreting a text.

6) In general formalism should be avoided in international procedure. Nippold 334; Feller in 25 AJ (1931) 502; A no. 2, 34; Scott, Judicial Settlement 486.

7) The existence of such a rule in Germany is often asserted. Stein-Jonas, II, 905. Cf. rule 69, where witnesses or experts whom it is desired to have heard by the summary chamber must be available to appear before the chamber when required. Cf. Caroli 337.

8) See Annex 5, *infra*.

9) Cf. ibid. Doubtless that suggestion is not mandatory, and in any case referred to action by the President, before the new rule requiring public hearing, where oral evidence certainly is permissible.

Court. All the modes of enlightenment provided for in articles 44, 49 and 50 of the Statute are available [1]).

10. The Court may make the indication of interim protection dependent upon applicant's furnishing adequate security against injury to other parties in case the request is subsequently shown to have been unjustified. This is not provided in any text, but may be implied. In the first place, it is a „general principle of law" that interim protection is an exceptional remedy, and is granted at the applicant's risk. Security is required in many legislations dealing with measures *pendente lite*. Moreover, since the Court can withhold relief entirely, it may impose conditions necessary in the interest of justice [2]). Interim protection is a matter resting within the discretionary power of the Court [3]), and not a right of the party requesting it. [4])

11. Other rules of procedure may be adopted by the Court if proposed jointly by the parties [5]). But the Court is free to reject such innovations if inconsistent with the Statute and Rules of Court [6]). The possibility of resorting to this procedure in connection with the indication of interim protection was mentioned by the Registrar during the course of the Belgian-Chinese affair [7]).

§ 73. (*B*) Requirements (*Voraussetzungen*).

1. *Circumstances* must require indication of interim measures.

[1]) Article 44 provides that the Court shall address itself directly to the government of the territory concerned in order to procure evidence on the spot. Article 49 provides that the parties may be asked to furnish information and explanations, note being taken of any refusal to do so. Article 50 empowers the Court to entrust any individual, body, bureau, commission or other organization with making an inquiry or giving an expert opinion. Likewise under rule 48 the Court may invite the parties to call witnesses. It would seem that in case of refusal to comply with such an invitation the Court may not summon the witness to appear at the public hearing, but must take steps under rule 49 (permitting it to take steps on its own initiative for examination of the witness out of court). Hammarskjöld in 49 RDILC (1922) 141 says that the sovereignty of the parties prevents the Court from citing witnesses. It is rather the fact that the Court is *not* sovereign which would prevent its compelling the attendance of a witness; but there would be nothing to prevent its summoning and hearing a witness willing and able to appear in court. Doubtless rule 48 simply expresses the principle of procedure according to which the parties are *dominus litis* and the Court does not seek truth on its own account (*Verhandlungsmaxime* as against *Offizialmaxime*. See Millar § 3). But under article 41 of the Statute the Court *does* have power to act *ex officio*.

[2]) This argument has been advanced to justify the practice introduced by President de Belleyme. See § 33 *supra*.

[3]) See p. 185 *infra*.

[4]) Cf. the situation in French law, § 31 *supra*. [5]) Rule 32.

[6]) Hammarskjöld in 49 RDILC (1922) 137. Rules proposed by the parties may contradict the Rules of Court, but must conform to the Statute. A no. 22, 12—3.

[7]) C no. 16-I, 305, Annex 5 *infra*.

Thus it is not necessary that applicant's jeopardy be due to the attitude of his opponent. The test is purely objective [1]).

The danger might arise from the action of a third state, not party to the proceedings. Is such a state, not participating in the litigation, bound by the Court's order to the same extent as the parties? It would seem that a state signatory to the Court Statute protocol would be so bound to recognize the legal effect of *all* official actions of the Court in virtue of that instrument, and not merely those in which it happens to be party to the record. A state which has accepted in advance the Court's obligatory jurisdiction under the optional clause is bound by proceedings instituted in cases covered by article 36 although at the moment when a particular dispute arises it does not manifest its assent to exercise of jurisdiction by the Court. Likewise article 41 binds all signatories, whether parties to the instant case or not.

2. The Court indicates provisional measures when circumstances so *require* („exigent"). Consequently no relief is granted when it is within the power of the applicant to protect himself by the exercise of due diligence [2]), or if other security or legal remedy is at hand [3]). It is not necessary that the measures be absolutely indispensable; it is sufficient if they serve as a safeguard against substantial and not easily reparable injury.[4]) The degree of necessity required varies with the nature of the measure. The more serious the hardship to defendant, the stricter the scrutiny of plaintiff's wants [5]). But the necessity, whatever its extent, must be a *legal* necessity. Interim measures protect actionable legal rights, not purely political interests unrecognized by international law [6]).

3. The measures must be purely conservatory, designed to *preserve* rights in question pending final judgment. Their function is not to accord in advance the relief to which applicant would be entitled on final judgment. They do not constitute a provisional judgment [7]). At best applicant can require only maintenance of

---

[1]) Cf. the subjective test in Austrian law as to pecuniary claims. EO § 379; Rintelen 48; p. 50 *supra*.

[2]) Cf. Ott 19. Nevertheless measures of self-help, such as seizure of enemy vessels before war is declared, should not be encouraged. Stowell 118, 511.

[3]) Ott 50; Rintelen 54; Stein-Jonas, II, 894. Pp. 149—150, *supra*, p. 185 *infra*.

[4]) Thus Austrian EO § 382 „vereitelt oder erheblich erschwert", p. 46 *supra*; Bern law of 7 July 1918 § 326 „erheblicher oder nicht leicht zu ersetzender Schaden oder Nachteil", p. 53 *supra*.

[5]) P. 186 *infra*. [6]) P. 155 *supra*. [7]) Pp. 23, 154 *supra*.

the last uncontested status quo [1]); he can not demand that his legal position be bettered. [2]) A seeming exception to the principle that interim protection should not amount to provisional execution occurs where the relief sought in the principal case is simply repressive, an exercise of „police jurisdiction" to forbid a flagrant wrong or violation of right, rather than an exercise of „judicial jurisdiction" to decide a truly doubtful question of law [3]). Since here the only object of the final judgment is to forbid the illegal act, definitively and with force of *res judicata*, it may well come to pass that the interim order temporarily prohibiting unlawful conduct threatening irreparable damage will in fact, though not in law, be equivalent to giving applicant the very same thing he hopes to secure by final judgment.

Being designed to preserve rights, and not to impose redress or punishment for past shortcomings [4]), interim protection looks to the future. *Non vivitur in praeteritum* [5]). If the harm is already done, the Court will not intervene [6]). Nevertheless measures to insure execution of a future judgment making adequate reparation for past wrongs may go so far as is useful and possible to undo a *fait accompli* [7]).

4. Interim measures protect *rights* of the parties, not the *evidence* by which a party expects to establish its rights, unless such evidence is indispensable and its loss would mean the loss of a right. In view of the wide range of available means of proof and the few restrictions imposed by the rules of international tribunals, it would seem that in most cases parties would be able to prove their case by other evidence, and a particular piece of proof need not be insisted upon.

It is possible also that by special agreement between the parties it might be provided that certain steps to preserve evidence should be taken. The right so created could be protected by interim measures.

Article 41 should be considered in connection with articles 44, 49 and 50 which deal with proofs [8]). Of course all these *mesures*

[1]) P. 187 *infra.*
[2]) Stein-Jonas, II, 892, 937; Ott 86; Ott, Zur Lehre 328—9.
[3]) § 6 *supra.*
[4]) Cf. Sarah Wambaugh in Proc. Am. Soc. Int. Law (1930) 111.
[5]) Roth 25. [6]) See p. 26 *supra.*
[7]) In order to give effect to the principle stated in note 2, p. 20 *supra.*
[8]) Note 1, p. 162 *supra.*

d'instruction depend for their effectiveness upon the good will of the states within whose territory evidence must be obtained. There is in the Statute no provision obliging even the parties to a disputes to facilitate the task of the Court in this respect [1]). From the very fact that parties submit a dispute to arbitration, however, may be implied an undertaking to furnish the tribunal a reasonable amount of material upon the basis of which to make its decision [2]); but no specific pieces of evidence are covered by this obligation.

The nature or content of the right is immaterial [3]), except that it must be actionable at law [4]) and its violation irreparable in money [5]). If it loses its quality of actionability, as by a decision that the Court has no jurisdiction, the interim measures cease to be effective. It is not necessary that the question of jurisdiction *in merito* be decided before protection *pendente lite* can be granted [6]). It is sufficient that want of jurisdiction is not obvious *prima facie*. If it is apparent that applicant can not succeed in his main action, preliminary relief will of course be denied. But jurisdiction to grant interim protection is separate and independent from jurisdiction over the action in chief [7]). According to article 36 of the Statute, the Court decides disputes as to the extent of its own jurisdiction. Consequently as soon as a proceeding is brought in which the Court considers it possible that it may ultimately decide in favor of its jurisdiction, and thereafter give judgment in favor of the party applying for interim protection, such measures may be indicated, if the other necessary requirements are present.

Likewise the possibility that the Court may decree *restitutio in specie* or *in pristinum* suffices to satisfy the requirement that pecuniary redress be inadequate [8]). *Certainty* that such relief will be given is not necessary. Consequently protection *pendente lite* is

[1]) Such a provision is usual in arbitration treaties. See, e.g. note 3, p. 100 *supra*.

[2]) P. 182 *infra*.

[3]) Rintelen 33; Neumann 1165; Stein-Jonas, II, 885.

[4]) Actual, not potential, justiciability is necessary. Note 9, p. 155 *supra*. There being no decision by the Court on the point, it is not certain whether justiciability in general suffices, as we have suggested, or whether protection is confined to rights (1) justiciable before the Court, and not another tribunal; or even to those (2) justiciable in the instant case pending before the Court.

[5]) Pp. 39, 116, 149—150 *supra*. [6]) See, e.g. case 21, § 64 *supra*. [7]) P. 186 *infra*.

[8]) Cf. A no. 9, 28; Guggenheim 12; Huber 561, note 3, p. 140 *supra*.

admissible, to ensure the possibility of executing the Court's final judgment, in all cases under the optional clause, where the Court has power to decide as to the nature and extent of reparation, or cases under a special agreement submitting that question to the Court. Of course, if it is agreed by the parties that reparation shall be made by indemnity, and only the amount to be paid is is issue, there would be no occasion for interim measures unless the solvency of defendant was in doubt [1]). Similarly if it is obvious from the nature of the case that restitutional relief is excluded, this ground of protection is absent, even if the optional clause is in force.

The object of interim remedies is to preserve real and substantial rights of the parties; that is, to guarantee effectually the possibility of bringing about in fact the situation of affairs called for by the law. It is not to protect rights *im juristischen Begriffshimmel*, as abstract entities apart from the factual possibility of concrete realization. Rights must be protected against actual menace in the external world, and not merely against juridical acts capable of legally extinguishing the right [2]).

§ 74. (*C*) Nature of measures indicated.

1. The interim measures indicated by the Court are not „suggestions", „proposals" or „recommendations", as sometimes said [3]). Their scope is limited by the legal situation as it would exist on the hypothesis that the contentions of both parties were well founded. The Court can not look beyond the legal rights of the parties and make suggestions which would facilitate solution of the controversy, such as that the foreign minister of one of the states involved should visit the capital of the other and be entertained lavishly; nor could it forbid smashing embassy windows or

---

[1]) P. 135 *supra*; cf. Politis, note 4, p. 159 *supra*, that states are presumed to be solvent and to act *bona fide*.

[2]) Thus if a building is seized by defendant state, which threatens (1) to transfer title to a purchaser so as to cut off the owner's rights *in rem* and possibility of recovering the property *in specie*; or (2) to burn it down, a distinction between the two cases with respect to the propriety of interim protection is untenable. It can not be said that in the latter case the owner's *right* to the house is not endangered, but merely the factual existence of the house; whereas in the former his legal ownership is threatened with extinction.

[3]) Statute, article 41 (2), English text; § 35 Secretariat draft rules, p. 145 *supra*; Guggenheim 62.

insulting the flag of one party by nationals of the other, even though such conduct might endanger the pacific settlement of the dispute. Measures indicated by the Court must have legal relevance to the questions at issue and the rights involved in the case [1])

2. Since interim measures do not constitute an advance decision of the merits of the case, but are granted only with a view to security, they should go no further than necessary to fulfil their purpose [2]). Of measures equally efficacious that which least harms defendant should be chosen [3]). Normally the Court will not grant relief *ultra petitum,* but since it has power to indicate interim protection *ex officio,* it must satisfy its own judgment that the measures requested by a party are adequate to safeguard rights upon which the Court's final judgment is to pronounce. It is desirable that the measures be indicated in definite and concrete form, so that the parties may be able to obey the law without doubts and hesitation [4]).

3. Interim measures afford protection not only against acts but also against omissions to act which threaten a right [5]).

Illustrations given as suitable occasions for protection *pendente lite* include: (1) Seizure of an object [6]). (2) Destruction of the subject matter of the dispute [7]). (3) Anticipation of the judgment [8]). (4) Invasion [9]).

As is shown by the last example, the Court may forbid acts of self-help and hostilities to the extent that such conduct interferes with the Court's functioning or jeopardizes execution of its judgment. Preservation of peace as such is not the task of the Court, but of the League of Nations. The Court may forbid only such fighting as impedes its own functioning. [10]). Other breaches

---

1) Compare the pacifying activity of a British diplomatic representative who paved the way toward settlement of the controversy between Argentina and Chile, which had been submitted to the arbitration of the English sovereign some six years before, by promoting friendly feeling between the litigants before the award was rendered. Politis, La Justice internationale, 1924, 65—6: „Le délégué brittanique.. sur place.. s'entremit pour amener une détente.... L'arbitre profita de cet heureux état d'esprit pour rendre sa sentence".

2) See p. 53 *supra.* 3) Pp. 49, 55 *supra.*

4) Guggenheim 62. Cf. annex 5, *infra.* The complaint is sometimes made against labor injunctions that they are too broad and vague. Chafee, The Inquiring Mind, 1928. 5) P. 145 *supra.*

6) De Lapradelle report of commission of jurists, Minutes 735.

7) Root in commission of jurists to amend statute, C. 166. M. 66. 1929. V, 64.

8) Ibid.

9) Note 6, *supra*; Negulesco and Guerrero in D no. 2, 2d add. 193, 195.

10) Guggenheim 39.

of peace, even if in contravention of international obligations, must be dealt with by other agencies.

Various sorts of measures may be found useful in protecting rights pending adjudication. Thus disputed territory may be placed in the hands of third parties [1]; or neutralized zones established between combatants [2]. In former times pledges and hostages served to sanction international obligations [3]. More recently, pecuniary security, or seizure of territory has been resorted to [4]. The Court may use its discretion in indicating any sort of measure which will attain the end desired and prove acceptable in practice.

§ 75. (*D*). Effect of interim measures.

1. Obligation to observe.

An order indicating interim protection does not have the force of *res judicata* [5]. Not only may it be modified *pendente lite* [6], but it is subject to review in the final judgment [7]. Although unlike the Bryan treaties the Statute confers on the Court a „power" and not a „mere faculty" to indicate measures [8], there is no question of a binding order [9]. Nevertheless, as we have seen, the Court

1) Dumas, Les Sanctions de l'Arbitrage international, 1905, 243.

2) Sir John Fischer Williams, Chapters, cap. V, Demilitarized Zones, 111—122.

3) Lammasch, Die Rechtskraft internationaler Schiedssprüche, 1913, 218; Muther, Sequestration 369.

4) Thus Greece made a deposit in a Swiss bank as security for indemnity to Italy during the Corfu incident; Italy alleged that the seizure of Corfu was for security. Conwell-Evans 79, 82. OJ (1923) 1304—5. But no proof of Greek insolvency was advanced. See p. 166 *supra*.

D. H. Miller, Secret Statutes of the United States, 1918, 5 refers to a law passed at a secret session of Congress providing for the seizure of certain territory adjacent to the United States, if circumstances should require; but the territory, though held by the United States for the time being, should remain the subject-matter of future negotiations. 3 U.S. Statutes at Large; law approved 15 January 1811.

5) Article 41 speaks of the measures as indicated „à titre provisoire", and contrasts them with „l'arrêt définitif". An *arrêt* has the force of *res judicata*, by article 60 of the Statute; an *ordonnance* has not. A no. 22, 13.

6) P. 156 *supra*.

7) Thus Mr. Root, after defining the duties of the President under former rule 57, says that in the final judgment the Court „devra examiner si les indications fournies par le président ont été l'expression exacte des obligations incombant aux parties. Il appartient au président de les indiquer, mais liberté est laissée aux parties de se conformer à cette indication". C. 166. M. 66. 1929. V, 64.

8) Guggenheim 56. It is difficult to see the exact nature of the distinction between the words „a le pouvoir d'indiquer" and „indiquera", „has the power to indicate" and „shall indicate", except that the Court's discretion to refuse measures is more clearly brought out in the former expression, used in the Statute. The Court's power stops short of that to issue an interim injunction. Bellot, Texts 32; Hudson 25.

9) Fernandes in the committee of jurists wished to introduce the word „ordonner", and Fromageot later at the time of amending rule 57 sought to use the word „pres-

does not merely „suggest" appropriate measures [1]). It would seem that the word „indicate" expresses exactly the Court's function, which is to *point out* what the parties must do in order to remain in harmony with what the Court holds to be the law. This was very lucidly stated by Judge Rolin-Jaequemyns [2]) and also by Mr. Root [3]), who explained that submission of a controversy to the Court implies certain obligations, such as that of not destroying the subject-matter of the controversy or anticipating the judgment. Article 41 states what are the duties of the parties. It is the task of the Court to indicate what it is necessary for the parties to do in order to fulfil their obligations under international law; but the parties remain free to observe such indication or not as they choose.

In other words, the Court's decision is really a special form of advisory opinion. It differs on the one hand from an arbitral award, in that it does not possess obligatory force (*Rechtskraft, res judicata*); but on the other hand it differs from the recommendations of the League Council or a conciliation commission in that it does not advance „proposals" of any sort which the Court may think wise and expedient, but is strictly confined to declaring what action is required by international law in order to safeguard legal rights of the parties. Though not formally binding, such a decision is of great weight, as being the solemn pronouncement of a learned and august tribunal acting in the course of its official duty.

It is hardly necessary to add that the orders of the Court have binding force if, in addition to the Statute, an arbitration treaty such as the Locarno agreements or the General Act [4]), providing that the parties agree to observe such measures, is applicable to the dispute.

2. Means of enforcing obedience.

Likewise if one confuses obligation to obey with the question of sanctions, relating to means for enforcing obedience and the

crire". Documents concerning, 134; D no. 2, 2d add. 182. Regret was expressed by a number of judges (van Eysinga, Guerrero, Rostworowski) that the power of the Court was so restricted. Ibid. 184—5.

Fromageot insisted that in any case there was a moral obligation to comply with the Court's indications. Ibid. 183.

[1]) Pp. 145, 166 *supra*.

[2]) „The Court told the parties what they must do in order to remain in harmony with what it held to be the law, and informed the Council accordingly. That was the whole duty laid upon it by the Statute in regard to measures of protection". Ibid. 199.

[3]) *Loc. cit.* note 7, p. 168 *supra*. [4]) P. 129 *supra*.

consequences of disobedience, one might say that interim measures indicated by the Court are in a measure obligatory because they are supported by the moral and political pressure which may be exerted by the League of Nations. [1]).

Article 41 (2) of the Statute provides that notice of the indication of interim measures shall be sent to the Council of the League [2]). The Statute thus seems to contemplate action by the Council of the League under article 13 of the Covenant [3]). Standing alone, that article refers to the execution of awards having the force of *res judicata*. But the Council may, if it sees fit, exercise powers attributed to it in virtue of another instrument than the Covenant [4]). Thus the effect of the two texts in question taken together may be to create a new competence in the Council. Moreover article 13 (4) of the Covenant may be interpreted so as to apply to interim protection. The task of the Council as there laid down is to propose with respect to judicial decisions measures to assure their having appropriate consequences, their proper effects. Now an order of the Court indicating interim measures is a sort of judicial decision; but not being identical in all respects with a final judgment, its appropriate effects would not be entirely the same as those of a final judgment.

The Council's function being that of taking action designed to ensure that each type of judicial decision shall produce the effects appropriate in view of its own peculiar characteristics, the measures proposed by the Council in the two cases would differ correspondingly [5]). In case of failure to comply with an order of the

[1]) Guggenheim 57.

[2]) As explained in the de Lapradelle report, „Mais tandis que, par les traités Bryan, l'indication des mesures à prendre à titre conservatoire était simplement transmise par la Cour aux parties, elle l'est naturellement, une fois donnée par une Cour de la Société des Nations, au Conseil, organe particulièrement compétent de cette Société pour proposer au regard des sentences arbitrales les mesures qui doivent en assurer l'effet". Minutes 736.

[3]) „Faute d'exécution de la sentence, le Conseil propose les mesures qui doivent en assurer l'effet — In the event of any failure to carry out such an award or decision the Council shall propose what steps should be taken to give effect thereto".

[4]) As in the case of the Mosul boundary. See also Capitant-Trotabas, L'Excès de Pouvoir du T.A.M. et la Compétence du Conseil de la S.D.N. dans l'affaire des Optants hongrois, 35 RGDIP (1928) 45—6.

[5]) For convenience calling the obligation incumbent on a party with respect to an interim order a moral obligation, we may say that there is nothing paradoxical about imposing upon one person a legal obligation to exert his best efforts to induce another person to perform a moral obligation. That the former person is also legally obliged to enforce legal obligations as well is immaterial. Doubtless the means used may differ according to the sort of obligation in question.

Court indicating interim measures the Council would doubtless bring to the attention of the delinquent state the serious responsibility it incurred by ignoring the decision of an authoritative tribunal in a matter within its jurisdiction, and would inquire what reasons led the state to take the course of action it was pursuing. If such grounds were obviously insufficient, or if there was a discrepancy between the professions and the conduct of the state in question, the Council would not fail to point out those circumstances. If the state were not moved by the moral force of international public opinion to abandon its attitude, it might nevertheless moderate the extremity of its views, mindful of the effects of its public admissions and declarations on the course of subsequent judicial proceedings; for it is to be remembered that in cases where orders for interim protection have been made, legal rights of the parties are involved, and await adjudication by the Court in its final judgment.

At all events, the Council may act under article 11 (2) of the Covenant, because failure to respect indications of interim measures is an act of disrespect for international law and international judicial authority which, if persisted in and made general, might lead to war. Any refusal to observe such indications is thus a circumstance affecting the peace of the world and the friendly relations between nations on which peace depends. Moreover in the particular case it may produce tension amounting to a threat of war. Action under article 11 (1) of the Govenant would thus be called for. Moreover, of course, a dispute arising between parties to the original dispute, with respect to the failure to observe interim measures, may, like any other international dispute, be made the object of League procedure or other modes of settlement by international tribunals [1]).

3. Consequences of disobedience.

Reference has already been made to the activity of the Council of the League of Nations in the matter of ensuring the observation of orders made by the Court. Judge de Bustamante has expressed the opinion that article 41 of the Statute made the Council the Court's executive agency, but that in its former rule 57, providing that a refusal to comply with an order should merely be put on record, the Court had adopted a contrary interpreta-

[1]) Guggenheim 58.

tion; for the Council would then have no means of knowing that the order had not been obeyed [1]). Nevertheless it would seem that the Council is not dependent upon the Court for information required by it in the discharge of its duties. The Council must act on its own responsibility. It can not shirk its task by saying that the Court has not notified it of failure to comply with the order. The Council has its own means of obtaining information and keeping in touch with current events. It must use such resources as it possesses. As a matter of fact, an application to the Council would probably be made by the injured state [2]). The function of the Council in enforcing orders of the Court indicating measures of interim protection was not diminished or affected, therefore, either by the adoption of the old rule 57 or the new rule striking it out.

It would seem quite logical, however, that if the Council is to be informed of the issuance of an order indicating interim measures, *a fortiori* it should be apprised of the grave circumstance that the order has been not complied with [3]). But it is quite true that the Statute in article 41 does not *require* such notice to be given. The Court's function is to make the order and notify it to the Council. It is the responsibility of the Council to set in motion the machinery for enforcing the Court's order [4]). Moreover it might be indiscreet to mention the possibility of disobedience [5]). In addition, Judges Anzilotti and Rolin-Jaequemyns pointed out a further difficulty, that procedure would be necessary in order to ascertain whether or not the order had been disregarded [6]). At all events, in view of these various reasons, no reference whatever to the consequences of disobedience to orders of the Court indicat-

[1]) De Bustamante § 205, p. 225—6. [2]) Cf. note 6 *infra*.

[3]) D no. 2, 2d add. 198—9. (van Eysinga, Schücking).

[4]) Anzilotti, Guerrero, Urrutia, Rostworowski. Ibid. 198. See also note 2, p. 169 *supra*.

[5]) Rostworowski, ibid. 187. The question is one of policy: should logical or psychological considerations prevail? In view of the absence of effective physical sanctions in international law, and the necessity of cultivating in every nation a sentiment of international amity and honorable fulfilment of duty, the Coué method of assuming the existence of those qualities may beget them, whereas threats might increase rather than diminish disobedience. But might not the prospect of publicity serve to strengthen the sentiments of honor and duty in time of temptation?

[6]) Ibid. 199. But as Judge Fromageot observed, the Court would probably receive a complaint from the party prejudiced by failure to carry out the order. Ibid. 200. To ascertain whether facts exist and whether they are in conformity with the law is not an unusual task for a court. Moreover the Court might notify the Council simply of the *alleged* violation, and leave the burden of investigation to that body.

ing interim protection is contained in the new version of rule 57.

Under the old rule 57 any refusal to comply with indications of interim measures was put on record. It has been suggested that a „refusal" is a definite act, solemnized with due formality [1]). A better interpretation regards the term as meaning any failure to comply with an order of the Court when compliance is within the power of the state in question, without requiring modification of its legislation or the collaboration of other states [2]). The effect of putting on record would seem to be that „account is taken" of such refusal in the final judgment, giving it „due legal weight" [3]). This may occur in several ways: (1) As a presumption, taking the place of evidence [4]). (2) Damages may be awarded on final judgment for injury caused by failure to comply with interim measures [5]). (3) The Court might withhold a decision in favor of a delinquent litigant. Compliance with previous orders of the Court may well be made the condition of invoking its aid [6]).

§ 76. (*b*) Interim protection in the absence of express norms.

Modern juridical science recognizes that law is made up of more than imperative, specific precepts [7]). It contains as well received ideals of justice and equity, general principles and doctrines, a traditional technique of legal thinking [8]). Definite rules laid down in express terms by the law-maker, prescriptions of immemorial

---

1) Ibid. 198. 2) Note 5, p. 126; note 1, p. 147 *supra*.

3) Hammarskjöld, in 49 RDILC (1922) 142; Nyholm, note 1, p. 147 *supra*.

4) P. 161 *supra*. This may be important where mental elements of intent are involved, as in determining good faith, aggression, etc.

5) Note 1 p. 147 *supra*; Guggenheim 67.

6) So article 61, Statute, as to revision of judgments. But see Salvioli, 16 Riv. (1924) 120.The Roman praetor resorted to that step. Keller, 6ed. 330; Bekker II, 42; Wetzell 201. Cf. McAdoo, address before Ohio State Bar Association, Toledo, January 1927; Bull v. Conroe, 13 Wis. 260 (1860). Thus the Mosul commission refused to proceed with its task until proper conditions were established. Conwell-Evans 145; C. 400. M. 147. 1295. VII, 9. Likewise the arbitration tribunal between Nicaragua and Honduras. § 43 *supra*. Cf. rules of Anglo-Austrian mixed arbitral tribunal, § 75.

The Permanent Court of International Justice will not give a judgment which the parties may render inoperative. A no. 24, 14; (cf. Anzilotti in A/B no. 41, 69—70 where the same question decided by the Court will come before the Council). Would not the same reluctance exist in case the parties *had already* rendered the judgment inoperative in fact? But see Hammarskjöld, Sidelights on the Permanent Court of International Justice, 25 Mich. L.R. (1927) 338.

7) Brierly, The Law of Nations, 1928, 44—5; Pound, Juristic Science and Law, 31 HLR 1060—2.

8) Pound, Theory of Judicial Decision, 36 HLR 645; The Ideal Element in American Judicial Decisions, 45 HLR 136—148.

custom, and generally accepted principles of juristic thought must all be taken into account as elements of the legal order. The inadequacy of attempts to define law in terms of one of its elements alone at the expense of the others has frequently demonstrated the futility of such a restricted outlook. The neglected aspects can only be overshadowed, but never completely eliminated [1]).

What has just been said holds good with respect to international law. International law is the application of the idea of law to the problems arising out of the international relations between states [2]). Thus nations agree that their relations shall be regulated by international law [3]) — which is based on good faith and justice [4]) — without always determining clear-cut rules in advance of particular cases. International law is made up only partly of definite precepts, and partly, even in the most weighty matters, of directive ideas and general principles [5]).

Law may be a seamless web, but it is not of uniform texture throughout. The hierarchical distinction between constitution, statute, ordinance, judgment in the individual case, is obvious [6]). Some rules are the expression of fundamental principles of legislative policy, while others are of minor importance [7]); some principles are procreative, while others linger on the way toward obsolescence and desuetude; „there are laws that wake and laws that slumber" [8]). So too some parts of the law admit of formulation in minute detail, others are more general; some are well settled, while others are beset by uncertainty. It would never occur to a lawyer to say that there was no law on a given point because he could not put his finger on a precise text, couched lucidly and of unshakeable authority [9]), or because application of a general standard such as good faith or reasonable conduct was called for [10]). Such a course would amount to repudiation of his professional function. Every lawyer in practice takes account of the

---

[1]) Pound, Theories of Law, 22 Yale LJ 114.
[2]) Verdross, Verfassung 61; Niemeyer, Völkerrecht, 1923, 10.
[3]) Hold-Ferneck, Lehrbuch 178.
[4]) Ibid. 200—1. [5]) Ibid. 214—5; Cereti 121.
[6]) Verdross, Verfassung §§ 4, 13.
[7]) D. H. Miller, Proc. Am. Soc. Int. Law (1930) 218.
[8]) Pollock, Essays in Jurisprudence and Ethics, 1882, 229.
[9]) Sir John Fischer Williams, Chapters, 26, 50—1.
[10]) John Dickinson, Administrative Justice and the Reign of Law, 1927, 215; Pound, Law and Morals, 56; Vinogradoff, Custom and Right, 1925, 14—5.

ideal element in law. He knows that existing, living law is not identical with previously formulated (i.e. past or ancient) law.

This unformulated element is part of the law itself. One must therefore regret the infelicitous terminology of a recent writer who introduces in this connection the expression „international equity law", and understands by the term a companion category of standards co-ordinate with international law, not a part of international law itself [1]. The word „equity" should not be used to designate that part of international law which does not rest upon express convention or palpable historically established custom. It means something else [2]. Likewise it is confusing to include this element under the rubric of customary law [3].

A number of writers have recognized that international law contains more than expressly formulated precepts. Thus Bruns regards as law not only what has been voiced explicitly, but also what follows by deduction from the presuppositions of the legal system [4]. A similar method [5] is employed by Liszt [6], who de-

[1]) Feilchenfeld, Public Debts §§ 279, 280: „What has been termed international equity law comprises not merely those rules which international tribunals admittedly base on equity, as distinguished from law, but also all those rules which, although described as international law, are not based on custom or general recognition".

[2]) „Equity" is either exercise of jurisdiction *juris corrigendi causa*, derogating from existing strict law as inadequate to the exigencies of justice and acting upon the basis of new rules introduced in its stead; or the exercise of jurisdiction disregarding the law altogether and deciding controversies in accordance with subjective considerations of justice or expediency. Aristotle, Nic. Eth. V, 14; J. B. Moore, International Adjudications, I, xlii, quoting Grotius, III, 20, 47, 2; Sir John Fischer Williams, Chapters, 63; Alvarez 118; Strupp, Das Recht des internationalen Richters nach Billigkeit zu entscheiden, 1930. Insistent that even what is really more in the nature of equity as we conceive it is part of the law is Huber 500: „Zwischen Staaten als solchen gilt nur Völkerrecht. Ein anderes allgemeines Recht an sich gibt es nicht, ausser für diejenigen die auf dem Boden des Naturrechts stehen. Wenn auf die Beziehungen zwischen Staaten Normen angewendet werden, die nicht als besondere völkerrechtliche Normen anerkannt sind, die aber in einem konkreten Fall als das richtige Recht erscheinen, als die den zwischenstaatlichen Verhältnissen adäquate Ordnung, so sind dies doch Normen des internationalen Rechts — denn diese — wie jede Rechtsordnung — trägt in sich das Streben nach Vollständigkeit und den Befehl an den Richter, die Lücken des Rechts zu ergänzen".

[3]) Cavaglieri in 14 Riv. di dir. int. (1921—2) 504 criticizes article 38 of the Statute of the Permanent Court of International Justice (see p. 176 *infra*) for repeating in the third paragraph what he considers already included in the second. Gianni 119, 159 describes „general principles of law" as „coutume dans le sens large" and true customs as „coutume dans le sens restreint". In both cases, according to Gianni, „elle est à base de conviction et non pas de consentement".

[4]) Bruns 1, 13.

[5]) Resembling Somló's method of finding fundamental principles necessarily common to every legal system, such as that a text must be interpreted without contradiction as part of a harmonious legal system. Somló 383.

[6]) Das Völkerrecht, 10 ed. 1917, 65: „Es handelt sich nicht um naturrechtliche

duces many rules of law from the presupposition of independent co-existence of states. Triepel also urges elaboration of new rules on the basis of existing materials [1]). So Strupp [2]) agrees with Anzilotti [3]) that presuppositions and consequences of established norms are likewise law, while rejecting „general principles of law" [4]).

The most important contribution to this topic has been made by Verdross [5]), who succeeds in clarifying the facts better than the other formulations just discussed. He finds it convenient to define as customary law only rules based upon actual ṭacit consent of states, a consent implied in fact and not in law, to use common law terminology [6]). Consequently he recognizes three sources of international law: treaty; customary law in the restricted sense mentioned; and general principles of law, which account for the positive international law which does not come from veritable consent of states [7]).

According to Verdross, article 38, paragraph 3 of the Statute of the Permanent Court of International Justice, which provides that the Court shall apply „the general principles of law recognized by civilized nations" simply codified and declared existing law [8]). According to Anzilotti [9]) this provision merely authorizes the Court, like the Roman praetor, to make law in cases submitted to it. Verdross [10]) argues that since this is a *general* provision for the guidance of the court in all cases, (and not a particular instruction like the three rules of the Alabama) [11]), it is unlikely that states would have consented that the Court in judging the parties

---

Trugbilde, sondern um Rechtsnormen, die nach dem Satze des Nichtwiderspruchs aus dem Begriff der Völkerrechtsgemeinschaft folgen und der Form ausdrücklicher Rechtssatzung nicht bedürfen, weil ohne sie ein Völkerrecht überhaupt nicht denkbar wäre".

1) Völkerrecht und Landesrecht, 1899, 95; 39 Niemeyers Zt. f. int. Rt. (1925) 188.

2) Eléments du droit international public, 2ed. 1930, I, 16.

3) Corso, 3ed. 1928, I, 64.

4) Gianni 69 observes: „Qu'est-ce que les principes généraux sinon les présuppositions et les conséquences logiques des normes établies?" Cf. Rabel 17.

5) Einheit 120—5; Verfassung § 16.

6) Spiropoulos, Die allgemeinen Rechtsgrundsätze im Völkerrecht, 1928, 63 overlooks this fact in his criticism of Verdross.

7) The doctrine recognizing three sources of law has not met with universal acceptance. Strupp, Recht des int. Richters 86. The orthodox view recognizes treaty and custom as sources of co-ordinate authority, as being the express or tacit consent of states.

8) Verfassung 59. 9) Corso, 3ed. 1928, 107. 10) Verfassung 61.

11) Triepel, Völkerrecht und Landesrecht, 1899, 74.

apply rules which the latter in their conduct were not obliged to observe [1]). „The Statute is essentially a code of procedure, and can not be interpreted as introducing a *new* definition of international law" [2]). It should be remembered that the Committee of Jurists were engaged in the task of drafting the charter of a court which was expected to have compulsory jurisdiction, and as Mr. Root observed, states would be hesitant to accept such a court unless its decisions were based on international law and nothing else [3]).

§ 77. „General principles of law" [4]) are not natural law [5]), or equity [6]), or, according to Verdross, general principles of *international* law [7]). They are arrived at by induction from a comparison

[1]) Strupp, Grundzüge des positiven Völkerrechts, 1928, 9—10 contends that the law applicable to cases pending before the court differs from that in force prior to the institution of proceedings.

[2]) Sir John Fischer Williams, Chapters, 20. The German-Portuguese arbitral tribunal in its decision of 31 July 1928 (8 TAM 409 at 413) considered article 38 as containing a definition of international law rather than special rules for the guidance of the Court.

[3]) Minutes of Committee of Jurists 308.

[4]) According to Scott, L'Universalité du Droit des Gens, 1 RDI (1927) 651, the expression „principes généraux de droit reconnus par les nations civilisées" is the Anglo-Saxon equivalent of the more elegant formula originally proposed by Baron Descamps: „Les règles de droit international telles que les reconnaît la conscience juridique des peuples civilisés". Cf. the preamble to the Hague convention of 1907 governing the conduct of land warfare: „En attendant qu'un code plus complet des lois de la guerre puisse être édicté, les Hautes Parties contractantes jugent opportun de constater que, dans les cas non compris dans les dispositions réglementaires adoptées par elles, les populations et les belligérants restent sous la sauvegarde et sous l'empire des principes du droit des gens, tels qu'ils résultent des usages établis entre nations civilisées, des lois de l'humanité et des exigences de la conscience publique".

[5]) Verdross in 11 Zt. f. öff. Rt. (1930) 130; Strupp, Das Recht des int. Richters, 87, 113. *Contra*, Cereti 165; Heller, Die Souveränität, 139—40. The former considers international law too vague a system to be completed as a comprehensive code may be interpreted and eked out, by deductions from the spirit of the legislator. Cereti 123. Heller distinguishes „allgemeine Rechtsgrundsätze" from „allgemeine Rechtssätze" only the latter being positive law, and article 38 (3) referring to the former. This opinion seems to be based on a misleading German translation of the text in question. As to a provision in Italian law resembling article 38 (3), see Del Vecchio, Sui Principi generali del Diritto, 1921.

[6]) Alvarez 113, 114, 118 distinguishes between general principles of law, of justice, and equity.

[7]) Verdross Règles 303; Strupp, Recht des int. Richters 113, Grundzüge 10. *Contra*, Anzilotti, Corso, 3ed. 1928, 106. The *argumentum a contrario* (Strupp Grundzüge 10, Verdross Verfassung 62) that paragraph 3 refers to what is not included in other paragraphs of article 38 is sound to the extent of indicating that that paragraph *includes* what is *not* in them. But the paragraph does not necessarily exclude everything which they *do* contain. As Anzilotti points out, the principles of the international legal order for the most part are identical with those in private law systems. He cites as an illustration the principle of international law that violation of an obligation entails a duty to make reparation. A no 9, 21.

of the internal law of different states. Not only must there be substantial unanimity in recognizing the principle *in foro interno* in practically all legal systems, but the principle must have juridical value, and be appropriate under the special circumstances of the international legal order [1]).

Examples of such principles given by Verdross are: that treaties are to be assimilated to contracts with respect to duress or error vitiating the expression of mutual assent, insofar as specific rules of international law have not grown up [2]); that self-defense must be conducted without the use of greater force than is reasonably necessary [3]); that delay may amount to denial of justice [4]); that foreigners must be accorded a certain generally recognized standard of treatment [5]).

Other examples that have been mentioned are: that plaintiff must prove his case [6]); that what is not forbidden is allowed [7]); that *in toto jure genus per species derogatur* [8]); that general principles of procedure, such as that the nature of the claim must not be varied during trial, must be observed [9]); that a party to a contract failing to fulfil obligations thereunder must make compensation [10]); that interest must be paid on delinquent debts [11]); that discretion or liberty must not be abused, and arbitrary action must be avoided [12]); that a party preventing fulfilment

[1]) Balladore-Pallieri I Principi, 73; Härle 234.

[2]) Verfassung 50. [3]) Règles 485.

[4]) Lectures at the Academy of International law at the Hague, August 1931, Le traitement des étrangers, cap. I.

[5]) Ibid. cap. III.

[6]) Lord Phillimore, in Minutes of the Commission of Jurists drafting the Statute, 316.

[7]) Ricci-Busatti, ibid. 314. [8]) Cavaglieri in 14 Riv. di dir. int. 498.

[9]) Sobolewski, Polish advocate, *arguendo*, C no. 13—I, p. 98; Lord Phillimore, Minutes 335. Thus the Corfu commission of jurists reported in favor of recognizing the dilatory exception of *lis alibi pendens* in procedure before the Council: „Il est conforme aux principes généraux de droit que le renvoi puisse être demandé et ordonné". OJ (1924) 524.

[10]) Sir John Fischer Williams, Chapters, 23; A no. 17, p. 29.

[11]) Strupp, Grundzüge 10; but the *rate* of interest is not prescribed.

[12]) Gerhard Leibholz, Das Verbot der Willkür und des Ermessensmissbrauchs im völkerrechtlichen Verkehr der Staaten, I Zt. f. aus. öff. Rt. u. Vrt. teil 1 (1929) 77—125, esp. 115—125. The author declares (77—8) „dass es auch im Völkerrecht unabhängig von Vertrags- und Gewohnheitsrecht Sätze gibt, die positivrechtliche Verpflichtungskraft für die Staaten besitzen. Dies sind die jeder Rechtsordnung immanenten Rechtssätze. Zu ihnen zählt sich vor allem der hier zur Diskussion gestellte, der Landesrechts- ebenso wie der Völkerrechtsordnung immanente Satz, dass kein Staat sich ausserhalb der Rechtsordnung stellen darf, dass Willkür verboten und rechtswidrig ist". He considers that „general principles", insofar as they are positive law should be on an equal footing with treaty and custom, and not occupy a subsidiary po-

of a condition may not take advantage of its absence [1]).

§ 78. A recent contribution of value is the work of Balladore-Pallieri [2]). He adopts the view that where a court has jurisdiction it can always decide the case; in this sense there are no gaps in the law [3]). Consequently he rejects the reasoning advanced by some members of the Committee of Jurists in support of article 38 (3). They deemed such a provision needful in order that the judge might decide every case and decide always according to law [4]). For Balladore-Pallieri the real problem is whether, in the absence of an applicable rule governing the case, the court shall apply the principle *pro libertate* (*nulla actio sine lege*), or may resort to analogy [5]). He rejects the view that in international law analogy is

sition. Leibholz seems to identify general principles with Somló's „juristische Grundlehre" as opposed to an „allgemeine Rechtslehre". But it would seem that article 38 (3) requires only that a principle actually be generally recognized, without the additional showing that such recognition is logically inescapable.

[1]) A no. 9, 31.

[2]) I principi, reviewed by Scerni in 23 Riv. di dir. int. (1931) 442—453.

[3]) As to gaps see Verdross, Verfassung § 19. There can really be no lack of law if there is jurisdiction and duty of the court to decide. Scott, Sovereign States and Suits 147. Likewise it would be *possible* for a court to be in a situation where it must reject all claims which are not supported by *treaty* provisions. The question is, what sources must the court investigate before being compelled to dismiss the claim for want of legal foundation? Cavaglieri in 18 Riv. di dir. int. (1926) 183 takes the view that recourse under article 38 (3) to the „novissimo jus gentium" is to be had only when there is no applicable international law and otherwise it would be necessary to decide against the complaint, „nella necessità di rigettare la domanda per mancanza di norme di diritto internazionale applicabili al caso concreto". This mode of expression seems to be inaccurate in that it regards the *Entscheidungsnorm* as something other than international law. Many writers have the unfortunate tendency to regard law as a finite number of rules, (See Brierly in BYB (1930) 127), an „Inventar bestehender Rechtssätze", (Guggenheim in 11 Zt. f. öff. Rt. (1931) 558), a bundle of paragraphs printed in a book. If one can not point to a text in the book there is no law. It is as if the judge's task were that of unlocking boxes brought to him by the parties by means of a certain number of keys on his key-ring. If none of the keys fits the particular box, he rejects the case.

[4]) P. 14: „Affinchè il giudice possa adempiere la sua funzione di giudicare in ogni caso e di giudicare sempre secondo il diritto".

[5]) Analogy is carefully distinguished from extensive interpretation. It cannot be said that there is no applicable rule, and hence occasion for resorting to analogy, when there is a rule which, when interpreted, is found to cover the case. When a court applies a certain rule by analogy, it does not apply the rule applied by analogy, but the rule authorizing resort to analogy. P. 33. A „general principle of law recognized by civilized nations" is not itself a norm of international law, but the existence of such a principle is a fact to which, pursuant to article 38 (3) (or a rule of customary law authorizing resort to analogy) legal consequences are attached by international law. If in one case the Permanent Court of International Justice applies a certain principle of law, and in another case does not, it has not applied a non-existent rule of international law or failed to apply an existing rule. It has merely interpreted and applied article 38 (3) incorrectly. P. 86—8. Of this view Scerni says in 23 Riv. di dir int. (1931) 452—3 that it is as if one said that in applying a treaty the court merely applied the rule *pacta sunt servanda*.

inapplicable. Two factors have upset that doctrine in modern times. In the first place, the conception of international law as a unified legal order based on a fundamental norm has replaced that which regarded it as an aggregate of disconnected consensual enactments [1]). In the second place, positive rules such as article 38 (3) authorize resort to analogy. Nothing in the nature of international law as compared with internal law makes for a different situation with respect to the problem. The solution must be sought by inquiring whether positive international law contains a rule authorizing analogy [2]). Balladore-Pallieri considers article 38 (3) as declaratory of a rule of customary international law to that effect [3]).

§ 79. From what has gone before it is evident that protection *pendente lite* is one of the „general principles of law" with which international lawyers must reckon. But this does not mean that every international tribunal is authorized by those principles to order measures of interim protection. We have seen that the action with a view to security is an independent judicial proceeding, a type of relief standing by itself [4]). It is therefore necessary that there be a tribunal with jurisdiction to entertain such an action. It is quite thinkable that a tribunal, though having power to decide the merits of a dispute, has no authority to extend protection *pendente lite* [5]). Indeed, in the early stages of international arbitration, when a special tribunal had to be constituted *ad hoc* (*post hoc* as well) there was no occasion for such a jurisdiction. Agreement to arbitrate was an indication of such a conciliatory mood on the part of the litigants that a *modus vivendi pendente*

---

[1]) Bruns 1; Verdross Verf. § 7, Fondement 297; Anzilotti, Corso, 3ed. 1928, 42.

[2]) Balladore-Pallieri, p. 39.

[3]) Ibid. p. 64. To demonstrate the existence of such a rule Balladore-Pallieri adduces: (1) the development of law regarding aviation and marine subsoil on the analogy of rules respecting territory or high seas; (2) the argument of Anzilotti, Corso 3ed. 1928, 456 to the effect that necessity of self-preservation justifies a state in not fulfilling its international obligations, when it would justify resort to war, a graver course; (3) the fact that at the time of the treaty of Westphalia when modern international law originated, there were few treaty provisions, and there had not been sufficient time for customs to grow up, yet nevertheless positive international law existed; (4) the fact that in numerous cases arbitral tribunals applied general principles of law, and no protest was made, whereas in cases where states felt that the tribunal had not decided in conformity with international law they did protest. Pp. 52, 54, 56, 58, 62.

[4]) See § 11 *supra.*

[5]) See 55 JW (1926) 378, note 1, p. 91 *supra.*

lite could be easily arranged, so far as it was of importance at that late date, for any irreparable injury against which interim protection would be useful had in all probability already occurred long before the arbitration tribunal was ready to do business. Interim protection presupposes the existence of a competent tribunal, capable of acting immediately, without preliminary negotiations, at the time when action is necessary and helpful. Not until such jurisdiction is expressed or implied in the provisions instituting the tribunal do the general principles of law which we have studied come into play.

Jurisdiction for purposes of interim protection, like every item in the jurisdiction of an international tribunal, must be affirmatively established. There is no presumption that such jurisdiction exists [1]). International tribunals do not have a general common law jurisdiction [2]). Not only does no particular tribunal have such a pre-eminence as against other tribunals, but it is not a rule of international law that disputes between states must be submitted to judicial procedure at all [3]).

Consequently, the mere fact that a tribunal has jurisdiction over the dispute in chief does not, without more, give it jurisdiction to order interim measures. Nor does the mere existence of a norm relating to the situation *pendente lite* and imposing on the parties obligations with respect thereto [4]), suffice to confer such jurisdiction. We have already seen that there may be a procedural norm without a jurisdiction to apply it [5]). Such remedial

[1]) Of course jurisdiction need not be conferred in express and indubitable terms. It is a question of interpreting the texts to ascertain the intention of the parties. The mere fact that weighty arguments may be adduced tending to show lack of jurisdiction is not sufficient to compel that conclusion, in the face of preponderant evidence to the contrary. A no. 9, 32. Cf. note 1, p. 28 *supra*.

[2]) Note 4, p. 30 *supra*.

[3]) Anzilotti, Corso, 3ed. 1928, 108 declares that article 38 (3), therefore, can not confer jurisdiction on the Court. Cf. A no. 9, p. 32.

„While judicial or semi-judicial methods have long been recognized by all nations as a suitable means of adjusting international controversies, it is, of course, not to be contended that custom or usage has as yet developed to the point where it requires the use of such methods to the exclusion of war. It cannot, however, be denied that many questions have been thus settled which might otherwise have led to war, and thus we see the beginning of a custom or usage which may ultimately ripen into a rule of law requiring such means to be used in all cases." T. R. White, Limitations upon the Initiation of War, Proc. Am. Soc. Int. Law, 1925, 104.

[4]) Such norms, directed to the parties and not to the tribunal, would not be regarded by Goldschmidt as forming part of procedural law. See p. 15 *supra*. They are included under our functional view. P. 17 *supra*.

[5]) See pp. 9, 93, 127 *supra*.

norms need not be expressly declared [1]), but may be implied from the very act of submitting a dispute to arbitration. The mere acceptance of judicial procedure creates certain obligations. Most important is that of executing the award [2]). Similarly there arises a duty to furnish the tribunal with the means of proof and evidence necessary to enable it to perform its function [3]).

Likewise there is implied the obligation to refrain from all acts tending to stultify the arbitration and render the decision nugatory. This conclusion flows inevitably from two weighty principles of international law with regard to the interpretation of agreements, that they must be interpreted in accordance with good faith and good sense. As to the first rule, it may be noted that even writers who reject the maxim *pacta sunt servanda* as an absolute and universal principle are insistent that treaties must be interpreted according to the requirements of good faith [4]). What could be more contrary to good faith than to provide that a question shall be submitted to arbitration, and then to wiggle out of that commitment by preventing the arbitration from taking its proper course? Likewise it is a well settled principle of international law that an interpretation is to be preferred that does not render the agreement meaningless or ineffective [5]). It will be presumed that foreign offices do not deal in futilities. States will not be deemed to have authorized a course of conduct frustrating their solemn decision that the dispute shall be settled by the tribunal.

What acts *pendente lite* fall within this prohibition? Obviously, in the first place, resort to war for the solution of a dispute referred to arbitration is repugnant to the obligations which the parties have assumed. An agreement to arbitrate would be nugatory if, after deciding that a dispute shall be settled by arbitration, parties remained free to settle it by war. Acts of hostility are certainly inconsistent with the expressed desire for peaceful solution of the controversy [6]).

[1]) For examples of such expressly declared norms see p. 127 *supra*.

[2]) Hague Convention of Pacific Settlement of 1907, § 3 7 (2); (Covenant, § 13).

[3]) Ibid. § 75; Anzilotti, Corso, (1915) III, 106. See also the enumeration of obligations resulting from resort to judicial procedure set forth by the Hungarian-Roumanian mixed arbitral tribunal. 5 TAM 955.

[4]) Hold-Ferneck, Lehrbuch 200—1.

[5]) Vattel, II, xvii, § 282—3; Gore's opinion in the Betsey, 1 Lapradelle-Politis, Recueil 67.

[6]) Guggenheim 39; van Boetzelar 16; Telders 6.

This conclusion follows *a fortiori* if it is admitted that invocation of one particular mode of settling a dispute precludes even resort to other means of *pacific* settlement [1]). Although parties who have invoked a particular tribunal are bound to conform to its rules of procedure applicable to the case in hand [2]), it would seem that they are free at any time to settle the dispute definitively by mutual agreement [3]).

It should be emphasized that the obligation not to resort to war in question here is entirely independent of legal limitations on warmaking as such [4]). It is not war *per se* which is illegal here; it is failure to live up to the promise to arbitrate [5]). Even without a general duty to refrain from war in all circumstances, states are not free to settle by war a particular dispute which they have agreed to settle otherwise.

But war is not the only form of action excluded by implication when an obligation to resort to arbitration is accepted. Any conduct unreconcilable with the arbitration agreement is forbidden. Self-help, destruction of the subject-matter of the controversy, and any action anticipating the decision are among the measures

---

1) General convention of inter-American conciliation of 5 January 1929, § 13 (23 AJ sup. 80); Conwell-Evans 220—5, Buell, International Relations, 1925, 596—7, OJ (1924) 524, as to Council; G. Ténékidès, L'Exception de litispendance devant les organismes internationaux, 36 RGDIP (1929) 502—527.

2) Proceedings once instituted must pursue their due course. See p. 150 *supra*.

3) Hence it might be argued, in accordance with the view of Lasson, Princip und Zukunft des Völkerrechts, 1871, 71—2 (that war is a means of negotiation in order to obtain a reasonable agreement based on political actualities), that parties might, without interfering with the arbitral procedure, wage war in order to come to a mutual agreement settling the dispute out of court. But the distinction between such a war and a war for the settlement of a dispute which parties have agreed shall be settled by arbitration, which latter kind of war we have seen to be forbidden, is almost impossible to perceive.

4) As to these, see Dumbauld, Legal Limitations on War-making, 18 Geo. LJ (1930) 83—91.

5) An agreement to arbitrate is a ban on war only *pro tanto*; only an agreement to arbitrate *all* disputes would amount to a general prohibition of war; even then war for other purposes than settling disputes would still be permitted. Pillet, La Guerre et le Droit, 1919, 58; Lasson, Princip und Zukunft des Völkerrechts, 1871, 67. Thus it might be argued that a state is free to make war to regain what it has given up in execution of an arbitral award, for the award confers no greater sanctity on the transfer of territory, for example, than a cession by treaty would possess, and a state having made such a cession is free to regain the ceded territory by war, in the absence of general prohibitions on warmaking. The state is bound by the arbitration agreement only to do no act *pendente lite* which would frustrate the proceedings, and *causa finita* to execute the award in good faith. What it does after that is not covered by the arbitration treaty and is governed by other international obligations of the parties.

banned [1]. In general, all acts are ruled out which tend to stultify the pacific procedure invoked.

On the other hand, instead of a remedial norm without a jurisdiction to apply it, there may be express or implied jurisdiction to grant interim protection without any express rules being laid down as to the scope and character of the measures authorized. The pertinent texts are generally couched in vague and summary terms, though usually some slight indication is given of the rules by which the court is to be guided (as by prescribing that the measures must be equitable and necessary, required to preserve rights of the parties, to fix the status quo, to ensure execution of the judgment, etc.). In practice tribunals have eked out those provisions by decisions evolving additional norms. Such rules spring from the „general principles of law" discussed above.

It will be useful to summarize some of the outstanding principles governing interim protection in international controversies which emerge from our survey of the provisions established in individual legal systems. Many principles have been expressly recognized in international law as well as internal law [2]; others become available for international law only in virtue of resort to „general principles of law" in the absence of specific international norms.

§ 80. CONCLUSIONS

1. Interim measures always constitute an exceptional remedy [3]. They derogate from the usual rule that a plaintiff can not obtain relief until he has thoroughly proved his case, and all defenses and objections of his adversary have been heard and considered [4].

Nevertheless realization of the fact that under certain cir-

---

[1]) According to Mr. Elihu Root's interpretation of article 41 of the Statute of the Permanent Court of International Justice, in the committee of jurists for amending the Statute. Document C. 166. M. 66. 1929. V. 63.

[2]) See note 7, p. 177 *supra.*

[3]) This was emphasized by mediaeval writers. See note 6, p. 39 *supra.*

[4]) Summary hearing of both parties should precede granting interim protection when urgency does not prevent. The Permanent Court of International Justice is more scrupulous than required by principle in requiring a hearing in all cases. P. 158—9 *supra.* French law denies a hearing in all cases, but this results perhaps from its conception of interim measures as a right of the applicant. Pp. 70—71, 74 *supra.* For the usual rule see note 3, p. 54; p. 131 *supra.*

cumstances delay is equivalent to denial of justice [1]), and that a remedy not available until expiration of the time required to obtain a final judgment in the normal course of proceedings is no remedy at all, has moved legislators universally to institute remedies *pendente lite*. Administration of justice according to law thereby extends its empire, and the scope of self-help is accordingly diminished [2]).

But special circumstances and adequate guarantees against injustice must be present in order to warrant such a departure from habitual practice [3]).

2. The plaintiff in a proceeding to obtain this exceptional remedy acts at his peril. A party not contented to await the results of normal judicial procedure must make good the harm caused by his impatience in case he is found to have been in the wrong. Not only is interim protection granted *periculo petentis*, but applicant may be required to furnish adequate security against damage resulting from the measures to be ordered [4]).

3. The power to exact adequate provision against harm to other parties as a condition of granting interim protection is only one manifestation of the general principle that the court has discretion of the widest possible character both as to the necessity and the nature of measures to be taken. It is impossible to enumerate in advance all the situations in which prompt action may be urgently required [5]).

In exercise of its discretion, however, the court must be mindful of the principle that interim measures should go no further than is indispensable in order to achieve the necessary protection and security. The slightest possible burden should be imposed upon the applicant's adversary [6]). The fact that the court has power to act at once instead of after a thorough trial of the case

[1]) Normal and inevitable delay is here meant. Cf. note 5, p. 159 *supra*.

[2]) § 40 *supra*.

[3]) If other protection is available, interim measures are refused. P. 163 *supra*; Austrian EO § 379 (1); cf. Druart 6.

[4]) See p. 162 *supra*. The Court might require the party asking for interim protection to make a deposit, (See pp. 131, 168 *supra*) or, as in the praetorian stipulations of old, to file a declaration accepting jurisdiction of the Court to award damages. Cf. the declarations which non-members of the League not mentioned in the annex to the Covenant of the League of Nations must put on record before being admitted to sue in the Court. Resolution of the Council of 17 May 1922, OJ (1922) 545—6.

[5]) Gianzana 19—20; German ZPO § 938; Bertin 15; pp. 59—60, 64, 77, 115; note 8, p. 168 *supra*. Cf. Hellwig 13, and p. 70—71 *supra*.

[6]) Pp. 49, 55, 132—3, 142, 167 *supra*.

does not mean that its action shall be taken primarily in the interest of one party alone [1]).

4. Indeed one of the most important principles in our matter is that that the court must weigh against each other the interests of the parties as affected by the relief sought. Each party's hardship and likelihood of ultimate victory in the main action must be considered and compared with the other's situation [2]).

5. Equally fundamental is rule that the principal proceeding (*Hauptsache*) is in no wise affected by interim measures. The action in chief and the action with a view to security are altogether independent of each other [3]). In rendering its final judgment the court is not bound by its interlocutory decision, and may disregard it entirely [4]).

6. Consequently jurisdiction to grant protection *pendente lite* is not dependent upon jurisdiction in the principal action [5]). From this it follows that interim measures may be granted before a plea to the jurisdiction is disposed of; [6]) and that one court may provide a remedy *pendente lite* in aid of an action of which another court has cognizance [7]).

7. Two main types of interim measures may be distinguished: those that facilitate functioning of the tribunal, by making it possible to carry on proceedings and execute the judgment; and

---

[1]) The court is on the surest possible ground when it confines itself to measures consistent with the legal theses of both parties, as in measures of pure conservation, since preservation of the property in dispute is in the interest of both parties, no matter which one wins. Pp. 21, 89 *supra*.

[2]) Garsonnet-Czar-Bru, VIII, 326; Bouchon 40, Druart 44—5, Caroli 110, Rintelen 88, Neumann-Ettenreich 409; pp. 60, 73. 142 *supra*.

[3]) § 11 *supra*. One must not, however, suppose that therefore the interlocutory order may not, in content, touch the same matters which are at issue in the main action. P. 23 *supra*.

[4]) P. 156 *supra*. The final judgment may find the interlocutory order to have been improper. Note 7, p. 168 *supra*; Salvioli, 16 Riv. (1924) 120.

[5]) Stern 40, Rintelen 113, Gianzana 530—1, 4, Thureau 10, Mérignac -Miguel 2ed. II, 149, Thureau 10, Meili, Das internationale Civilprocessrecht, 1906, 453; Schücking-Wehberg 2ed. 589; Schüle 8; note 2, p. 54, pp. 91, 144, 165, 181, *supra*.

[6]) Pp. 144, 165 *supra*; RGZ 50, § 81, 342 at 346, 23 November 1901; „Für das Arrestverfahren ist das Gericht, bei welchem die Hauptsache anhängig ist, zunächst auch das zuständige Gericht der Hauptsache. Eine abgesonderte Prüfung seiner Zuständigkeit für die Hauptsache ist in dem Arrestverfahren ausgeschlossen".

[7]) Pp. 121, 155, 165 *supra*. The rights for which protection is sought must be actionable at law. If action is not pending, it must be brought within a short time, as interim protection is designed to supplement the ordinary legal remedy in urgent cases and not to affect the legal relations of the parties permanently. German Z PO § 926; Austrian EO § 391 (2); pp. 6, 66, 80, 131 *supra*.

those that regulate for the time being a situation which by reason of natural or social exigencies requires regulation, but because of the pending litigation cannot receive a definitive solution before the final decision in the case is rendered [1]). The classical case of the second situation occurs in a boundary dispute. Assuming that neither party intends to make any important or damaging alterations in the status of the territory in dispute, there is no necessity for measures designed to ensure execution of the judgment; the land will still be there when the decision is rendered. *Who* shall enjoy possession *pendente lite* is, in that respect, a matter of absolutely no importance. But that *someone* must administer the litigated area is inevitable [2]). That the temporary line should be drawn clearly and peaceably is highly desirable. Since the court's action in fixing the status in which the parties must remain pending its decision is here directed merely at removing uncertainty and preventing strife, and not at achieving justice and protecting jeopardized rights, the mechanical rule of preserving the *status quo ante litem motam* applies. It should be noted that the status quo thus sanctioned is not that at the time of the judgment, or at the date suit is brought, but the last uncontested status prior to the controversy [3]). Often the two types of interim measures overlap. It would seem that the Permanent Court of International Justice is empowered to grant both sorts of protection *pendente lite* [4]).

---

[1]) § 14 *supra*.

[2]) P. 29.

[3]) Pp. 35, 61, 84, 88, 98, 164 *supra*. Cf. A no. 24, 16, where in deciding whether circumstances had changed since a treaty was made, any changes due to French acts which Switzerland held to be in violation of the treaty were not taken into account. Conwell-Evans 58 states that parties are expected to cease hostilities when appealed to by the Council, at the spot where they are then fighting, and can not claim that so long as the invaders are not expelled continued resistance is legitimate.

[4]) Such was undoubtedly the intention of Fernandes, the author of article 41, and the traditional provision in American treaties, which inspired him. Pp. 95, 101, 144—5 *supra*. The text supports that conclusion if too restricted an interpretation of the word „rights" is not adopted. See note 2, p. 26 *supra*. Judges Negulesco and Schücking considered that the Court had power to fix the status quo. D no. 2, 2d add. 193.

BIBLIOGRAPHY

ALVAREZ, La Codification du Droit international, 1912.

ANZILOTTI, Corso di Diritto internazionale, I, 3ed. 1928; III, 1915.

——, La Riconvenzione nella Procedura internazionale, 21 Riv. (1929) 309—327.

ARNOLD, The Rôle of Substantive Law and Procedure in the legal Process, 45 HLR (1932) 617—647.

AMIRA, Das altnorwegische Vollstreckungsverfahren, 1874.

——, Nordgermanisches Obligationenrecht, 1885—1892.

ARENA, JACOBUS DE, Tractatus de Sequestrationibus. (See Cludius).

AVERARA, Sequestro, in Enciclopedia giuridica Italiana, XV, pt. II, (1915) 710—829.

BALLADORE-PALLIERI, I „Principi generali del diritto riconosciuti dalle Nazioni civili" nell' art. 38 dello Statuto della Corte permanente di Giustizia internazionale, 1931.

——, La Forza obbligatoria della Consuetudine internazionale, 20 Riv. (1928) 338—374.

LE BARON, De l'Acte d'Administration en Droit civil français, 1916.

BASDEVANT, in 16 RGDIP (1909) 99—107.

BAUR, Das summarische Verfahren nach zürcherischem Recht, 1927.

BAYER, Theorie der summarischen Processe, 1859.

BAZOT, Des Ordonnances sur Requête et des Ordonnances de Référé, 1876.

BEKKER, Die Aktionen des römischen Privatrechts, 1871—3.

DE BELLEYME, Ordonnances sur Requêtes et sur Référés, 3ed. 1855.

BELLOT, Texts illustrating the Constitution of the Supreme Court of the United States and the Permanent Court of International Justice, 1921.

BELLOT, Loi sur la Procédure civile du Canton de Genève, suivie de l'Exposé des motifs (cited Bellot).

BERTIN, Ordonnances sur Requête, 1874; Ordonnances de Référé, 1875

BETHMANN—HOLLWEG, Der Civilprocess des gemeinen Rechts in geschichtlicher Entwicklung, II, der römische Civilprocess, 1865.

BILHAUD, Traité des Référés en France, 1834.

BINDER, Prozess und Recht, 1927.

BISHOP, International Arbitral Procedure, 1930.

BLUMENSTEIN, Handbuch des schweizerischen Schuldbetreibungsrechtes, 1911.

van Boetzelar, Les Arbitrages internationaux néerlandais de 1581 à 1794, 1929.
Bonjean, Traité des Ordonnances sur Requête et sur Référé, 1899.
Bonnard, Le Séquestre d'après la Loi fédérale sur la Poursuite pour Dettes et la Faillite, 1914.
Borchard, Judicial Relief for Peril and Insecurity, 45 HLR (1932) 793—854.
Borel, L'Acte général de Genève, 27 Rec. 1929-II, 501—592.
Bort, Tractaet handelnde van Arresten, in Alle de Wercken, 3ed. Utrecht 1745.
Bouchon, Les Saisies conservatoires, 1889.
Bourjon, Le Droit commun de la France et la Coutume de Paris, nouvelle éd. 1770.
Briegleb, Einleitung in die Theorie der summarischen Processe, 1859.
Brierly, The Law of Nations, 1928.
Brodeau, Commentaire sur la Coustume de la Prévosté et Vicomté de Paris, 1658.
Brown, La Conciliation internationale, 1925.
Bruns, Völkerrecht als Rechtsordnung, 1 Zt.f.aus.öff.Rt.u.Vrt. (1929) Teil 1, 1—56.
Buckland, A Text-book of Roman Law from Augustus to Justinian, 1921.
Bülow, Die Lehre von den Processeinreden und den Processvoraussetzungen, 1868.
Star Busman, Hoofdstukken van Burgerlijke Rechtsvordering, 2ed. I 1924.
De Bustamante, The World Court, 1925.
Carnelutti, in 1 Riv. di dir. pr. civ., pt. II (1924) 87—97.
——, in 2 Riv. di dir.pr.civ., pt. II, (1925), 185—205.
——, Lezioni di Diritto processuale civile, 1929.
Caroli—Meyers, Het kort Geding, I, 1906; II, 1915.
Cavaglieri, La Consuetudine giuridica internazionale, 1907.
Cereti, La Tutela giuridica degli Interessi internazionali, 1929.
Chiovenda, Principii di Diritto processuale civile, 3ed. 1923.
Cludius, Tractatus de Jure Sequestrationis, cui demum in eodem Argumenti Generis accesserunt alii duo Tractatus Jacobi de Arena, Francisci Curtii, editio nova, Coburg 1700.
Commissione reale per la Riforma dei Codici, Cod. di Pr. Civ. Progetto, 1926.
Complaint of Costa Rica against Nicaragua, 1916.
Complaint of Salvador against Nicaragua, 1916.
Comunicaciones cruzadas entre la Corte Suprema de Justicia Centroamericana y el Gobierno de El Salvador con Motiva del reciente Conflicto Hondureño, 1908.
Conference on Central American Affairs, 1923.
Conferencia de Paz Centro-Americana. Recopilación de los Tratados, Actos y Documentos.

Coniglio, Il Sequestro conservativo, 1926.
——, La Riforma del Sistema cautelare nel Diritto processuale civile, 4 Riv. di dir.Pr.civ., pt. II, (1927) 3—23.
Conwell Evans, The League Council in Action, 1929.
Coops, Grondtrekken van het Nederlandsche Burgerlijk Procesrecht, 1927.
Corpus Iuris canonici, ed. Richter 1867; ed. 1917.
Corpus iuris Civilis, ed. Krueger-Mommsen 1895.
Curet, La Juridiction des Référés, 1907.
Curtius, Tractatus Sequestrorum. (See Cludius).
Cynus, Super Codice, and Super Digesto veteri, Leyden 1547.
Dalloz, Répertoire pratique de Législation, de Droit et de Jurisprudence, t. X, *sub voce* saisie etc.
Degenkolb, Einlassungszwang und Urteilsnorm, 1877.
Demanda de la Républica de Costa Rica contra la Nicaragua ante la Corte de Justicia Centroamericana, 1916.
Demanda del Gobierno de El Salvador contra el Gobierno de Nicaragua ante la Corte de Justicia Centroamericana, 1916.
Demanda intentada por el Gobierno de Honduras contra el Gobierno de la Républica de El Salvador y contestación definitiva dada por éste ante la Corte de Justicia Centroamericana, 1908.
Descamps, Le Droit international nouveau. L'Ère juridique sans Violence et l'Avènement du Pacigérat positif, 56 RDILC (1929) 159—216.
Desmaze, Le Châtelet de Paris, 2ed. 1870,
Diana, Le Misure conservative interinali, 1909.
Dorendorf, Arrest und einstweilige Verfügungen nach dem deutschen Civilprozessrecht, 1884.
Druart, La Saisie conservatoire du Droit commercial, 1928.
Dumbauld, Automatic Arbitration, 12 World Tomorrow (1929) 72—74.
——, Legal Limitations on War-making, 18 Geo. L.J. (1930) 83—91.
——, Towards a self-governing World: Five Functions of the League of Nations, 40 Int. J.Ethics (1929) 92—104.
Durantis, Speculum Judicialis. Frankfort 1612.
Eichhorn, Die einstweilige Verfügungen in ihrem Verhältnis zum Arrest, 1909.
Enger, Zwangsverwaltung durch einstweilige Verfügung, 1911.
Entscheidungen des Reichsgerichtshofes in Zivilsachen.
Eyma, La Cour de Justice centre-américaine, 1928.
Fachiri, The Permanent Court of International Justice, 1925.
Boneval Faure, Het Nederlandsche Burgerlijk Procesrecht, 3ed., I, 1893.
Feilchenfeld, Public Debts and State Succession, 1931.
Ferarriis, Johannes de Petrus de, Practica singularis ac perutilis, Leyden 1515.
Ferrière, Corps et Compilation de tous les Commentateurs anciens et modernes sur la Coutume de Paris, 2ed. 1714.

FRITZSCHE, Gesetzgebung und Rechtsprechung der Schweiz auf dem Gebiet des Zivilprozessrechts, 1 Zt.f.aus.u.int.Privatrecht (1927) 379—395.

GAILL, Tractatus de Manuum Injectionibus, sive Arrestis Imperii, in Practicarum Observationum, etc., Cologne 1626.

GALLUS, L'Acte général d'Arbitrage, 57 RDILC (1930) 190—246, 413—472, 878—925.

GARSONNET, Traité théorique et pratique de Procédure, 1883. 2ed. Cézar-Bru, 1904.

GIANNI, La Coutume en Droit international, 1931.

GIANZANA, Del Sequestro giudiziario e conservativo, 3ed. 1884.

GIRARD, Manuel élémentaire de Droit romain, 7ed. 1924.

GLASSON, Etude historique sur la Clameur de Haro, 1882.

GLASSON—TISSIER, Précis théorique et pratique de Procédure civile, 2ed. 1908; 3ed. Morel, 1925.

GOLDSCHMIDT, Zivilprozessrecht, 1929.

——, Zwei Beiträge zum materiellen Ziviljustizrecht, in Festschrift für Heinrich Brunner, 1914.

GOLDSCHMIDT, Etude sur l'Acte d'Administration en Droit civil français, 1898.

GRALINSKI, Le Règlement pacifique obligatoire des Différends internationaux suivant le Pacte de la Société des Nations, 1925.

GROTIUS, De Jure Belli ac Pacis Libri Tres, 1625.

MICHEL DE LA GROTTE, Les Affaires traitées par la Cour permanente de Justice internationale pendant la Période 1926—1928, 56 RDILC (1929) 225—276.

GÜTHE, Voraussetzungen und Inhalt der antizipierten Zwangsvollstreckung, 24 ZZP (1898) 346—414.

GUGGENHEIM, Les Mesures provisoires de Procédure internationale et leur Influence sur le Développement du Droit des Gens, 1931.

HABICHT, Post-War Treaties for the Pacific Settlement of International Disputes, 1931.

HÄRLE, Die allgemeine Rechtsgrundsätze im Völkerrecht, 11 Zt.f.öff. Rt. (1931) 206—246.

HAMMARSKJÖLD, Le Règlement de la Cour permanente de Justice internationale, 49 RDILC (1922) 125—148.

HEINSHEIMER, in 55 JW (1926) 378—9.

HELLWIG, Klagrecht und Klagmöglichkeit, 1905. (Cited Hellwig).

——, System des deutschen Zivilprozessrechts, 1912.

HOLD-FERNECK, Lehrbuch des Völkerrechts, I, 1930.

HUBER, Die Fortbildung des Völkerrechts auf dem Gebiet des Prozess- und Landkriegsrechts durch die II. Internationale Friedenskonferenz im Haag 1907, 2 Jahrbuch des öffentlichen Rechts der Gegenwart (1908) 470—611.

HUDSON, The Permanent Court of International Justice, 1925.

The International Conference of American States on Conciliation and Arbitration, 1929.

JAEGER, Bundesgesetz betreffend Schuldbetreibung und Konkurs, 2ed. 1905.
JAHN, Darf der STGH einstweilige Verfügungen erlassen? 59 JW (1930) 1160—3.
JENKS, A short History of English Law, 4ed. 1928.
JERUSALEM, Die Staatsgerichtsbarkeit, 1930.
JUSTER, Der Anspruch als materielle Voraussetzung der einstweiligen Verfügung, GZ 1902, nr. 49, 426—8, 437—8, 452—3.
KARLOWA, Der römische Civilprocess zur Zeit der Legis Actionen, 1872.
KELLER, Der römische Civilprocess, 6ed. Wach, 1883.
KISCH, Der deutsche Arrestprozess, 1914.
KLEIN, Die Aufnahme des référé in das Ungarische Prozessrecht, GZ 1911, nr. 41, 321—5.
KLEIN—ENGEL, Der Zivilprozess Oesterreichs, 1927.
KLEINFELLER, Lehrbuch des deutschen Zivilprozessrechts, 3ed. 1925.
KOHLER, Prozessrechtliche Forschungen, 1879.
KRAINZ-PFAFF-EHRENZWEIG, System des österreichischen allgemeinen Privatrechts, 1925.
KUNZ, Die intrasystematische Stellung des Art. XI des Völkerbundpaktes, 1931.
VAN KUYK, Rechtsingang en verstek in de middeleeuwschstedelijke procedure in verband met het recht der Republiek, 71 Themis (1910) 363—425.
LAMMERS, in 55 JW (1926) 376—8.
LAMMERS—SIMONS, Rechtsprechung des Staatsgerichtshofs für das deutsche Reich und des Reichsgerichtshofs auf Grund Artikel 13 Absatz 2 der Reichsverfassung, 1929.
LAPRADELLE—POLITIS, Recueil des Arbitrages internationaux, I, 1905.
League of Nations Documents are cited by their official numbering.
VAN LEER, Het Verbod van Eigenrichting, 1909.
LEUCH, Die Zivilprozessordnung für den Kanton Bern, 1922.
LOYSEL, Institutes coutumières, 1846.
MAGYARI, Die internationale Schiedsgerichtsbarkeit seit dem Weltkrieg, 1927.
MAITLAND, Justice and Police, 1885.
MARTIN, Histoire de la Coutume de la Prévôté et Vicomté de Paris, I (1922); II, fasc. 1 (1926), fasc. 2 (1930).
MEILI, Der Zivil und Strafprozess des Kantons Zürich und des Bundes, 1882.
MERIGNAC-MIGUEL, Traité théorique et pratique des Ordonnances sur Requête et des Référés, 2ed. 1923.
MERKEL, Uber Arrest und einstweilige Verfügungen nach dem geltenden deutschen Prozessrecht, 1880.
MERULA, Manier van Procederen, ed. Haas, Leyden 1741.
MILLAR, A History of Continental Civil Procedure, 1928.

MILLER, Secret Statutes of the United States, 1918.
——, The Drafting of the Covenant, 1928.
——, The Geneva Protocol, 1925.
MITTERMAIER, Die summarischen Verfahrungsarten des gemeinen deutschen bürgerlichen Prozesses, 1840.
——, Über den Ursprung und das Verhältniss des sogenannten summarischen Prozesses zum ordentlichen Prozess, 7 Archiv für die zivilistische Praxis (1824) 369—405.
MOLINAEUS, Commentaria in consuetudines Parisienses, tit. II, gloss I in verbo arrest ou brandon, ad § 74, vol. I in Omnia quae extant Opera, Paris 1681.
MOORE, International Adjudications, Modern Series, vol. I, 1929.
——, Law and Organization (1914), reprinted in International Law and some current Illusions, 1924.
MORELLI, La Sentenza internazionale, 1931.
MORENO, Historia de las Relaciones interstatuales de Centroamérica, 1928.
MORGENTHAU, Die internationale Rechtspflege, 1929.
MORTARA, Commentario dei Codice e delle Leggi di Procedura civile, 2ed. 1910.
——, Manuela della Procedura civile, 9ed. 1921.
MUCK, Die einstweilige Verfügung, 1900.
MÜNZ, Betrachtungen über die einstweiligen Verfügingen in Theorie und Praxis, GH 1902 nr. 31—2, 341—3, 351—3.
MUNRO, The five Republics of Central America, 1918.
MUTHER, Sequestration und Arrest im römischen Recht, 1856.
——, Zur Lehre von der römischen Actio, dem heutigen Klagrecht, etc. 1857.
NERON, Les Edicts et Ordonnances des tres-Chrestiens Roys François I Henry II Charles IX Henry III Henry IV Louis XIII et Louis XIV sur le faict de la justice & abreviation des Procez, 1656.
NERON-GIRARD, Recueil d'Edits et d'Ordonnances royaux, 1720.
NEUMANN, Kommentar zur Exekutionsordnung, 3ed. 1929.
NEUMANN—ETTENREICH, Einstweilige Verfügungen, GZ 1900, nr. 50, 407—412.
NEUNER, Prozessrecht und Privatrecht, 1923.
NICARAGUA, Ministerio de relaciones exteriores. Documentos oficiales referentes á la guerra entre Nicaragua y Honduras de 1907, y á la participación de El Salvador.
——, Memoria de relaciones exteriores, 1906—7.
NIPPOLD, Die Fortbildung des Verfahrens in völkerrechtlichen Streitigkeiten, 1907.
OERTMANN, Grundriss des deutschen Zivilprozessrechts, 1930.
OTT, EMIL, Zur Lehre von den besonderen Verfahrensarten, 30 Grünhuts Zt. (1903) 273—336.
OTT, EUGEN, Das Arrestverfahren nach dem Bundesgesetz über Schuldbetreibung und Konkurs vom 11. April 1889, 1900. (cited Ott).

OTT, FRITZ, Die Rechtsverfolgung in der Schweiz, 1915.
OUDEMANN, Het Nederlandsch Wetboek van burgerlijke Regtsvordering, 3ed., III, 1863.
PANORMITANUS, Commentaria Primae Partis in Secundum Decretalium Librum, Leyden 1636.
PASQUIER, Etude sur les Actes conservatoires, 1910.
PECKIUS, Tractatus de jure sistendi et manuum injectione quam vulgo arrestationem vocant, in Opera Omnia, Antwerp 1647.
PERMANENT COURT OF INTERNATIONAL JUSTICE:
Permanent Court of International Justice, Advisory Committee of Jurists. Documents presented to the Committee relating to existing plans for the establishment of a Permanent Court of International Justice. (cited Documents presented).
Permanent Court of International Justice. Advisory Committee of Jurists. Procès-verbaux of the Proceedings of the Committee June 16th-July 24th 1920 with annexes. (cited Minutes)
League of Nations, Permanent Court of International Justice. Documents concerning The action taken by the Council of the League of Nations under article 14 of the Covenant and The adoption by the Assembly of the Statute of the Permanent Court (not including material collected for, or the minutes of, the advisory committee of jurists) 1921. (cited Documents concerning)
Publications of the Permanent Court of International Justice. Series D. Acts and Documents concerning the organisation of the Court. No. 2. Preparation of the Rules of Court. Minutes of Meetings held during the Preliminary Session of the Court, with Annexes. (January 30th to March 24th 1922). (cited D no. 2)
Permanent Court of International Justice. Series D. Acts and Documents concerning the organization of the Court. Second addendum to no. 2. Modification of the Rules, 1931. (January 21-February 20. Cited D no. 2, 2d add.)
Publications of the Court include series A, B, A/B, C, D, E and F; citations beginning with those letters refer to publications of the Court.
PETERS, Arrest und einstweilige Verfügung nach preussischem Recht, 1884.
PHILIPSE, Le Rôle du Conseil de la Société des Nations dans le Règlement pacifique des Différends internationaux, 1928.
PIGEAU, La Procédure civile du Châtelet de Paris, 1787.
PLANCK, Das deutsche Gerichtsverfahren im Mittelalter, 1879.
PLANITZ, Grundlagen des deutschen Arrestprozesses, 1922.
——, Studien zur Geschichte des deutschen Arrestprozesses, Zt.Sav. St.Germ., 34 : 49—140 (1913); 39 : 223—308 (1918); 40 : 87—198 (1919).
PLÓSZ, Beiträge zur theorie des Klagrechts, 1880.
POLENAAR, Schets van het Nederlandsche Burgerlijke Procesrecht, 6 ed 1925.

POLLAK, System des Österreichischen Zivilprozessrechtes mit Einschluss des Exekutionsrechtes, 2 ed., III, 1932.

POLLOCK-MAITLAND, The History of English Law before the time of Edward I, 1895.

POTHIER, Coutumes des Duché, Bailliage et Prévôté d'Orleans et ressort d'iceux, 1776.

——, Traité de Procédure civile, (Oeuvres posthumes t. VII), 1778.

POUILLET, Traité théorique et pratique des Brevets d'Invention et de la Contrefaçon, 4 ed. 1899.

——, Traité théorique et pratique de la Propriété littéraire et artistique et du Droit de Réprésentation, 3 ed. 1908.

POUND, Introduction to the Philosophy of Law, 1922.

——, Juristic Science and Law, 31 HLR 1047—63.

——, Law and Morals, 2ed. 1926.

——, The End of Law as developed in legal Rules and Doctrines, 27 HLR 195—234.

——, The End of Law as developed in juristic Thought, 27 HLR 605—628; 30 HLR 201—225.

——, The ideal Element in American judicial Decision, 45 HLR (1931) 136—148.

——, The Theory of judicial Decision, 36 HLR 641—662.

——, The Spirit of the Common Law, 1921.

——, Theories of Law, 22 Yale LJ 114 (1912).

RABEL, Rechtsvergleichung und internationale Rechtsprechung, 1 Zt.f. aus.u.int. Privatrecht (1927) 5—47.

RAMIREZ, Cinco Anos en la Corte de Justicia Centroamericana, 1918.

RAPPARD, The Geneva Experiment, 1931.

RINTELEN, Die einstweilige Verfügung, 1905.

RIPERT, Droit maritime, 3ed. 1929.

ROSENBERG, Lehrbuch des deutschen Zivilprozessrechts, 1927.

ROTH, Über einstweilige Verfügungen auf Geldleistungen nach dem deutschen Zivilprozess. Diss. Frankfort-am-Main.

SALVADOR, Ministerio de relaciones exteriores. El Golfo de Fonseca y el Tratado Bryan-Chamorro, Documentos oficiales, 1917.

SALVIOLI, La Corte permanente de Giustizia internazionale, 1928. (cited Salvioli).

SALVIOLI, Storia della Procedura civile e criminale, 1927.

SAUER, Grundlagen des Prozessrechts, 2ed. 1929.

SCHINDLER, Les Traités de Conciliation et d'Arbitrage conclus par la Suisse, 52 RDILC (1925) 816—875.

SCHÜCKING-WEHBERG, Die Satzung des Völkerbundes, 2ed. 1924.

SCHÜLE, Das Problem der einstweiligen Verfügung in der deutschen Reichsstaatsgerichtsbarkeit, 1932.

SCHULTE, Eine Untersuchung über das Erkenntnisverfahren bei Arrest und einstweiliger Verfügung, 1930.

SCHULTZE, Privatrecht und Process in ihrer Wechselbeziehung, 1883.

SCHURTER-FRITZSCHE, Das Zivilprozessrecht des Bundes, 1924.

SCOTT, L'Universalité du Droit des Gens, 1 RDI (1927) 637—657.

——, Judicial Settlement of Controversies between States of the American Union, 1919.

——, Sovereign States and Suits before arbitral Tribunals and Courts of Justice, 1925.

——, The Project of a Permanent Court of International Justice, Resolutions of the advisory Committee of Jurists, 1920.

——, Treaties for the Advancement of Peace, 1920.

Sentencia en el Juicio promovido por la República de Honduras contra las Repúblicas de El Salvador y Guatemala, 1908.

SEUFFERT, Kommentar zur Zivilprozessordnung 10 ed. 1908.

SMITH, JEREMIAH JR., The Preservation of Peace. (Phi Beta Kappa oration at Harvard 24 June 1927).

SOMLÓ, Juristische Grundlehre, 1917.

STEIN, Grundriss des Zivilprozessrechts und des Konkursrechts, 3ed. Juncker 1928.

——, Über die Voraussetzungen des Rechtsschutzes, insbesondere bei der Verurteilungsklage, in Festgabe für Hermann Fitting, 1902.

STEIN-JONAS, Die Zivilprozessordnung für das deutsche Reich, 1926.

STERN, Arrest und einstweilige Verfügung nach der deutschen ZPO, 1912.

STOWELL, International Law, 1931.

STRÄULI, Gesetze betreffend zürcherische Rechtspflege, II Teil, 1915.

STREY, Die Lehre von den Arresten und dem Arrestverfahren nach preussischem Recht mit Bezugnahme auf das gemeine deutsche Recht, 1859.

STRISOWER, Der Krieg und die Völkerrechtsordnung, 1919.

STRUPP, Eléments du Droit international public, 2ed. 1930.

——, Grundzüge des positiven Völkerrechts, 4ed. 1928.

——, Das Recht des internationalen Richters nach Billigkeit zu entscheiden, 1930; Le Droit du Juge international de statuer selon l'Equité, 33 Rec. 1930-III, 357—478.

Systematic Survey of the Arbitration Conventions and Treaties of mutual Security deposited with the League of Nations, 2ed., to 15 December 1927. C. 653.M.216.1927.V.29.

TAMBOUR, Des Voies d'Exécution sur les Biens des Débiteurs dans le Droit romain et l'ancien Droit français, 1856.

TELDERS, De juridieke waardeering van den oorlog, 1931.

THIEME, Die Fortbildung der internationalen Schiedsgerichtsbarkeit seit dem Weltkrieg, 1927.

THOMASIUS, Philosophia Juris ostensa in Doctrina de Obligationibus et Actionibus, Dissertatio Academica IIII, Halle 1773.

THUREAU, De la Saisie-arrêt en Droit international privé, 1897.

TRASBOT, L'Acte d'Administration en Droit privé français, 1921.

United States Foreign Relations, 1907, part 2.

DEL VECCHIO, Sui Principi generali del Diritto, 1921.

VERDROSS, Die allgemeine Rechtsgrundsätze als Völkerrechtsquelle, in Gesellschaft, Staat und Recht (*Festschrift* for Kelsen) 1931.

——, Die Einheit des rechtlichen Weltbildes, 1923.
——, Le Fondement du Droit international, 16 Rec. 1927-I, 251—319.
——, Règles générales du Droit de la Paix, 30 Rec. 1929-V, 275—503.
——, Die Verfassung der Völkerrechtsgemeinschaft, 1926.
Paul de Vineuil, La Cour permanente de Justice internationale en 1929, 57 RDILC (1930) 125—148.
Vizioz, Observations sur l'Etude de la Procédure civile, in Revue générale du Droit, de la Législation et de Jurisprudence, 51 : 161—185, 254—268 (1927); 52 : 20—33, 88—102, 181—187 (1928); 53 : 2—27, 161—192 (1929); 54: 81—101, 161—175 (1930).
van Vollenhoven, Du Droit de Paix (de Jure Pacis) 1932.
Wach, Der Arrestprozess in seiner geschichtlichen Entwicklung. Der italienische Arrestprozess, 1868.
Wenger, Institutionen des römischen Zivilprozessrechts, 1925.
Werner, Das Recht des Arrestes im Civilprozesse, 1884.
Wetzell, System des ordentlichen Civilprozesses, 3 ed. 1873.
Williams, Sir John Fischer, Chapters on Current International Law and the League of Nations, 1929.
——, Treaty Revision and the Future of the League of Nations, 10 Int. Aff. (1931) 326—351.
World Peace Foundation Pamphlets, VII, no. 1, (1917), Central American League of Nations.
Wrede, Das Zivilprozessrecht Schwedens und Finnlands, 1924.
Der Zivilprozess. Vier Vorträge, von Adolf Wach, Wilhelm Kisch, Albrecht Mendelssohn-Bartholdy, Friedrich Stein. 1922.

ANNEXES

ANNEX 1

(a) *Phillimore draft convention*, § 12. „Any one of the Allied States having a dispute pending may apply to the Conference to be relieved from the moratorium imposed by article 1(b) on the ground that there is a continuing injury, or on the ground that unless some prompt provision for reparation or restitution is made the injury will be irreparable. The Conference shall, without deciding in any way upon the merits of the dispute, forthwith consider this application, and may relieve the applicant State from the provisions of the moratorium, or may suggest terms of temporary arrangement as a condition of not relieving the applicant State from the moratorium, and may from time to time consider the application of the terms which should be imposed. In the event of relief from the provisions of the moratorium being granted under this article, any of the Allied States may, notwithstanding the provisions of Article 1, come to the assistance of the state so relieved." D. H. Miller, Drafting, II, 5.

(b) *Phillimore report of March 20, 1918*. „16. Article 12 is a substitutional provision for that power of injunction which has been recommended by many English and American writers. It has been felt that if there is to be a moratorium, there may be cases of continuing or irreparable injury to which the injured State can not be expected to submit. In order to meet this difficulty these writers have taken an idea from the legal procedure common to Great Britain and the United States. But in applying this procedure to international matters the following objections seem to arise:

a. If final awards or recommendations are not to be the subject of enforcement by the League, it would seem illogical that interlocutory awards or recommendations should be so enforced.

b. The aggressive State would certaintly resent such an infringement of its sovereignty and struggle to prevent the use of an injunction and the proceeding would almost necessarily be so prolonged, particularly if the injunction is to be the work of the whole Conference, that the interlocutory decision would hardly be reached sooner than the final one, and the mischief would have been done;

c. It may be added that such knowledge as any of the members of the committee have of such foreign jurisprudence as is founded on the

Code de Napoléon, leads them to doubt whether the procedure which most nearly approaches to the Anglo-American injunction has received the same development or occupies the same position of importance which it has with us.

17. The committee have, therefore, rejected the idea of injunction, and submit this Article as a corrective for hardship which might otherwise be worked by the moratorium." Ibid, I, 7—8.

ANNEX 2

Bruns in 1 Zt. f. aus. öff. Rt. u. Vrt. (1929) 1 teil, 35—6: „Einen besonders naiven Ausdruck hat die Auffassung, dass ein internationales Organ sich von jedem Eingriff in die Souveränität eines Staates fernzuhalten habe, in einigen Urteilen des Deutsch-Polnisches Gemischten Schiedsgerichts gefunden. Der Versailler Vertrag gibt in seinem Artikel 305 dem Schiedsgericht Kompetenz, der „partie qui aura subi de ce chef un préjudice" eine Reparation zuzuerkennen, wenn durch eine Entscheidung des polnischen Liquidationskommittees, die die beteiligten Regierungen wie das Schiedsgericht als ein „jugement d'un tribunal" im Sinne dieses Artikels ansehen, eine Bestimmung über das Liquidationsrecht verletzt wird. Das Gericht verweigerte eine einstweilige Verfügung gegen den polnischen Staat unter anderem, weil die Liquidation zwar verfügt, aber noch nicht völlig beendet sei. Der Staat hatte das Grundstück beschlagnahmt, und dem Eigentumer das Verfügungsrecht entzogen, sich selbst aber noch nicht das Eigentum angeeignet. Das Gericht erklärt, selbst wenn die Liquidation in dem eingeklagten Falle nach dem Versailler Vertrag unzulässig sei, dürfe es nicht in die im Gang befindliche Liquidation eingreifen. Wenn das Gericht das Recht hat, einem Staat, der eine Vertragsbestimmung verletzt hat, zum Schadenersatz und damit zu Wiederherstellung des Zustandes, wie er ohne den rechtswidrigen Ergriff bestanden haben würde, zu verurteilen, so muss es ihm auch im Wege der einstweiligen Verfügung die Fortsetzung der begonnenen Rechtsverletzung untersagen können, vorausgesetzt, dass seine Prozessordnung die einstweilige Verfügung als Rechtsinstitut kennt. Das Gericht hat in anderen Fällen *nach* Beendigung der Liquidation dem polnischen Staat durch einstweilige Verfügung untersagt, über das Grundstück, das er sich im Wege der Liquidation angeeignet hatte, zu verfügen, wie wenn dieses Verbot nicht ebenfalls einen Eingriff in die Souveränität des polnischen Staates darstellte. Die Meinung des Gerichts beruht auf einer völligen Verkennung des Wesens der einstweiligen Verfügung sowie der Verletzung einer Völkerrechtsverpflichtung."

ANNEX 3

Franco-German rules of 2 April 1920, 1 *TAM 49—50.*

Art. 31. A la requête d'une partie ou d'un agent, le tribunal peut ordonner, en dehors des mesures conservatoires déjà prévues par le traité, toute mesure conservatoire ou provisoire qui lui paraît équitable et nécessaire pour garantir les droits des parties.

Art. 32. Les mesures conservatoires peuvent être demandées et ordonnées en tout état de cause, même avant le dépôt de la requête introductive de l'instance. Dans ce dernier cas, l'instance doit être introduite dans le plus bref délai possible.

Art. 33. La partie contre laquelle des mesures conservatoires sont requises doit être entendue, si possible.

La partie qui n'a pas pu être entendue peut demander au tribunal de revenir sur sa décision. Cette demande n'est pas suspensive.

Art. 34. Dans tous les cas où les mesures conservatoires seraient de nature à porter préjudice au droit d'un tiers, celui-ci aura la faculté d'y faire opposition au moyen d'une requête présentée au tribunal.

Les dispositions de la procédure ordinaire sont applicables à l'instruction et au jugement de cette requête.

Celle-ci n'est pas suspensive.

Art. 35. La partie requérante peut être tenue de fournir une caution ou de faire un dépôt pour garantir les dommages qui peuvent résulter des mesures conservatoires.

Art. 36. La décision de mesures conservatoires détermine leur étendue et leurs conditions. Elle est notifiée aux parties et a la même force exécutoire qu'une sentence du tribunal.

Le tribunal peut requérir l'agent compétent de faire exécuter cette décision, avant même toute notification, celle-ci devant être faite dans les huit jours qui suivent l'exécution.

ANNEX 4

Statute and Rules of the Permanent Court of International Justice.

Article 41: „La Cour a le pouvoir d'indiquer, si elle estime que les circonstances l'exigent, quelles mesures conservatoires du droit de chacun doivent être prises à titre provisoire.

„En attendant l'arrêt définitif, l'indication de ces mesures est immédiatement notifiée aux parties et au Conseil."

English text: „The Court shall have the power to indicate, if it considers that circumstances so require, any provisional measures which ought to be taken to (p) reserve the respective rights of either party.

„Pending the final decision, notice of the measures suggested shall forthwith be given to the parties and the Council."

By an obvious slip, „reserve" instead of „preserve" appears in the text as published. See Manley O. Hudson in 35 HLR 263, note 69.

Original rule 57: „Lorsque la Cour ne siège pas, l'indication des mesures conservatoires est faite par le Président.

„En cas de refus de la part des parties de se conformer aux indications de la Cour ou du Président concernant les mesures conservatoires, il en est pris acte."

English text: „When the Court is not sitting, any measures for the preservation in the meantime of the respective rights of the parties shall be indicated by the President.

„Any refusal by the parties to conform to the suggestions of the Court or of the President, with regard to such measures, shall be placed on record."

Amended rule 57: „Une requête adressée à la Cour par les parties ou par l'une d'entre elles en vue de mesures conservatoires, a la priorité sur toutes autres affaires. Il est statué d'urgence et, si la Cour ne siège pas, elle est à cette fin convoquée sans retard par le Président.

„En l'absence d'une requête, si la Cour ne siège pas, le Président peut convoquer la Cour pour lui soumettre la question de l'opportunité de semblables mesures.

„Dans tous les cas, la Cour n'indique des mesures conservatoires qu'après avoir donné aux parties la possibilité de faire entendre leurs observations à ce sujet."

English text: „An application made to the Court by one or both of the parties, for the indication of interim protection, shall have priority over all other cases. The decision thereon shall be treated as a matter of urgency, and if the Court is not sitting it shall be convened without delay by the President for the purpose.

„If no application is made, and if the Court is not sitting, the President may convene the Court to submit to it the question whether such measures are expedient.

„In all cases, the Court shall only indicate measures of protection after giving the parties an opportunity of presenting their observations on the subject."

ANNEX 5

Extract from letter of the Registrar to the Belgian agents, of 20 December 1926:

„Laissant de côté la question de savoir si la Requête du 25 novembre 1926, en comprenant parmi les conclusions auxquelles elle aboutit une demande visant l'indication de mesures conservatoires, n'a pas cherché en s'inspirant de l'article 32 du Règlement, à obtenir que la Cour plénière indique les mesures dont il s'agit à l'exclusion du seul Président, celui-ci a compris la demande comme tendant à provoquer une application par la Cour ou par le Président du pouvoir qu'ils possèdent aux termes des dispositions que je me suis permis de rappeler ci-dessus.

„Or, au vu des documents qui ont été déposés jusqu'ici dans l'affaire, le Président n'a pu acquérir la conviction, que les circonstances exigent' l'indication des mesures conservatoires à prendre dans la présente affaire. C'est pourquoi je suis chargé de porter à votre connaissance que, jusqu'à nouvel avis, il ne saurait donner suite à la demande que formule la Requête du 25 novembre 1926, et qui tend à obtenir l'indication de mesures conservatoires en attendant l'arrêt définitif.

„Le Président a pris cette décision sous réserve de toute conclusion différente à laquelle il pourrait arriver si le Gouvernement belge estimait utile de faire valoir des circonstances qui, à son avis, exigent que des mesures conservatoires soient indiquées pour la sauvegarde des droits qui seraient éventuellement reconnus à la Belgique ou à ses ressortissants. Les considérations que le Gouvernement belge désirerait, le cas échéant, soumettre à cet égard, devraient sans doute mentionner la nature des mesures qui, selon lui, pourraient être utilement indiquées, et être accompagnées, en outre, des preuves documentaires appropriées. Elles pourraient être présentées, par exemple, dans le Mémoire du gouvernement belge sur le fond, mais en aucun cas après l'expiration du délai fixé pour le dépôt de ce document." C no. 16-I, 305—6.

INDEX

STELLINGEN

1. Art. 828 C.P.C. eischt niet de van waarde verklaring van eene „*saisie-gagerie*" of „*saisie-revendication*".

2. Een vreemd vonnis, ofschoon niet executoir in Nederland heeft kracht van gewijsde zaak.

3. Een slaaf was een juridisch persoon in het romeinsche recht.

4. Het is niet juist, dat alle staatsverdragen behalve degenen die uitdrukkelijk voor oorlogstijd bedoeld zijn, door den oorlog buiten werking worden gezet.

5. De Nederlandsche rechter behoort het Haagsch verdrag van 12 Juni 1902 analogisch toe te passen in een echtscheidingsproces tusschen onderdanen van niet toegetreden staten.

6. De toekenning van het bezit van alle goederen der nalatenschap aan een executeur-testamentair kan rechtsgeldig geschieden ook indien er legitimarissen zijn.

GPSR Compliance

The European Union's (EU) General Product Safety Regulation (GPSR) is a set of rules that requires consumer products to be safe and our obligations to ensure this.

If you have any concerns about our products, you can contact us on ProductSafety@springernature.com

In case Publisher is established outside the EU, the EU authorized representative is:

Springer Nature Customer Service Center GmbH
Europaplatz 3
69115 Heidelberg, Germany

Batch number: 10824476

Printed by Printforce, the Netherlands